The 300 CLUB

Have We Seen the Last of Baseball's 300-Game Winners?

By Dan Schlossberg

With a Foreword by Wayne Hagin

www.ascendbooks.com

10 9 8 7 6 5 4 3 2 1

Printed in the United States of America

ISBN-13: 978-0-9841130-3-3
ISBN-10: 0-9841130-3-7

Library of Congress Control Number: 2010923348

Editor: Lee Stuart
Design: Randy Lackey

www.ascendbooks.com

The
300
CLUB

Have We Seen the Last

of Baseball's 300-Game Winners?

Dedication

To Sophie, a future Olympic
swimmer who can light
my fire anytime.

Table of Contents

Acknowledgments

This book would not have been possible without the help of many friends and professional colleagues.

First on the list is Bob Ibach, former publicist and publications director for the Chicago Cubs, and a friend and colleague for nearly 25 years (time flies when you're having fun!). Bob came up with the concept, found a perfect publisher, and provided unlimited support and encouragement throughout the project.

Thanks also to Bob Snodgrass, publisher of Ascend Books and a partner in three of my previous projects. A good guy who knew he'd be getting a good book well before deadline, Bob believed in this book and was a pleasure, personally and professionally.

I can't say enough about Lee Stuart, a book editor who not only loves baseball but loves lighting up the Internet with pun-filled comments as chapters are submitted. Hey, Lee, did you get that tube of Vaseline that accompanied the Gaylord Perry chapter? My computer told me it slid through cyberspace safely.

Publication Coordinator Kerry Comiskey, who bears the name of a celebrated old ballpark, was on top of things from the start and helped make this volume so attractive.

So did Ronnie Joyner, the best baseball cartoonist since Pap, whose handsome cartoons also appeared in some of my previous books, including *Baseball Bits* and *Baseball Gold*. Thanks, Ronnie, for drawing new cartoons on 300-game winners.

And, speaking of artwork, the images of goodsportsart.com, supplied by Bill Goff, always turn a type-heavy baseball book into a work of art. Bill commissions a bevy of artists from his base in Connecticut and produces the handsome "Hallowed Ground" calendar that always hangs above my home computer. Bill should feel flattered: his calendar won a close race for a prime spot with a poster of Counselor Troi from *Star Trek: The Next Generation*.

Baseball cards, always part of Bill Goff's portfolio, are a part of this book, too.

Special thanks go to Clay Luraschi of Topps for again providing reprint permission – plus annual factory sets and special issues at All-Star FanFest. You're a good friend, Clay.

Bill Menzel, who answers to the old Bill Murray nickname of "Mr. Bill," supplied open access to his exceptional photography portfolio both for this book and *Baseball Bits*. He and I have worked together on various projects and often travel together to baseball events from New York ballparks to All-Star and World Series venues. Relatively new on the scene, Bill is an undiscovered talent – and a big one – who deserves his own book.

Like Mr. Bill, the staff at the Baseball Hall of Fame couldn't have been nicer during the compilation process. Jeff Idelson, a long-time friend and lifetime good guy who now reigns as president of the Hall, and Brad Horn, who succeeded Jeff as media relations mogul in Cooperstown, were more than supportive, with Brad even writing personal notes urging 300-game winners already in the Hall of Fame to cooperate with interviews.

Photo archivist Pat Kelly not only provided a very reasonable price but asked Freddy Berowski to prepare in advance two wheeled carts containing more than 150 files of the 24 pitchers with 300 victories. Jim Gates and Tim Wiles also lent encouragement during the day-long process, while Bob Faller of The Otesaga provided a fantastic place to stay – right on Otsego Lake – plus a great radio interview promoting his venerable property.

Once the photo-gathering was finished, the search for interview subjects started. Finding active players during the off-season isn't easy, but finding retired players with Cooperstown credentials is even harder.

Acknowledgments

Although I thought it would be impossible to talk to all 10 of the living 300-game winners, I actually did it – though setting up the interviews required considerable sleuth work to land phone numbers, find agents who would contact their clients, and show up at card shows featuring former stars.

Special thanks go to the Hendricks brothers, agents for Roger Clemens, and Tiffany at the Clemens Foundation; Barry Meister, the Chicago-based representative of Randy Johnson; and especially Gregg Clifton, who not only arranged a Tom Glavine phone interview but also called and emailed multiple times on both ends to be sure everything went smoothly (how could it not with a client who is so polite, thoughtful, and sensitive?).

Thanks also go to Billy Tooma of Icon Independent Films, LLC, and Mike Ross, attorney for MAB Celebrity Services of Fairfield, New Jersey, who graciously allowed me to interview pitchers who participated in their 20-game winners show last October. And thanks to Bob Ibach for urging me to show up with tape recorder in hand. I had almost given up on Tom Seaver, but managed to land him after he completed a lengthy signing session.

During that weekend, I also managed to sit down with Gaylord Perry, another guy with whom I'd been playing telephone tag; Bert Blyleven, whose exclusion from the Hall of Fame remains a major mystery; and four guys I'd had as guests on my baseball theme cruises: Ralph Branca, Bob Feller, Fergie Jenkins, and Jim Kaat (there's an "Almost, But Not Quite" chapter for guys who flirted with 300 wins).

Thank you, Don Sutton, for sitting with me in the CitiField pressbox and talking about The 300 Club for 45 minutes. You enlightened me on many things and provided intimate details of your career that I'd never read before.

Except for Seaver and Perry, everybody else was done by phone but gave generously of their time and thoughts.

Greg Maddux remains humble and low-key but friendly and frisky, as well as a fountain of knowledge about pitching. He's virtually certain to follow his brother, Mike, as a respected major-league pitching coach. Randy Johnson, the most recent 300-game winner, was honest, forthcoming, and perfectly polite and professional – contrary to his previous public persona. Roger Clemens, the only man to win the Cy Young Award seven times, took his time and provided intimate details about his career.

Poetry-writing pitcher Phil Niekro, who preferred polka dancing to running as a workout regimen, talked about the obstacles he faced with a trick pitch nobody could catch. He said he's especially proud of the record he and his late brother, Joe, share for victories by brothers. They beat out Gaylord and Jim Perry, the only brothers who both won Cy Young Awards.

And then there's Nolan Ryan, who pitched more no-hitters and struck out more batters than anybody in baseball history. The soft-spoken Texan, who now serves as president of the Texas Rangers, wrote the foreword for my previous autobiography of Astros broadcaster Milo Hamilton and was cooperative with this venture as well.

As Gary Sheffield said last September, "Nobody was like Nolan Ryan. I think he stands alone. When I hear about guys throwing 97-98 miles an hour, I don't really believe it. I don't think anybody threw harder than Nolan Ryan."

Sheffield, Chipper Jones, Keith Hernandez, Bobby Cox, Dallas Green, Joe Morgan, Gary Matthews, and Phillies broadcaster Chris Wheeler all deserve thanks for sharing their thoughts. So do Hall of Famer Robin Roberts, whose phone call followed a request from long-time Philadelphia publicist Larry Shenk, and Cooperstown candidate Tommy John, who pitched almost as long as Ryan, but still waits for the call. Thanks to Ira Silverman, an old pal from my Syracuse University days, for getting the old left-hander on the horn.

Two active radio broadcasters, Wayne Hagin of the New York Mets and Milo Hamilton of the Houston Astros, were active participants in this project and their help was much appreciated. Hagin, who has broadcast for teams in all four time zones, shared his thoughts for the foreword, while Hamilton passed along memories from a baseball broadcasting career now in its seventh decade (take that, Julio Franco!).

Other baseball personalities who merit mention include long-time Florida Marlins traveling secretary Bill Beck; John Blundell of Major League Baseball; MLB.com writers Barry Bloom and Mark Bowman; author Peter Golenbock; Braves publicist Brad Hainje; Dave Kaplan, director of the Yogi Berra Museum and Learning Center in Montclair, New Jersey; Julio Pabon of LatinoSports.com; Joe Pinto of Roger Dean Stadium in Jupiter, Florida; Phillies historian and author Rich Westcott, who wrote a previous paperback on 300-game winners; and PR chief Jason Zillo of the New York Yankees.

There are too many friends to list from the Society for American Baseball Research (SABR), but three who deserve special mention are Evelyn Begley, chair of the Casey Stengel chapter in New York, and long-time friends Doug Lyons, a fun-loving historian and fellow author when not tackling his real job as a criminal attorney, and David Vincent, an author and home run guru who somehow tolerates an assignment as official scorer for the Washington Nationals.

I also enjoyed talking baseball with Bob Muscatell, a silver-tongued deejay at simulcasting Connecticut radio stations WLIS Old Saybrook and WMRD Middletown, and Kal London, whose "Travel With Kal" show airs weekday mornings.

Heartfelt thanks also go to a trio of female friends who kept my head and heart in the right place: Maggie Linton of Sirius XM Satellite Radio, Radburn aerobics instructor Linda Rosen, and across-the-street neighbor Joy Goldstein Zaken, whose ability to transcribe long interview tapes and copy pages from dozens of books saved my neck (and other body parts) from my editor's chopping block.

I would be remiss if I did not thank Sean Forman, founder and gatekeeper of the enormously helpful website Baseball-almanac.com, for his generous reprint permission and the NMC company for its invaluable support in providing extra eyes for the tedious process of proofreading.

And finally, thank you so much to family and friends who put up with long absences that consumed weekends and holidays, not to mention every waking moment since the project began shortly after the 2009 All-Star Game.

Dan Schlossberg
April 2010

Foreword

Winning 300 games is one of the toughest feats in baseball; so many great pitchers never achieved it.

To reach 300 wins, a pitcher has to stay healthy. He has to be on a decent team. And he has to have tenacity, the ability to say, "I'm going to go out there and win that game."

I remember the great Warren Spahn quote: "When you go out there as a starting pitcher, 85% of the time, you have your best stuff. What's tough is the other 15%, when you have to bob and weave and make your way through it."

As an announcer, I was lucky enough to broadcast a game in which a great pitcher won his 300th. I was working for the St. Louis Cardinals on June 13, 2003, when Roger Clemens, pitching for the New York Yankees, got his 300th.

The preparation for an event like that is different. You have to do something special, much more than just giving the background of the pitcher. Vin Scully always taught me that the first inning should be dedicated to the starting pitcher. You tell as much as you can about that guy and then get into the flow of the game.

On that Friday night at Yankee Stadium, we talked about Roger and the impact he made, not just with the Red Sox, where he started, but all the way back to the University of Texas before he turned pro. It was a different and more comprehensive preparation for me.

What I remember most about that night is that Roger reached two milestones in one game: 300 wins and 4,000 strikeouts. Edgar Renteria, not easy to strike out in those days, was No. 4,000 and I thought he must have felt terrible to be that part of history. But years from now, when he looks back, he might be proud to be remembered as No. 4,000 just as Rickey Henderson will be remembered as strikeout victim No. 5,000 for Nolan Ryan.

It happened before a crowd that used to hate Roger when he was with the Red Sox, but that rooted for him once he wore Yankee pinstripes. They were as much of the story as Roger was. That generation had seen so much history in Yankee Stadium in the 20th century; but now, in the 21st century, it was Roger Clemens, an old enemy, who claimed a special night at Yankee Stadium.

Roger was the second pitcher to win his 300th in the old ballpark: Tom Seaver had done it eight years earlier while pitching for the Chicago White Sox. The Yankee fans understood history and actually rooted for Tom to win. I never thought a former Met would be accepted like that in the Bronx, but the fans were celebrating. They wanted to be able to say, "I was in the stands for something monumental."

As an announcer, you can't get caught up in what your team is doing. There are nights when the opposition just beats you. And there are those special nights when someone is pursuing a milestone.

Tony Gwynn flew his mom from Indiana to St. Louis to see his 3,000th hit, but he just couldn't get it. He may have been an eight-time batting champ, but the pressure just got to him. That tells you what it must be like for a pitcher on the brink of getting his 300th win.

There's a lot of pressure we don't know about. We don't know what it's like to wake up in the middle of the night thinking, "Omigosh, tomorrow's my start and I have to get my 300th."

That's why a lot of guys don't get it on the first try, or sometimes not even on their second, third, or fourth tries.

It would also be nice if the pitcher pursuing it could win his 300th for the team where he spent most of his career. But that rarely happens, partly because of free agency, but also because most 300-game winners move from team to team as they near the end of their careers.

With the exception of the Phillies' Steve Carlton, nine of the 10 living 300-game winners won their 300th while pitching for teams who employed them only briefly. I saw all 10 of those pitchers.

The pitching feat of the postwar era was Warren Spahn winning 363 games – more than any left-handed pitcher and more than any pitcher after World War II. Even though only a few of his Braves teams were champions (1948, 1957, 1958), Warren succeeded in an era when it was tough to win. There were more great players, divided among many fewer teams.

Phil Niekro, who joined the Milwaukee Braves just as Spahn was leaving, won by becoming the best pitcher ever who relied on a knuckleball. It was a great pitch that a lot of people couldn't hit or catch. And Phil could throw a first-pitch knuckleball strike and get a swing; he got lots of swings and misses. He won well over 300 games, mostly with really bad Braves teams.

Shortly after Niekro left, the Braves added Tom Glavine, another pitcher who didn't throw hard. He never had any fear of a hitter or fear of a ballpark. He may be the only pitcher ever to throw two complete-game shutouts at Coors Field in Denver. When Coors first opened, everybody was very dismissive of it, saying it would mess pitchers up. But Glavine said, "I'm not changing for the ballpark. I'm just going to pitch my game."

After Greg Maddux joined the Braves as a free agent in 1993, the Braves had a rotation headed by three future Hall of Famers. Both Glavine and Maddux won 300 games, and John Smoltz might have if he hadn't spent several seasons as a closer.

Another 300-game winner who pitched for the Braves was Gaylord Perry. I was in college in San Diego when he was pitching for the Padres. The turning point in his career had come in New York when he worked 10 scoreless innings of relief for the San Francisco Giants in a 23-inning game against the Mets. Jim Lang, who was then the host of *The Dating Game*, had a morning show for KSFO in San Francisco the next morning and had to leave New York early. He flew cross-country, against the headwinds, and when he landed, the game was on the radio. He thought it was a tape-delay, but it was live. The game was still going.

Don Sutton, now a Braves broadcaster, made his mark pitching for the Dodgers. To me, his intelligence and perfectionist makeup were ideal attributes to succeed at the major-league level. I remember when he pitched for the Brewers on the last day of the season and beat Jim

Palmer to put Milwaukee in the playoffs. I realized then just how good he was. That game personified his internal courage: he knew how big it was to him and to his team.

Nolan Ryan was a completely different kind of pitcher. He pitched in the majors for 27 years, a record for any player, by taking care of himself. Even after he threw a no-hitter, he'd ride his exercise bike after the game before addressing the media. What I remember about him is that he grunted, a terrifying sound for certain hitters. Late in his career, he'd check out the foul lines before the game. He'd walk down the third-base line and then walk down the first-base line. When a young player asked about Ryan's ritual, Carney Lansford, then with the A's, said, "What he just told you is that you're not going to be bunting on him." When Willie Wilson, Oakland's leadoff hitter, tried to bunt, the next pitch hit him in the leg and he was out for six weeks.

I never saw anybody more dominating than Nolan Ryan. He not only had the great fastball and curveball, but late in his career, he added a little bit of a split, a little change-up, and a little off-speed pitch. It was almost impossible to hit him no matter how old he was.

Ryan had more no-hitters (seven) and more strikeouts (5,714) than anyone, but never won a Cy Young Award, while Carlton, Maddux, and Clemens combined for 15 Cy Youngs without ever throwing a no-hitter. Randy Johnson, who won his 300th in 2009, did both: he won five Cy Youngs and threw two no-hitters, including a perfect game. Nobody liked to face The Big Unit.

I doubt if we'll ever have another 300-game winner. There's no way Jamie Moyer (258 wins) will get there, even if he pitches into his 50s, and Andy Pettitte (229), at 37, has to stay healthy. CC Sabathia took seven years to get to 100 victories, and Roy Halladay (148) has an outside chance, but I don't see Johann Santana (122) pitching that long.

Players are compensated so well now that they just don't hang around. Mike Mussina is a great example; he felt comfortable leaving with 270 wins. Money is a big factor for this generation of ballplayers.

You won't see guys pitching at age 47, as Jamie Moyer has. They'll retire to go spend time with their families.

In addition, the game has changed. It's a manager's game now, with all kinds of specialists for the late innings. The starters don't hang around that long. A pitcher used to be able to tell the manager he could pitch another inning. And most managers would let him.

There are very few complete games anymore and very few 20-game winners. The bullpens have taken over. That's just how the game has evolved.

Of the 24 members of the 300-win club, only a handful worked in the era of set-up men and closers. In fact, only half spent the better part of their careers after World War II.

That makes the 300 Club a vanishing breed, the last vestige of baseball as it was played through the first half of the 20th century.

Make no mistake: The men who won 300 did something rare and extraordinary. And my friend Dan Schlossberg did something rare and extraordinary, too: He paints vivid portraits, through detailed research and exclusive interviews, of a fraternity whose doors may be closed forever.

WAYNE HAGIN
Flushing, New York
September 23, 2009

Wayne Hagin has worked behind a big-league microphone for the A's, Giants, White Sox, Rockies, and Cardinals before joining the Mets radio team in 2008.

Introduction

To win 300 games, a pitcher needs 20 seasons of 15 wins or 15 seasons of 20 wins. To put it mildly, that is a Herculean task.

Consider the long list of accomplished athletes who fell short. Bob Feller, one of the best pitchers of any era, finished at 266 because he lost four prime years while serving in the U.S. Navy during World War II. Robin Roberts, whose career overlapped Feller's, fell 14 wins short. Fellow Hall of Famers Bob Gibson, Jim Palmer, and Ferguson Jenkins aren't on the list, either. Nor are Bert Blyleven, Tommy John, or Jim Kaat, all of whom were fewer than 20 wins away.

In fact, only 17 pitchers from baseball's modern era, which began with the creation of the current two-league structure in 1901, were able to win 300. Add six men who worked exclusively in the 19th century plus Cy Young, whose career spanned the century's turn, and the list grows to 24 – still just a tiny fraction of all the men who have stood on a major-league pitching mound.

Randy Johnson, the most recent man to gain admission the club, got his 300th win on June 4, 2009. He joined Greg Maddux, Tom Glavine, and Roger Clemens as 300-game winners of recent vintage, all joining the group in the 21st century.

Whether anyone else will join them is questionable at best. Mike Mussina retired with 270 victories after the 2008 season and Andy Pettitte, his teammate with the New York Yankees, is a long shot because of his age. Jamie Moyer, the oldest man in the majors in 2009, is even less likely to join the elite fraternity of 300-game winners.

Such talents as CC Sabathia, Roy Halladay, and Johann Santana all face enormous obstacles. All work in five-man pitching rotations, rather than four, and work in an era when starters seldom finish games. With at least four days between starts, and with managers juggling relief pitchers over the final innings, even the best starters seldom win 20 games in a season, with 2009 a prime example: Adam Wainwright and CC Sabathia led the majors with 19 wins.

In addition, pitchers are paid so well for their work that few have the incentive to remain active long enough to reach 300 wins.

Before the advent of free agency in 1976, things were different: Pitchers working for one-year contracts often pitched through pain for fear of losing their jobs. They also took pride in going all the way – completing games they started.

The first 300-game winners finished their starts as routinely as rolling out of bed. Pitching rules changed almost annually and pitching staffs, for the most part, did not exist. That meant every pitcher had to be a workhorse, not only finishing every game he started but working almost every day.

Although the National League celebrated its debut season in 1876, Pitchers were obliged to throw underhand (submarine style) until 1881 and faced numerous other restrictions that remained in force until 1884. Batters could even "order" their own pitches well into the 1880s and runners were allowed to interfere with gloveless fielders trying to make plays.

The distance from pitcher to batter was only 45 feet until 1881, and then 50 feet before settling at the present 60'6" in 1893 when a surveyor misread the mandated "0" for a "6." Proximity to home plate allowed pitchers to work more because they didn't have to throw the ball as far. It also allowed them to last longer.

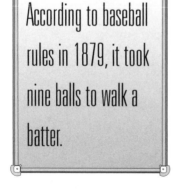

According to baseball rules in 1879, it took nine balls to walk a batter.

According to BaseballLibrary.com, it took nine balls to walk a batter in 1879, eight in 1880, seven in 1881, six in 1884, five in 1886, and finally the present-day four in 1889. Two experimental rules, valid in 1887 only, forced pitchers to throw four strikes for a strikeout and awarded batters with hits when they walked.

Restrictions on a pitcher's motion were lifted in 1884 but the pitching rubber did not appear until 1893, when it replaced the old pitcher's box. The rubber was enlarged to its present size of 24" x 6" in 1895, the first year a batter was charged with a strike on a foul tip.

The first balk rule, aimed at protecting baserunners, appeared in 1898 but was amended a year later.

Pitchers hardly had time to learn one rule when another surfaced. But they still had enormous advantages over batters, especially during the Dead Ball Era that lasted the first two decades of the 20th century. The dead ball, plus a permissive attitude that allowed pitchers to apply saliva or other substances that made balls drop, yielded a golden age of pitching when 30-win seasons were routine.

All that changed with the advent of the lively ball in 1920, when owners suffering from the Black Sox Scandal thought Babe Ruth and other sluggers would bring a box office bonanza. Nobody asked permission from the pitchers.

Schedules changed, too, with the National League increasing from 63 games in 1876, to 84 in 1880, to 98 in 1882, to 134 in 1887, to 154 in 1904, and to 162 in 1962. With each increase, more pitching help was needed (the original National League teams of 1876 carried only two pitchers among the 10 or 11 players on their rosters).

The first pitchers threw as many as 600 innings per year, with Will White falling just 20 innings short of 700 in 1879. Neither he nor Old Hoss Radbourn, who won a record 60 games five years later, had a pitching coach or a pitch count.

Neither did Matt Kilroy, who struck out 513 hitters in 583 innings in 1886 while pitching in the American Association, which was then a major league.

Just to show how different the game was then, starting pitchers completed 97.8 percent of the games they started from 1885-88. But they were often victimized by fielders who either wore no gloves or didn't have enough protection. The first padded catcher's mitt appeared in 1884, the same year Jack Clements wore a secret chest protector, but the first shin guards did not show up until 1907. In fact, most position players did not use gloves until 1893.

Ten years later, the pitcher's mound was legalized, with a maximum height restriction of 15 inches. At the same time, the strike zone was officially described as between the batter's shoulders and knees.

Both rules have changed many times since – making it even more difficult to compare 300-game winners across the history of baseball.

Most historians agree, however, that the Golden Age of Pitching occurred from 1903-20, when Cy Young, Walter Johnson, Grover Cleveland Alexander, and Christy Mathewson all enjoyed their peak seasons.

The golden age of research occurred much later, with the advent of the Internet and the establishment of the Society for American Baseball Research (SABR). As a result, there is disagreement over the lifetime win totals of several 300-game winners, including Johnson, and over the single-season record for wins held by Radbourn. Some sources say 59, while others say 60.

There is even disagreement over the exact dates early pitchers notched their 300th victories, though all sources agree on the years. In one case, three different games were cited for the same pitcher's 300th win.

To resolve conflicts, this author chose to use material supplied by SABR sources or members, as well as such recognized historians as Rich Westcott.

One thing is certain: There were 24 pitchers who won 300 games and a half-dozen who came close. The pages that follow tell how they got there.

DAN SCHLOSSBERG
Fair Lawn, New Jersey
November 23, 2009

First to 300

Pud Galvin – 361 wins

Tim Keefe – 342 wins

Mickey Welch – 307 wins

Long before the advent of the airplane, radio, or women's suffrage, a handful of young men pitched well enough and often enough to win 300 games in the major leagues.

There was no bullpen phone in the earliest days of baseball, not only because there was no bullpen, but also because there was no telephone. Never mind the lack of trainers, coaches, or managers who liked to manipulate pitchers like pawns on a chessboard.

Nineteenth century rules were different too – for the game and for the individuals who played it. Even after the founding of the National League in 1876, pitching regulations changed often. Pitchers had to face batters and were banned from throwing overhand until 1884. In addition, the distance from home plate to the pitcher's box increased from 45 feet to 50 feet before settling at the modern measurement of 60'6" in 1893.

Those were the conditions that greeted **James Galvin**, a compact right-hander born three years before the Civil War began.

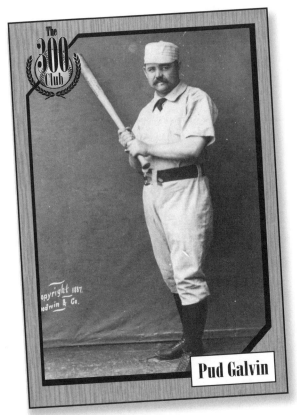

Photo courtesy of National
Baseball Hall of Fame Library

Cooperstown, N.Y.

Pud Galvin

Galvin had three claims to fame:

☞ He was "Walter Johnson" before the real Walter Johnson, a mild-mannered pitcher whose fastball had such frightening velocity that he was nicknamed for a locomotive.

☞ He was also called "Pud," shortened from pudding, the quivering confection that hitters who faced him felt was in their stomachs.

☞ He was the first pitcher to win 300 games.

Galvin pitched only 14 seasons, but still managed to win 361 games, more than any 19th century pitcher, thanks to a regimen that required him to pitch virtually all of his team's games – or so it seemed to both the pitcher and the teams who faced him.

Known for his hard fastball, baffling changeup, and proficient pickoff move, Galvin also helped himself with his fielding ability, even though players of his era wore minimal, if any, protection on their hands.

Galvin earned his nickname because of his reputation for turning opposing hitters into pudding. He was also called the "Little Steam Engine," a forerunner of Walter Johnson's "Big Train" moniker, and "Gentleman Jeems," for his mild-mannered disposition. He was neither an umpire baiter on the field nor a drinker off it.

An "illusionist" who once picked off all three batters he walked in an inning, Galvin impressed rival catcher Buck Ewing. "If I had Galvin to catch," he said, "no one would ever steal a base on me. That fellow keeps 'em glued to the base and also has the best control of any pitcher in the league."

Though he used his curve only as an occasional backup to his high-velocity heat, Galvin's rivals named it the "cannonball curve" because of his off-season occupation as a blacksmith.

Even for a small man, he had the brawn of a blacksmith. On May 2, 1877, Galvin yielded only one hit, and delivered the game's lone run with an eighth-inning home run that actually cleared the fence – a prodigious feat, especially for a pitcher.

He pitched a pair of no-hitters and threw 57 shutouts en route to a career total of 361 wins.

Although some sources list June 4, 1888, as the date of his 300th win, most agree that Galvin became the first man to reach 300 on October 5, 1888, when he stopped the Washington Nationals, 5-1, on a four-hitter. The game took only 90 minutes to play, primarily because both pitchers went the distance and combined for only one walk.

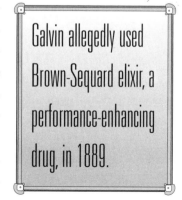

Galvin allegedly used Brown-Sequard elixir, a performance-enhancing drug, in 1889.

Because teams of the 19th century changed cities and leagues even more often than official baseball changed pitching rules, Galvin's career path seems confusing to casual observers.

At the age of 18 in 1875, he pitched briefly for the St. Louis Brown

Stockings in the short-lived National Association, the first major league. When the league folded, Galvin shifted to the St. Louis Red Stockings, an independent club, for whom he promptly pitched two no-hitters, including a perfect game. That performance attracted the attention of Allegheny, a new entry in the International Association, the first minor league. While working for that club, the first professional team in Pittsburgh's history, Galvin once pitched four shutouts in 19 days.

To support his growing family, the father of 11 moved again in 1878, signing with the Buffalo Bisons, another team in the International Association.

A year later, when Buffalo joined the three-year-old National League, he was ready. Galvin went 37-27, worked 593 innings, and completed 65 of his 66 starts during his team's 78-game schedule. Those statistics would have made him Rookie of the Year if the award had existed at that time.

With one-year contracts in vogue at the time, Buffalo made Galvin an offer to retain his services. But the pitcher rejected it and jumped across country to San Francisco of the California League. When the pitcher who had replaced him struggled in Buffalo, team management wanted him back so desperately that it enlisted his wife in the persuasion process. Galvin consented, but his new employers didn't, refusing to release him. He left anyway, hopping an eastbound train that left him 23 miles short of the Nevada state line with California police in hot pursuit. He covered the rest of the distance on foot, burning his feet on the desert sand, but received a huge welcome when he finally shuffled back to Buffalo.

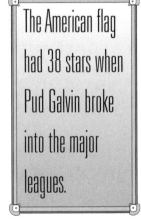

The American flag had 38 stars when Pud Galvin broke into the major leagues.

Back in time to work 58 games in 1880, the pitcher with the handlebar moustache was just getting warm, winning 28 times in both 1881 and 1882. Then, proving durability beyond description, he led the 1883 National League with 75 starts, 72 complete games, and 656 $1/3$ innings pitched!

Galvin led the league in games, starts, complete games, innings, and shutouts but not in victories – Old Hoss Radbourn, with 60, and Charlie Buffington, with 48, won more.

In his peak years of 1883 and 1884, Galvin won 92 games – 46 in each season – and pitched 17 shutouts. Three of those shutouts, including a no-hitter, came against Detroit between August 2 and August 8, 1884. That was also the year Galvin stopped two streaks simultaneously: 20 wins by Providence and 18 straight by Radbourn, who would win 60 that summer.

The pitcher also befriended a local lawman named Grover Cleveland, a future president whose name would be given to a future 300-game winner (Grover Cleveland Alexander). Years later, when a delegation of ballplayers visited the White House, Cleveland would ask, "How's my friend Jimmy Galvin?"

Galvin's time in Buffalo included both of his no-hitters, in 1880 and 1884, and an 1882 doubleheader in which he started and won both games. But that was easy duty for a pitcher who once pitched 22 consecutive games and completed all of them.

Galvin stayed with Buffalo until 1885, the city's last as a National League franchise. After getting off to a bad start as both a pitcher (13-19) and a manager (7-17), he was sold to Allegheny of the American Association, then a major league, for $2,500. He won 29 games in 1886, teaming with Cannonball Morris, who won 41 of his own, in a potent 1-2 punch that helped the team finish second.

Galvin stayed with the club when it joined the National League in 1887 and, except for his one-year switch to the Pittsburgh Burghers of the Players League in 1890, was still there after it became the Pittsburgh Pirates (a name that came about allegedly because the organization signed players who belonged to other teams).

During his last three seasons, Galvin had four matchups with Tim Keefe, the second pitcher to reach 300 wins. Galvin won the first, 8-2, and one of the last three. After their last duel, on July 21, 1892, no other active 300-game winners met until Don Sutton faced Phil Niekro in 1986.

The only 300-game winner never to pitch from the modern pitching distance, Galvin retired among the lifetime leaders in wins, losses, innings pitched, and complete games. Although he won at least 20 games in 10 seasons and was the first major-leaguer with 50 shutouts, he never pitched for a team that finished first. Nor did he ever lead his league in any categories of the pitching Triple Crown – wins, strikeouts, or earned run average.

Box Score of 300th Win

Galvin Box Score
Pittsburgh Alleghenys 5, Washington Nationals 1

Game played on Friday, October 5, 1888

Pittsburgh	ab	r	h	Washington	ab	r	h
Miller c	4	1	0	Hoy cf	4	0	1
McShannic 3b	4	0	0	Myers 2b	4	0	1
Smith 2b	4	0	0	Wilmot	4	0	0
Coleman 1b	4	1	1	O'Brien 1b	4	0	0
Kuehne ss	4	0	1	Mack c	4	1	0
Fields, lf	4	2	1	Dailey rf	3	0	0
Maul rf	4	0	1	Donnelly 3b	4	0	1
Nichols cf	3	1	0	Shoch ss	3	0	0
Galvin p	4	0	0	Haddock p	3	0	1
Totals	35	5	4	Totals	33	1	4

Pittsburgh	0	2	0	0	0	0	0	2	1	–	5
Washington	0	1	0	0	0	0	0	0	0	–	1

Pittsburgh	IP	H	R	ER	BB	SO
Galvin (W)	9	4	1	0	0	1

Washington	IP	H	R	ER	BB	SO
Haddock (L)	9	4	5	1	1	0

DP–Pittsburgh 2. **E**-McShannick 2, Smith 3, Myers 2, Wilmot 1, O'Brien 1, Donnelly 1, Shoch 3, Haddock1. **3B**-Coleman, Kuehne, Fields, Maul. T-1:30

Even on those rare days when he wasn't pitching, Galvin found a way to get into the lineup. He played 51 games in the outfield and even appeared at shortstop twice. He wasn't there for his bat – he

Career Statistics

GALVIN, Pud	James Francis "Pud, Gentle Jeems, The Little Steam Engine" Galvin b: 12/25/1856, St. Louis MO D: 3/7/1902, Pittsburgh PA BR/TR, 5'8", 190 lbs. Debut: 5/22/1875; HOF: 1965														
YEAR	TM-L	W	L	PCT	G	GS	CG	SH	SV	IP	H	R	HR	SO	ERA
1875	StL-n	4	2	0.667	8	7	7	1	1	62	53	...	0	7	1.16
1879	Buf-N	37	27	0.578	66	66	65	6	0	593	585	299	3	136	2.28
1880	Buf-N	20	35	0.364	58	54	46	5	0	458	528	281	5	128	2.71
1881	Buf-N	28	24	0.538	56	53	48	5	0	474	546	250	4	136	2.37
1882	Buf-N	28	23	0.549	52	51	48	3	0	445	476	255	8	162	3.17
1883	Buf-N	46	29	0.613	76	75	72	5	0	656	676	367	9	279	2.72
1884	Buf-N	46	22	0.676	72	72	71	12	0	636	566	254	23	369	1.99
1885	Buf-N	13	19	0.406	33	32	31	3	1	284	356	204	8	93	4.09
	Pit-a	3	7	0.300	11	11	9	0	0	88	97	64	2	27	3.67
1886	Plt-a	29	21	0.580	50	50	49	2	0	434	457	229	3	72	2.67
1887	Pit-N	28	21	0.571	49	48	47	2	0	440	557	259	12	76	3.29
1888	Pit-N	23	25	0.479	50	50	49	6	0	437	446	190	9	107	2.63
1889	Pit-N	23	16	0.590	41	40	38	4	0	341	392	230	19	77	4.17
1890	Pit-P	12	13	0.480	26	25	23	1	0	217	275	192	3	35	4.35
1891	Pit-N	15	14	0.517	33	30	23	2	0	246	256	143	10	46	2.88
1892	Pit-N	5	6	0.455	12	12	10	0	0	96	104	51	0	29	2.63
	StL-N	5	6	0.455	12	12	10	0	0	92	102	47	4	27	3.23
	Year	10	12	0.455	24	24	20	0	0	188	206	98	4	56	2.92
TOTAL	14	361	308	0.540	697	681	639	56	1	5941	6419	3315	122	1799	2.87

batted only .202 lifetime – but because he was well-liked and considered both a gate attraction and a good-luck charm.

Unfortunately, his luck didn't last forever. Plagued by excess weight, a bad finger, and a leg injury suffered in a collision with superstar Cap Anson, Galvin couldn't continue after 1892, though he tried resurrecting his career for Buffalo, then a minor-league team. After an unsuccessful one-year stint as a National League umpire, he spent his retirement years running a saloon in Pittsburgh and recounting tales of his storied career.

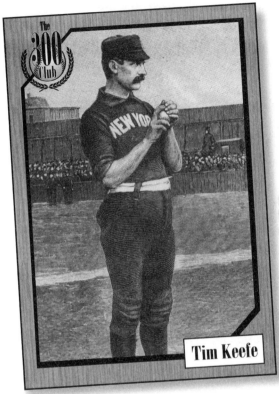

Photo courtesy of National Baseball Hall of Fame Library Cooperstown, N.Y.

Tim Keefe

Although Galvin won more games than any pitcher who worked exclusively in the 19th century, **Tim Keefe** came close.

From 1880, when he began his big-league career at age 22 in Troy, New York, through 1893, when he finished it with Philadelphia of the National League, he racked up 342 wins, placing him in the game's all-time Top Ten.

Like Galvin, he was small in stature (5'10" and 185 pounds), but tall in talent. He also carried a reputation as a gentleman respected by rivals as well as teammates.

The father of a pitch known today as the change of pace, Keefe catapulted to 300 wins by working and winning often. In 1883, while going 41-27 in his fourth major-league season, he completed all 68 of his starts, striking out 359 men while working 615 innings. All of those figures were the best of his 14-year career.

Although Keefe was raised not far from Harvard yard in Cambridge, Massachusetts, his father, Patrick, had roots in the South. A builder by trade, Patrick was an Irish immigrant who was jailed for three years after refusing conscription into the Confederate Army during the Civil War. Two brothers were killed fighting for the North while Patrick was forced into forging bullets for the South.

Tim Keefe would later be throwing bullets with a baseball. Intrigued by the game at age 9, he overcame the objections of his parents – who wanted him to pursue something more substantial – and soon displayed unusual versatility. He played both infield corners, as well as shortstop and center field, before turning to pitching in his first professional season, in Utica, New York. A strong hitter, Keefe later played some third base in the majors.

A teenaged sandlot standout who later played for semipro and minor-league clubs, Keefe made his big-league debut in 1880, the same debut season as future 300-game winners Mickey Welch and Old Hoss Radbourn. Although he had a losing record (35-53) during his three years with the hapless Troy Haymakers (also called Trojans), Keefe did manage to win both ends of a doubleheader on July 4, 1883. He yielded only three hits, one in the morning and two in the afternoon.

Plagued by bad weather, poor crowds, and a small population base, the Troy franchise fizzled, yielding its spot in 1883 to the team that later became the New York Giants. Because tobacco merchant John Day owned New York teams in both the National League and the American Association, which was also a major league at the time, Troy's players were divided between the two clubs.

Keefe went to the AA team, known as the Metropolitans, and promptly pitched them to the league title. During an 1884 postseason series against Providence, where Old Hoss Radbourn was en route to 300 wins, Keefe lost two games to Radbourn and umpired a third.

After watching the Metropolitans lose the series, Day decided to boost the more established Giants by reassigning Keefe to the National League franchise. The owner's reasoning was rational: since National League clubs charged 50 cents admission per game, but

American Association teams charged half of that, he would make more money if Keefe pitched as well for the Gothams as he did for the Mets.

It was a move made in heaven for Keefe, who was reunited with Welch, his former Troy teammate. It was also a move made in heaven for manager Jim Mutrie, who not only accompanied Keefe but openly admired a spectacular defensive play by his team. When he shouted, "My Giants! My Giants!" a sportswriter overheard him and a new team nickname was born.

He could have called the team the Twins: In a five-year stretch that started in 1885, the Keefe-Welch tandem averaged 400+ innings each per year and won 325 games (172 for Keefe and 153 for Welch). The game's first great pitching tandem, they also pitched the Giants to pennants in 1888 and 1889.

Keefe was well-paid for the time (his $4,500 salary in 1889 topped the Giants' payroll), but he felt sorry for fellow players who weren't. He also was the brother-in-law of John Montgomery Ward, not only a colleague, but also the founder of the Brotherhood of Professional Baseball Players. Like Galvin, Keefe was quick to join Ward when he broke with the National League and American Association to found the Players League of 1890 – but just as quick to return to the established National League after the one-year experiment fell apart. The settlement resulted in the demise of the AA and the expansion of the National League to 12 teams, a number it would reach again 77 years later.

Unconcerned with changes in league size or rules, Keefe managed to pitch for New York clubs in three different leagues – enabling him to appear in 47 ballparks – and lead his league in wins, strikeouts, and complete games twice each. During the five-year period that began in 1883, the workhorse right-hander *never* yielded to a relief pitcher. In order, his total of complete games was 68, 58, 46, 64, and 56.

The first pitcher to strike out 2,000 hitters, Keefe won the most games of his 14-year career when he went 46-20 in 1886, but he posted his best winning percentage, a league-leading .745, with a 35-12 mark two years later. That same season, he won the Triple Crown of pitching, leading the league in wins, strikeouts, and earned run average. He also won 19 games in a row, a streak that stood for 24 years. Keefe led his league in lowest opponents' batting average six times, twice finishing below .200.

Keefe suffered arm problems only in his last season. He worked 4,103 innings in his first nine years – putting him well on the road to 300 wins.

He reached that plateau in his 10th year, on June 4, 1890, with a 9-4 win over the Boston Reds, a Players League rival. Though he returned to the Giants for eight games in 1891, Keefe spent most of his last three seasons in Philadelphia. His last hurrah as a player came in 1892, when he went 19-16 and finished 31 of his 38 starts.

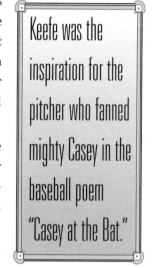

Keefe was the inspiration for the pitcher who fanned mighty Casey in the baseball poem "Casey at the Bat."

The soft-spoken star was so gentle that he once suffered a nervous breakdown after inadvertently beaning a batter with a fastball. He overcame that incident, which occurred in 1887, to recapture his form.

Keefe showed talents beyond pitching. The owner of his own sporting goods firm, he designed and sold the ball used by the Players League and the white-on-black shirts worn by the Giants when they faced the St. Louis Browns in a forerunner of the World Series in 1888 (Keefe won four of the 10 games played). He also learned shorthand, figuring the skill could make him a more valuable employee as a civilian.

A hero as a player, Keefe failed to receive the same adulation as an umpire. After an especially difficult afternoon with irate fans, who pelted him with debris and epithets, Keefe quit as an umpire after three seasons. Longing for quieter pursuits, he found them as a realtor and as a college baseball coach at Princeton, Harvard, and Tufts.

Box Score of 300th Win

**Keefe Box Score
New York Giants 9, Boston Reds 4**

Game played on Wednesday, June 4, 1890

Boston	ab	r	h	New York	ab	r	h
Brown cf	5	0	1	Gore cf	4	3	3
H. Richardson lf	5	0	1	Ewing c	4	3	2
Stovey rf	4	1	1	Connor 1b	3	0	1
Nash 3b	3	1	0	O'Rourke rf	5	0	1
Brouthers 1b	3	0	0	D. Richardson 2b	4	1	1
Murphy c	4	1	1	Slattery lf	5	0	2
Irwin ss	3	1	1	Shannon ss	5	1	2
Quinn 2b	4	0	2	Hatfield 3b	5	1	2
Madden p	1	0	0	Keefe p	5	0	0
Gumbert p	3	0	1	Totals	40	9	14
Totals	35	4	8				

Boston	0	0	0		1	3	0		0	0	0	–	4
New York	3	0	1		0	1	3		0	1	X	–	9

DP–Boston. E-Brouthers, Murphy 2, Irwink, Madden 2, Bumbert 3, Shannon 1, Keefe 4. **2B**-Gore 2, Shannon Hatfield, Irwin. **3B**-Shannon, Gumbert. **SB**-Stovey, Shannon, D Richardson. Earned Runs –Boston 1, New York 3. Base on Balls-Madden 2, Gumbert 3, Keefe 2. Strikeouts-Madden 1, Gumbert 1, Keefe 7. WP-Keefe.. T-2:05.

Career Statistics

KEEFE, Tim	Timothy John "Smiling Tim, Sir Timothy" Keefe; B: 1/1/1857, Cambridge, MA; D: 4/23/1933, Cambridge, MA; BR/TR, 5'10.5"/185 lbs.; Debut: 8/6/1880; HOF 1964

YEAR	TM-L	W	L	PCT	G	GS	CG	SH	SV	IP	H	R	HR	SO	ERA
1880	Tor-N	6	6	0.500	12	12	12	0	0	105	68	27	0	39	0.86
1881	Tor-N	18	27	0.400	45	45	45	4	0	403	434	243	4	103	3.24
1882	Tor-N	17	26	0.395	43	42	41	1	0	376	367	221	4	111	2.49
1883	NY-a	41	27	0.603	68	68	68	5	0	619	488	244	6	359	2.41
1884	NY-a	37	17	0.685	58	58	56	4	0	483	380	196	5	334	2.25
1885	NY-N	32	13	0.711	46	46	45	7	0	400	300	154	6	227	1.58
1886	NY-N	42	20	0.677	64	64	62	2	0	535	479	250	9	297	2.56
1887	NY-N	35	19	0.648	56	56	54	2	0	476	536	260	11	189	3.12
1888	NY-N	35	12	0.745	51	51	48	8	0	434	317	140	5	335	1.74
1889	NY-N	28	13	0.683	47	45	39	3	1	364	319	212	9	225	3.31
1890	NY-N	17	11	0.607	30	30	23	1	0	229	225	137	6	89	3.38
1891	NY-N	2	5	0.286	8	7	4	0	0	55	70	57	1	30	5.24
	Phi-N	3	6	0.333	11	10	9	0	1	78	82	55	2	34	3.91
	Year	5	11	0.313	19	17	13	0	1	133	152	112	3	64	4.46
1892	Phi-N	19	16	0.543	39	38	31	2	0	313	279	142	4	136	2.36
1893	Phi-N	10	7	0.588	22	22	17	0	0	178	202	131	3	56	4.40
TOTAL	14	342	225	0.603	600	594	554	39	2	5049	4546	2469	75	2564	2.62

Mickey Welch

Photo courtesy of National
Baseball Hall of Fame Library
Cooperstown, N.Y.

Mickey Welch and Keefe were the perfect pair personally as well as professionally. The man called "Smilin' Mickey" because of his cheery disposition disdained drinking, smoking, swearing, and even the customary wearing of facial hair by men of the Victorian era.

Welch, who stood only 5'8", threw a fastball, but used it mostly for show. He was a finesse pitcher, tantalizing batters by changing speeds and mixing a variety of breaking pitches. "I had to use my head," he once said, explaining his philosophy of pitching.

Although he started his career with Keefe in Troy, Welch didn't win quite as often. When he did win, though, he won in huge numbers: 39-21 in 1884, 44-11 in 1885, and 33-22 in 1886.

Welch completed 525 of 549 starts, most of them for the New York Giants – before and after they had that nickname. After spending his first three years in Troy, Welch wandered south when the franchise shifted to New York and stayed there 10 seasons before retiring.

The two New York teams shared the Polo Grounds, with a canvas fence separating the two diamonds. Fans in the upper bleachers could watch both games and players could hit balls from one field to the other.

It was a strange arrangement, but it didn't seem to wipe the smile off the face of Welch. The right-hander liked to laugh often. He was being facetious when he once cited beer as the source of his pitching prowess.

Welch, who played sandlot ball in his native Brooklyn, wallowed through three years of minor-league ball before breaking into the big leagues with Troy.

A workhorse who topped 400 innings six times, Welch worried that overuse would burn him out too quickly. So he negotiated a contract clause that prevented the Giants from pitching him in consecutive games. The manager responded by playing Welch in the outfield on his "off-days."

Though plagued by periods of wildness (he led the National League in walks three times), Welch still pitched well enough and often enough to become the third 300-game winner in baseball history. On July 28, 1890, he beat Pittsburgh, 4-2, with a five-hitter for his 15th win of the season. Welch, who once pitched 105 consecutive complete games, went all the way that afternoon.

Welch picked up two of his 307 wins on his birthday, July 4, in 1881. The Independence Day baby bested Buffalo twice, 6-0 and 6-2, in a true test of his arm. Three years later, he became the only pitcher in baseball history to strike out the first nine men he faced in a game. Tom Seaver, a future 300-game winner, became the first major-leaguer with 10 straight strikeouts in 1970. But even he didn't strike out the first nine batters of the game.

Welch won at least 20 games in a season nine times, seven of them in succession. He won 17 straight in 1885, when he and Keefe combined for 76 wins, and helped the Giants to postseason series wins in both 1888 (against St. Louis of the American Association) and 1889 (against Brooklyn).

Welch helped himself with his bat, topping .200 in his first eight seasons, including a .287 mark as a rookie. He lashed 92 doubles among his 492 hits.

Welch worked the first game for the home team in the original Polo Grounds, then located north of Central Park, and showed loyalty to the Giants (who paid him a handsome $4,000) by refusing to follow the exodus to the Players League – even though he was a supporter of the fledgling union that sparked the revolt.

An injury to regular catcher Buck Ewing might have shortened the pitcher's career. Unable to adjust to Ewing's replacement, Welch struggled so mightily in 1891 that he wound up with a 5-9 record. New manager Pat Powers let him go after one unsuccessful start in 1892. He went back to Troy, but could not recapture his youth.

Welch worked as steward of the Elks Club in Holyoke, Massachusetts, before returning to New York as a security guard for the Giants during the John McGraw era. He outlasted the Hall of Fame manager, keeping his job as gatekeeper even after the start of World War II.

Like Galvin and Keefe, Welch was elected to the Hall of Fame by the Veterans Committee. Just as he was the last of the three to win 300, he was the last of the three picked for Cooperstown. Keefe went in first, in 1964, followed by Galvin in 1965, and Welch in 1973.

Box Score of 300th Win

Welch Box Score
New York Giants 4, Pittsburgh Infants 2
Game played on Saturday, July 28, 1890

New York	ab	r	h		Pittsburgh	ab	r	h
Tiernan cf	3	1	2		Decker c	4	0	1
Hornung 1b	4	0	0		Miller 3b	3	1	1
Bassett 2b	4	0	0		Laroque 2b	4	0	0
3Burkett cf	3	1	1		Hecker 1b	4	1	1
Glasscock ss	4	1	2		Berger rf	4	0	1
Denny 3b	4	1	3		Osborne lf	4	0	0
Henry lf	3	0	1		Sales ss	3	0	1
Clark c	3	0	1		Wilson cf	2	0	0
Welch p	3	0	0		Baker p	2	0	0
Totals	31	4	10		Totals	30	2	5

New York	1	0	0		0	0	3		0	0	0	–	4
Pittsburgh	2	0	0		0	0	0		0	0	0	–	2

New York	IP	H	R	ER	BB	SO
Welch (W)	9	5	2	2	2	3

Pittsburgh	IP	H	R	ER	BB	SO
Baker (L)	9	10	4	2	2	1

DP-Pittsburgh. **E**-Hornung, Welch 3, Decker, Baker 2. **2B**-Hecker. **3B**-Tiernan. **SB**-Miller. **PB**-Decker. **HBP**-Wilson (by Welchs). T-2:00

Career Statistics

WELCH, Mickey	Michael Francis "Smiling Mickey" Welch; B: 7/4/1859, Brooklyn, NY; D: 7/30/1941, Concord, NH; BR/TR, 5'8"/160 lbs.; Debut: 5/1/1880; HOF 1973

YEAR	TM-L	W	L	PCT	G	GS	CG	SH	SV	IP	H	R	HR	SO	ERA
1880	Tro-N	34	30	0.531	65	64	64	4	0	574	575	321	7	123	2.54
1881	Tro-N	21	18	0.538	40	40	40	4	0	368	371	186	7	104	2.67
1882	Tro-N	14	16	0.467	33	33	30	5	0	281	334	221	7	53	3.46
1883	NY-N	25	23	0.521	54	52	46	4	0	426	431	271	11	144	2.73
1884	NY-N	39	21	0.650	65	65	62	4	0	557	528	275	12	345	2.50
1885	NY-N	44	11	0.800	56	55	55	7	1	492	372	170	4	258	1.66
1886	NY-N	33	22	0.600	59	59	56	1	0	500	514	279	13	272	2.99
1887	NY-N	22	15	0.595	41	40	39	2	0	346	430	191	7	115	3.36
1888	NY-N	26	19	0.578	47	47	47	5	0	425	328	156	12	167	1.93
1889	NY-N	27	12	0.692	45	41	39	3	2	375	340	196	14	125	3.02
1890	NY-N	17	14	0.548	37	37	33	2	0	292	268	145	5	97	2.99
1891	NY-N	5	9	0.357	22	15	14	0	1	160	177	136	7	46	4.28
1892	NY-N	0	0	...	1	1	0	0	0	5	11	9	0	1	14.40
TOTAL		13 307	210	0.594	565	549	525	41	4	4802	4679	2556	106	1850	2.71

Early Workhorses

Kid Nichols – 361 wins

John Clarkson – 328 wins

Old Hoss Radbourn – 309 wins

Because he was the best pitcher of the 1890s, **Kid Nichols** was the youngest man to reach 300 wins. It was after his 30th birthday – and the turn of the 20th century – that Nichols achieved the milestone on July 7, 1900. He gave up a dozen hits but no earned runs in the game, an 11-4 victory for the Boston Beaneaters over the Chicago Orphans (the Boston Braves and Chicago Cubs nicknames were introduced a few years later).

With 20 wins in every year of the 1890s, Nichols dominated the decade more than any other pitcher en route to a career victory total of 361. As a result, the Beaneaters won three pennants in his first four seasons and five titles during his nine-year tenure.

Neither Cy Young nor Amos Rusie, the other most prominent pitchers of the period, pitched for a single championship team, let alone five of them.

But Nichols was different. Armed with little more than a live fastball and uncanny control, he did something during the 1890s unequalled even by the five pitchers ahead of him on the career victories list: he won at least 30 games seven times in eight seasons from 1891-97. Neither Young nor Walter Johnson, the only pitchers with

Photo courtesy of National Baseball Hall of Fame Library Cooperstown, N.Y.

Kid Nichols

400 wins, nor Christy Mathewson, Grover Cleveland Alexander, Warren Spahn, or Pud Galvin, came close.

The 60-win season of Old Hoss Radbourn was old news by the time Nichols reached the majors with the 1890 Boston Beaneaters. But the philosophy of riding the arm of a star pitcher was prevalent throughout the game.

As a result, Nichols pitched at least 400 innings in each of first five seasons, all with Boston, then topped 300 innings for the next five seasons. He finished what he started, completing 532 of his 562 career starts and tossing 48 shutouts.

Nichols was only a kid when he started pitching. After winning praise for his work with the Blue Avenue Club, an amateur club in Kansas City, he joined the local Western League team in 1887 and won 21 games. He split the next year between Kansas City and Memphis, then hooked on with Omaha of the Western Association in 1889.

When Frank Selee, his manager there, left for Boston, he invited Nichols, who was coming off a 36-12 season. Selee convinced Boston to offer $3,000 for the 19-year-old pitching prodigy. The offer was accepted.

Working from a no-windup delivery that proved particularly difficult for right-handed hitters, Nichols rejected persistent efforts to alter his style. "It's a useless exertion of the arm that interferes with control of the ball," he said. "As far as confusing the batter, it doesn't always work."

Nichols confused batters without a windup or any other deception. A 30-game winner in his second year, he later struck out 15 batters in a 17-inning game, pitched two complete games on the same day, and won 11 games by 1-0 scores. He never threw a no-hitter, but he came close.

In his rookie year of 1890, Nichols battled Amos Rusie for 13 innings of a scoreless tie before yielding a home run to Mike Tiernan at New York's Polo Grounds. Seven years later, his 31-11 mark made the difference as Boston edged Baltimore by two games in the National League pennant chase.

"We were required to work 40 or 50 full games in a season," said Nichols. Although he had fewer strikeouts and a higher earned run average when the pitching distance increased from 50 feet to 60'6" in 1893, few people paid attention. Nichols still went 34-14 in 425 innings, spread over 52 games (44 of them starts). When he didn't start, the 5'11" right-hander was always available in relief.

"You never heard of anyone with a sore arm in my day," he said in 1948, 42 years after his career ended. "When we weren't pitching, we either played in the outfield or doubled as ticket takers. The biggest strain my arm ever underwent was at the Polo Grounds one afternoon when I counted 30,000 tickets."

Nichols was much more proficient with baseballs than tickets. He won 27 games in his first year, 273 games in his first 10 seasons, and had 10 consecutive winning records. He led the National League in wins three times, and in games and innings pitched once each.

"In my day," he said years after his retirement, "if you won only 20 games the club owner would say, 'You didn't do so good this year. We are going to cut your salary for next year.'"

Nichols played for the love of the game – literally – since the National League of the 1890s had a salary cap of $2,400. Only in 1899, when given a $235 bonus for winning the pennant the previous season, did he earn more – but not without provoking a press corps that dubbed him "Nervy Nick."

According to Nichols, "I wanted to pitch every day so we could win more games than the other guy. It wasn't for the money, but for the glory of winning.

"If I was overworked, it didn't affect my arm. I spent 17 years in organized ball. If my arm got sore, I went out and pitched until the soreness left. Otherwise, I would have been dropped from the team. Nothing short of a broken leg could have kept us out of uniform."

Just six years after underhand pitching was no longer required by rule, Nichols dominated batters with an overhand pitch that he called his "jump" fastball. He changed speeds on that pitch and placed the ball brilliantly. "I had no fancy curves," he said. "Speed, change of pace, and control are all any pitcher needs – if he masters them."

Durability personified, he once pitched both ends of a double-header, winning both, and pitched three complete games in three different cities on three consecutive days.

"We worked hard, but I wouldn't say we were overworked," said the Wisconsin native. "During my 12 years with Boston, I took part in 517 games and averaged 27.3 wins per season. You stayed in there and worked. My objective was to have the batter hit at the first one, and the second one, and the third one. By that time, barring fouls, I figured he was either out or had made a hit."

At a time when players had little longevity with a single team, Nichols was a notable exception. He left Boston only after buying a piece of the Western Association's Kansas City franchise, where he doubled as pitcher and manager. Lured back to the majors by the cross-state St. Louis Cardinals, Nichols won 21 games during his first season in St. Louis. But the team was struggling – giving ownership an opportunity to oust Nichols.

"I always felt Stanley (Robison) had an in for me," said Nichols, referring to one of two brothers who owned the team. "Firing me as manager was only the beginning of our troubles. In Cincinnati one day, Stanley ordered me to work one of the gates. Players had to make themselves useful in more ways than one and he wanted me to keep an eye on the tickets to see that we got an honest count. I had pitched the day before and told Stanley I wasn't going to work the gate – I was going to the race track. He got mad and released me."

Acquired off waivers by Philadelphia, Nichols got instant revenge when he beat the Cardinals, 2-1, in his first start for the Phillies. After winning only 10 more games over the next two years, he knew he was through.

During the 1890s, Nichols won 30 more times than Young and 64 more than Rusie. He had four more years of double-digit wins during the 20th century.

Always considered a gentleman, Nichols stayed active in retirement by becoming an accomplished bowler at the alley he managed in Kansas City. He coached college baseball, tried his hand at real

Career Statistics

NICHOLS, Kid		Charles Augustus Nichols; B: 9/14/1869, Madison, WI; D: 4/11/1953, Kansas City, MO; BB/TR, 5'10.5"/175 lbs.; Debut: 4/23/1890; HOF 1949												
YEAR	TM-L	W	L	PCT	G	GS	CG	SH	SV	IP	H	R	HR	SO	ERA
1890	Bos-N	27	19	0.587	48	47	47	7	0	424	374	175	8	222	2.23
1891	Bos-N	30	17	0.638	52	48	45	5	3	425	413	219	15	240	2.39
1892	Bos-N	35	16	0.686	53	51	49	5	0	453	404	211	15	192	2.84
1893	Bos-N	34	14	0.708	52	44	43	1	1	425	426	222	15	94	3.52
1894	Bos-N	32	13	0.711	50	46	40	3	0	407	488	308	23	113	4.75
1895	Bos-N	26	16	0.619	48	43	43	1	3	389	429	220	15	147	3.33
1896	Bos-N	30	14	0.682	49	43	37	3	1	372	387	211	14	102	2.83
1897	Bos-N	31	11	0.738	46	40	37	2	3	368	362	152	9	127	2.64
1898	Bos-N	31	12	0.721	50	42	40	5	4	388	316	136	7	138	2.13
1899	Bos-N	21	19	0.525	42	37	37	4	1	343	326	155	11	108	2.99
1900	Bos-N	13	16	0.448	29	27	25	4	0	231	215	116	11	53	3.07
1901	Bos-N	19	16	0.543	38	34	33	4	0	321	306	146	8	143	3.22
1904	StL-N	21	13	0.618	36	35	35	3	1	317	268	97	3	134	2.02
1905	StL-N	1	5	0.167	7	7	5	0	0	51	64	47	1	16	5.40
	Phi-N	10	6	0.625	17	16	15	1	0	138	129	47	1	50	2.27
	Year	11	11	0.500	24	23	20	1	0	190	193	94	2	66	3.12
1906	Phi-N	0	1	0.000	4	2	1	0	0	11	17	16	0	1	9.82
TOTAL	15	361	208	0.634	621	562	532	48	17	5066	4924	2478	156	1880	2.95

estate, and even sold movie film in a partnership that involved Chicago Cubs star Joe Tinker. He lived to see his plaque posted in the Baseball Hall of Fame gallery in 1949.

Box Score of 300th Win

Nichols Box Score
Boston Beaneaters 11, Chicago Orphans 4

Game played on Saturday, July 7, 1900

Boston	ab	r	h	Chicago	ab	r	h
Hamilton cf	5	2	2	McCarthy lf	5	0	1
Collins 3b	4	2	2	Childs 2b	5	0	2
Stahl lf	5	1	2	Mertes 1b	5	0	4
Tenney 1b	5	0	3	Ryan rt	4	0	1
Freeman rf	5	0	1	Green df	3	2	2
Lowe 2b	5	1	3	Clingman ss	4	0	0
Long ss	5	1	2	Bradley 3b	4	1	2
Clarke c	3	2	2	Donahue c	4	0	0
Nichols p	5	2	2	Callahan p	3	1	0
Totals	42	11	19	Totals	37	4	12

Boston	0	7	0	0	0	3	0	1	0	–	11
Chicago	0	2	1	0	0	0	0	1	0	–	4

Boston	IP	H	R	ER	BB	SO
Nichols (W)	9	12	4	0	2	2

Chicago	IP	H	R	ER	BB	SO
Callahan (L)	9	19	11	4	1	0

DP-Boston 1, Chicago 1. **LOB**-Boston 7, Chicago 9. **E**-Lowe, Long, Bradley. **2B**-Bradley 2, Collins, Tenney, Lowe. **HR**-Green. **SB**-Tenney, Green. **SF**-Collins. **HBP**-Ryan (by Nichols), Clarke (by Callahan). T-2:12

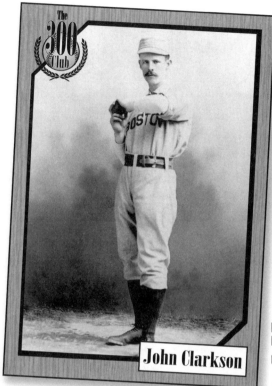

John Clarkson

Photo courtesy of National
Baseball Hall of Fame Library
Cooperstown, N.Y.

John Clarkson's sinker worked wonders against 19th century hitters: it helped him win 328 games in only 12 seasons.

One of three brothers who pitched in the majors, Clarkson spent his entire career in the National League during a time when players changed their teams as often as their socks. He broke in with Worcester in 1882, moved to Cap Anson's Chicago White Stockings, then finished with five years in Boston and four in Cleveland, then a National League city.

Anson, who always had an eye for talent, found Clarkson as a teenaged prodigy pitching in Saginaw, Michigan, in the Northwestern League. A one-time schoolboy catcher, Clarkson had already had a stint in the majors, with Worcester of the National League in 1882, but succumbed to shoulder problems that ruined his season. He won only once in Worcester, then went home to nurse his ailing arm.

Once he got well, Clarkson quickly showed why Anson wanted him.

A stringbean in stature – he stood 5'10" but weighed only 155 pounds – Clarkson collected strikeouts like a kid collecting candy on Halloween. He topped 300 in both of his first two full seasons, finishing with a career total of 1,978.

He led the league in wins, games, starts, and complete games in three different seasons, including one year (1889) when he led in all three components of the pitching Triple Crown: wins (49), strikeouts (284), and earned run average (2.73).

Old Hoss Radbourn, Tim Keefe, and Clarkson were the only 300-game winners of the 19th century who also won the pitching Triple Crown.

Clarkson was probably the best prepared of the bunch. Like later 300-game winner Greg Maddux, whose knowledge of opposing hitters prompted his "Professor" nickname, Clarkson knew the tendencies of the men he faced. Also like Maddux, he was a control artist whose pet pitch, then called a drop-curve, induced many ground balls.

If one of his pitches didn't work on a given day, another one would. Clarkson came armed with an extensive arsenal: straight fastball, sinking fastball, changeup, and several varieties of curveball.

That repertoire, plus a reputation for avoiding injury, enabled Clarkson to win 53 games – trailing only Radbourn's 60 among single-season leaders – in 1885, his first full year with Anson's White Stockings (the future Cubs). He not only completed 68 of 70 starts, but threw shutouts in 10 of them, while working a career-best 623 innings. Thanks to an earned run average of 1.85 and solid support behind him, Clarkson posted a record of 53-16 and a winning percentage of .768.

It was the first of five straight seasons in which he won at least 33 games and the first of two straight seasons that the Cubs – yes, the

Cubs — won the National League pennant. But their euphoria was short-lived.

One year after selling catcher Mike (King) Kelly to Boston for the outlandish figure of $10,000, the Cubs sold Clarkson to Boston for the same price, prompting a sportswriter to dub them "the $20,000 battery." Reuniting with Kelly gave a kick-start to Clarkson's career.

When the Cubs sold Clarkson, they sold a pennant, too. The 1891 Boston Beaneaters won the National League flag because of their 1-2 pitching punch of Clarkson (33-19) and Kid Nichols (30-17), then in his second season. When Clarkson retired three years later, he had more wins than any National League pitcher.

"John Clarkson never had a superior as a pitcher and never will," teammate Fred Pfeffer once said. "He was a master of control who could put the ball where he wanted it nine times out of 10. His speed was something terrific and he could throw any curve. His favorite pitch was a drop, something like the spitball."

The pitcher also had a psyche that needed soothing on a regular basis.

Anson was the man most responsible for manipulating the pitcher's moods.

According to Anson, "Many people regard (Clarkson) as the greatest, but not many know of his peculiar temperament and the amount of encouragement needed to keep him going. Scold him, find fault with him, and he could not pitch at all. Praise him and he was unbeatable.

"In knowing what kind of ball a batter could not hit and in his ability to serve up just that kind of ball, I don't think I have ever seen the equal of Clarkson."

Arthur (Dad) Clarkson and Walter Clarkson never escaped their brother's shadow. They won 39 and 18 games, respectively — hardly enough, even combined with John's 328, to challenge the fraternal wins record of the Perrys or Niekros. But the Clarksons did claim third place on the list of victories by brothers.

John Clarkson pitched a no-hit game against Radbourn, beating Providence, 4-0, on July 27, 1885, and another against Detroit in 1886. Since he didn't walk a man in the Providence game, only bad defense (five errors) separated Clarkson from a perfect game.

Clarkson earned his 300th win on September 21, 1892, with a 3-2 win for the Cleveland Spiders over the Pittsburgh Pirates.

After being sold to Boston, Clarkson supplemented his meager baseball salary ($2,000 in 1889) by coaching at Harvard, his alma mater.

That college job, more than anything else, dissuaded Clarkson from joining the Players League in 1890. As a result, he was treated like a strike-breaking scab the rest of his career.

Clarkson felt at home in Boston: he and his brothers were born in suburban Cambridge during the Civil War era. Pitching rules were in a state of flux and neither leagues nor teams had much stability. Only one thing was a constant: without lights, teams played all their games in daylight.

As a result, contests were often curtailed by darkness. One gloomy afternoon, Clarkson thought the umpires were late in halting the action. He retrieved a lemon from the clubhouse, went out to the mound, and threw the lemon instead of the baseball. When the

Career Statistics

CLARKSON, John				John Gibson Clarkson; B: 7/1/1861, Cambridge MA; D: 2/4/1909, Belmot MA; BR/TR, 5'10"/155; Debut: 5/2/1882; HOF 1963;											
YEAR	TM-L	W	L	PCT	G	GS	CG-SHO	SV-BS	IP	H	R	HR	SO	ERA
1882	Wor-N	1	2	0.333	3	3	2	0	24	49	31	0	3	4.50
1884	Chi-N	10	3	0.769	14	13	12	0	118	94	64	10	102	2.14
1885	Chi-N	53	16	0.768	70	70	68-10	0	623	497	255	21	308	1.85
1886	Chi-N	36	17	0.679	55	55	50-3	0	466	419	248	19	313	2.41
1887	Chi-N	38	21	0.644	60	59	56-2	0	523	513	283	19	237	3.08
1888	Bos-N	33	20	0.623	54	54	53-3	0	483	448	247	17	223	2.76
1889	Bos-N	49	19	0.721	73	72	68-8	1	620	589	280	16	284	2.73
1890	Bos-N	26	18	0.591	44	44	43-2	0	383	370	186	14	138	3.27
1891	Bos-N	33	19	0.635	55	51	47-3	3	460	435	244	18	141	2.79
1892	Bos-N	8	6	0.571	16	16	15-4	0	145	115	65	4	48	2.35
	Cle-N	17	10	0.630	29	28	27-1	1	243	235	132	4	91	2.55
	Year	25	16	0.610	45	44	42-5	1	389	350	197	8	139	2.48
1893	Cle-N	16	17	0.485	36	35	31	0	295	358	240	11	62	4.45
1894	Cle-N	8	10	0.444	22	18	13-1	0	150	173	109	6	28	4.42
TOTAL	12	328	178	0.648	531	518	485-37	5	4536	4295	2384	159	1978	2.81

umpire called a strike on the batter, Clarkson instructed his catcher to show the umpire the fruit. The game was stopped.

Like Christy Mathewson, a later 300-game winner, Clarkson lost his life to disease at a young age. He was only 47 when he died of pneumonia in 1909. The Veterans Committee of the Baseball Hall of Fame enshrined him in 1963.

Box Score of 300th Win

Clarkson Box Score Cleveland Spiders 3, Pittsburgh Pirates 2							
Game played on Wednesday, September 21, 1892							
Pittsburgh	**ab**	**r**	**h**	**Cleveland**	**ab**	**r**	**h**
Donovan rf	4	0	1	Childs 2b	3	2	1
Farrell 3b	4	0	0	Burkett lf	4	0	0
Miller c	4	0	1	Davis 3b	2	1	0
Beckley 1b	4	1	1	McKean ss	4	0	1
Smith lf	4	0	0	Virtue 1b	3	0	0
Bierbauer 2b	2	1	1	McAleer cf	3	0	0
Shugart ss	3	0	0	O'Connor rf	4	0	0
Terry p	2	0	0	Zimmer c	3	0	0
Kelly cf	3	0	1	Clarkson p	3	0	0
Totals	30	2	5	Totals	29	3	2

Pittsburgh	0	0	0		0	0	0		0	1	1	–	2
Cleveland	0	0	0		0	0	1		0	0	2	–	3

Pittsburgh	**IP**	**H**	**R**	**ER**	**BB**	**SO**
Terry (L)	9	2	3	0	5	8

Cleveland	**IP**	**H**	**R**	**ER**	**BB**	**SO**
Clarkson (W)	9	5	2	2	2	3

E-Donovan. **2B**-Berkley. **3B**-Childs. **SB**-Davis, Berkley2. **SF**-Burkett, Virtue, McAleer, O'Connor, Shugart. **PB**-Miller. T-1:55.

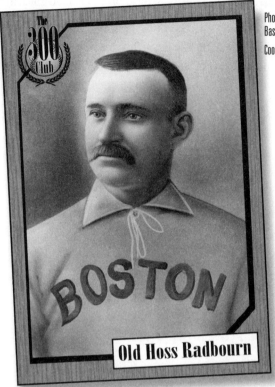

Old Hoss Radbourn

Charles Gardner (Old Hoss) Radbourn took only 11 seasons to win 310 games. Winning a record 60 times in a single season certainly helped.

A little guy with a big taste for booze, Radbourn had a temper to match his talent. Paranoid and self-centered, he was suspended briefly during the 1884 season because he detested the attention given to his teammate, 21-year-old rookie pitcher Bill Sweeney. Radbourn didn't like Sweeney and failed to keep his feelings quiet.

Accused of lack of effort by his own team, Radbourn compounded the problem by sometimes showing up inebriated.

After he cursed out his catcher and knocked him down with a baseball thrown at him deliberately, Radbourn was suspended by Providence manager Frank Bancroft for "improper conduct." The suspension didn't last long, however, because Sweeney decided to jump to St. Louis of the Union Association, a rival league, in mid-season.

Most clubs carried two pitchers, but Providence was down to one. They reinstated Radbourn only after agreeing to his terms: more money plus the right to leave as a free agent after the season ended.

Banking on its one-man pitching "staff," Providence pitched Radbourn almost every day (a few position players appeared as pitchers on occasion). Although overhand pitching was legalized that season, Radbourn relied on his submarine-style delivery, working 678 $^2/_3$ innings, an inning-and-a-third short of Will White's 1879 record, and winning the first Triple Crown of pitching with a 60-12 record, 441 strikeouts, and a 1.38 earned run average. He completed all of his starts, shutting out the opposition 11 times. During the stretch drive, Radbourn pitched 35 times in 37 games, confusing batters by blending curveballs and changeups.

The enormous workload took its toll: rumors circulated that Radbourn could not lift his right arm in the morning but recovered in time to pitch every afternoon. But for whatever reason, Radbourn was the primary force behind the 20-game winning streak that helped Providence win the 1884 National League pennant and postseason series that followed. Including the three complete-game victories that Radbourn pitched in New York, clinching the playoff, the pitcher actually had 63 wins in one season!

No wonder he described himself as an Old Hoss. It was during that 1884 season that Radbourn gave himself that nickname. Warming up in the outfield before a game, he blurted, "Old Hoss is ready!" The nickname stuck.

Paid all of $3,000 for his record-setting season, Radbourn relied on a unique training regimen. It included rolling an iron ball underhand for a few minutes a day, relaxing his sore muscles with 60-minute hot towel treatments, and playing pre-game long toss, gradually increasing the throwing distance until it matched the regulation pitching distance of the day.

Radbourn spent his first five seasons in Rhode Island, then moved north after the Providence franchise folded. He spent four years with the Boston National League team and then joined the Boston Players League club in 1890. After placing second among Players League pitchers with a .692 winning percentage, he returned to the National League to complete his career with Cincinnati a year later.

He led his league in victories, strikeouts, and winning percentage twice each, and in earned run average, innings, and shutouts once. He also pitched a no-hitter against Cleveland in 1883, when he led the National League with 48 wins.

He had enormous ability – when he wanted to show it.

According to Bancroft, the Providence manager: "No pitcher ever had the weaknesses of the batsmen who faced him down to a finer point than Old Rad. He could throw the ball where he wanted to and that was just where the batsman did not want it. He had wonderful grit and perfect command."

Born in Rochester, New York, but raised in Bloomington, Illinois, Radbourn learned to pitch on the family farm. As a teenager, he pitched semipro ball in his hometown, then signed with the Peoria Reds, an independent professional team. A right fielder and relief pitcher for both Peoria, where he launched his pro career in 1878, and Dubuque of the Northwestern League in 1879, Radbourn ranked second in batting both years. That convinced Buffalo of the National League to sign him for 1880. He made his National League debut in right field on May 5, 1880, collecting a single in a lopsided 23-3 loss, but soon injured his arm. Radbourn requested and received his release, allowing him to sign with Providence a year later.

Even with Providence, he played the outfield often, alternating with John Montgomery Ward as a pitcher and right fielder. Radbourn, who won his pitching debut on May 5, 1881, with a 4-2 win over Boston, made his biggest impression as a rookie by throwing two one-hitters. A year later, on Aug. 17, 1882, he ended a scoreless 18-inning game by hitting a ball through a hole in the left-field fence – an inside-the-fence home run. Ward was the winning pitcher.

Radbourn reached 300 wins quickly, not only because of the 60-win season (listed as 59 by some sources), but also because he won 20 games in nine different seasons.

He earned his 300th win on June 2, 1891, with a 10-8 victory for the Reds over the Boston Beaneaters. Radbourn even contributed a single to Cincinnati's 16-hit attack.

Radbourn won 167 games in his first four seasons, but only 144 more in his final seven. The combination of too much pitching and too much drinking took a heavy toll.

After retiring from the game, Radbourn owned a pool hall and went hunting in his spare time. But after losing an eye and the ability to speak in the wake of a hunting accident, the old pitcher seldom faced the public again. Plagued by health problems, he died at age 42. But his famous handlebar moustache lived on. It was immortalized in the Baseball Hall of Fame, where it graces the Radbourn plaque that was added to the Cooperstown gallery in 1939.

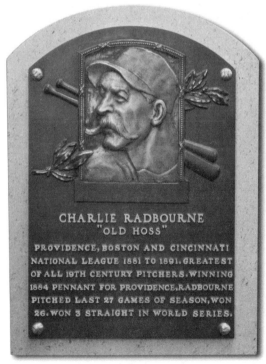

Radbourn's Hall of Fame plaque

Photo courtesy of National Baseball Hall of Fame Library, Cooperstown, N.Y.

Box Score of 300th Win

Radbourn Box Score
Cincinnati Reds 10, Boston Beaneaters 8

Game played on Tuesday, June 2, 1891

Cincinnati	ab	r	h	Boston	ab	r	h
McPhee 2b	5	0	1	Brodie cf	5	1	1
Latham 3b	4	2	1	Sullivan lf	4	0	1
Marr rf	5	2	2	Long ss	2	0	0
Holliday lf	4	4	3	Nash 3b	5	0	0
Reilly cf	4	1	2	Quinn 2b	5	3	3
Keenan 1b	4	1	2	Lowe rf	5	0	2
Smith ss	4	0	3	Tucker 1b	4	3	1
Clark c	4	0	1	Ganzel c	4	1	2
Radbourn p	4	0	1	Staley p	1	0	1
				Clarkison p	3	0	0
Totals	38	10	16	Totals	38	8	11

Cincinnati	3	0	1	0	4	0	2	0	0	–	10
Boston	0	3	1	0	2	0	1	1	0	–	8

DP–Cincinnati1, Boston 1. **E**-McPHee, Clark, Long, Nash, Tucker. **2B**-Marr, Tucker. **3B**-Reilly, Ganzel, Quinn. **HR**-Latham. **SB**-Holliday 2, Quinn 2, Tucker, Ganzel. Earned Runs–Cincinnati 4, Boston 3. **Base on Balls**-Radbourn 4, Clarkson 1. **Strikeouts**-Radbourn 4, Clarkson 2. **WP**-Staley. **HBP**-Ganzel (by Radbourn), Sullivan (by Radbourn). **W**-Radbourn. **L**-Clarkson. T-1:50.

Career Statistics

RADBOURN, Charley	Charles Gardner "Old Hoss" Radbourn; B: 12/11/1854, Rochester, NY; D: 2/5/1897, Bloomington, IL; BR/TR, 5'9"/168 lbs.; Debut: 5/5/1880; HOF 1939

YEAR	TM-L	W	L	PCT	G	GS	CG	SH	SV	IP	H	R	HR	SO	ERA
1881	Pro-N	25	11	0.694	41	36	34	3	0	325	309	162	1	117	2.43
1882	Pro-N	33	20	0.623	54	51	50	6	0	466	422	213	6	201	2.12
1883	Pro-N	48	25	0.658	76	68	66	4	1	632	563	275	7	315	2.05
1884	Pro-N	59	12	0.831	75	73	73	11	1	678	528	216	18	441	1.38
1885	Pro-N	28	21	0.571	49	49	49	2	0	445	423	209	4	154	2.20
1886	Bos-N	27	31	0.466	58	58	57	3	0	509	521	300	18	218	3.00
1887	Bos-N	24	23	0.511	50	50	48	1	0	425	638	305	20	87	4.55
1888	Bos-N	7	16	0.304	24	24	24	1	0	207	187	110	8	64	2.87
1889	Bos-N	20	11	0.645	33	31	28	1	0	277	282	151	14	99	3.67
1890	Bos-N	27	12	0.692	41	38	36	1	0	343	352	183	8	80	3.31
1891	Cin-N	11	13	0.458	26	24	23	2	0	218	236	149	13	54	4.25
TOTAL	11	309	195	0.613	527	502	488	35	2	4527	4461	2273	117	1830	2.68

One Who Won 500, and Another Who Won 400

Cy Young – 511 Wins

Walter Johnson – 417 Wins

In baseball, 400 is a magic number, an elusive achievement for pitchers (400 career victories) or batters (a .400 average in a season).

Only two pitchers have won 400 games, succeeding long before the lively ball, night games, artificial turf, jet-lag, pitch counts, and relief pitching diminished anyone's ability to amass such an astronomical win total.

Early in the game's history, teams carried only a handful of pitchers, counting on them to pitch as often and as long as they could. With trainers, doctors, and body-building equipment not even figments of the imagination for major-league teams in the early years, pitchers with bad arms, elbows, or shoulders suffered in silence to save their jobs.

Photo courtesy of National Baseball Hall of Fame Library Cooperstown, N.Y.

When **Cy Young** pitched, batters suffered. Blessed with a resilient right arm fortified by off-season farm chores, he completed 92 percent of his starts (749 of 815), averaging more than eight innings per game during his 22-year career.

"I usually pitched with just two days' rest and sometimes one," said Young, who blended pinpoint control with a pair of curves and a fastball of considerable velocity. "My arm would get weak and tired at times, but never sore. In the spring, I ran constantly for three weeks before I ever threw a ball. I ran regularly to keep my legs in shape. And I worked hard all winter on my farm, from sunup to sundown, doing chores that were not only good for my legs, but also for my arms and back. I needed only a dozen pitches to warm up for a ballgame."

Able to make a smooth adjustment when pitching rules changed in 1893, Young was the only pitcher whose performance stood out both before and after the turn of the century. Pitching for teams in both leagues, he finished with 511 wins, but was not a 300-game winner in either. He finished with 222 American League victories and 289 in the National League.

"I had excellent control, throwing with four different deliveries and wheeling on the batter to hide the ball," said Young, who worked 7,356 innings in 906 games and went over the 400-inning mark in five different seasons. "I saw some fast ones – Amos Rusie, Walter Johnson, Lefty Grove, and Bob Feller – but I was among them, too. My favorite pitch was a whistler right under the chin. And I had a couple of curveballs, an overhand pitch that broke sharply down, and a sweeping, sidearm curve."

The game was vastly different when the 23-year-old Young, once a semi-pro third baseman, reached the majors with the National League's Cleveland Spiders in 1890. Several infielders played without gloves, catchers had minimal protection, and Young himself didn't don a mitt during his first six seasons.

"When the glove came in, players began to depend upon the gloved hand to stop the ball and the right hand to hold it," Young remembered. "Naturally, their range and reach improved."

Pitching rules also changed. The distance from the pitcher's location to home plate increased from 50' to 60'6" in 1893 and a raised mound, complete with a rectangular slab made of rubber, replaced the flat pitcher's box. Young, not missing a beat, still won 34 games, the second of his five 30-win seasons.

He had more 20-win seasons (16) than anyone, but led his league in victories only four times: in 1895, when he had 35 of Cleveland's 84 wins in the National League race, and in the first three years of the American League's existence, 1901-03, all with Boston.

Because he was the seventh pitcher to reach the 300-victory plateau, neither teammates nor newspapers made a big deal of Young's 5-3 victory for the Boston Pilgrims over the Philadelphia Athletics on July 5, 1901. Thanks to the weak competition in the infant

American League, Young needed only three years to reach 400 wins, a mark he achieved on August 22, 1904.

Win No. 500 was a 5-4, 11-inning win for the Cleveland Indians against the Washington Senators on July 19, 1910 – still during the Dead Ball Era when home runs were scarce.

Denton True Young, whose middle name was the surname of the soldier who saved his dad during the Civil War, acquired his nickname while working out for Canton, Ohio, of the Tri-State League in 1890. One of his pitches smacked into the wooden backstop, ripping out some boards, and the incredulous batter murmured something about the kid pitcher doing more damage than a cyclone. A native of Gilmore, Ohio, 50 miles away, Young was 23 when he launched his pro career at Canton for $60 a month. He pitched so well that the club shipped him to Cleveland for $250 and a new suit. It was the biggest steal since native tribesmen sold the island of Manhattan for $24 in the first Dutch treat.

The 6'2" right-hander won 10 games in limited action that first season, then at least 20 for the next 14 seasons in succession. He threw no-hitters in 1897, 1904, and 1908.

"The reason I was good," he told *Washington Star* writer Burt Hawkins in 1943, "was because I had great control and a lot of good stuff on the ball. The secret of my pitching success was being able to get all that stuff over the plate. I could throw anything with a count of 3-2 on the batter and be reasonably certain of pitching a strike."

Young's nickname was Cy because he could throw like a cyclone.
Photo courtesy of National Baseball Hall of Fame Library, Cooperstown, N.Y.

Such control – he averaged just over one walk per nine innings during his long career – enabled Young to throw a perfect game against long-time rival Rube Waddell on May 5, 1904.

"The biggest thrill I ever got out of baseball was pitching that perfect game," said Young, whose winter wood-chopping hardened his back and shoulders. "I never realized what a nice game I had pitched until it was over. The fellows on the bench never said anything about it and when we got into the late innings, I just never realized nobody had gotten on base."

The first perfect game pitched from the modern pitching distance (60'6") was payback for Young, who had lost to Waddell a week earlier and once lost a 20-inning game to the Philadelphia star. When Waddell boasted before the game that he would beat him again, Young turned his game up a notch. After it was over, the normally-unflappable Young shouted to the A's ace, "How did you like *that*?"

Connie Mack, the owner-manager of the Athletics, appreciated the effort even though his team finished on the wrong end. Mack, who managed the A's for 50 years, always called Young's perfect game the greatest exhibition of pitching he had ever seen.

Young was at the top of his game in 1904. He hurled 24 consecutive hitless innings, still a record, and 45 straight innings without yielding a run. He walked only 29 batters in 380 innings. And he finished with a flourish, hurling shutouts in his last three starts to help the Americans edge the New York Highlanders in a tight pennant race.

There was no World Series, though, because New York Giants manager John McGraw, miffed over continuing player raids by the American League, refused to engage the upstarts.

Young was left with only one World Series on his resume – the first ever played. Pitching the odd-numbered games in the best-of-nine series in 1903, he went 2-1 with a 1.85 earned run average, helping Boston beat Pittsburgh, after declining a gambler's offer of $20,000 to throw the classic. "If you put any value at all on money," he reportedly said, "bet on me to win."

Young was always a good bet. In 1908, he came within a whisker of pitching a second perfect game – a feat never accomplished by anyone. Young walked New York leadoff hitter Harry Niles, who was caught stealing, and then retired the next 26 men in a row. At age 41, he was the oldest man to throw a no-hitter before 44-year-old Nolan Ryan, who had just become a 300-game winner, did it in 1991.

Blessed with an arm that was younger than his birth certificate suggested, Young finished the 1908 season with 21 wins and a 1.26 earned run average, among the Top 10 single-season marks in baseball history.

Young pitched for five different teams in three cities. After spending his first nine seasons with the Cleveland Spiders, he was one of several stars transferred to the St. Louis Perfectos by the Robison brothers, who owned both clubs. After sweating out two steamy summers marked by a rib injury and an altercation with a heckler, Young yearned to go north and increase his salary at the same time.

Ban Johnson, trying to lure stars into the infant American League, made Young an offer he couldn't refuse: a chance to escape St. Louis and his $2,400 paycheck, then the maximum allowed by the National League's salary cap.

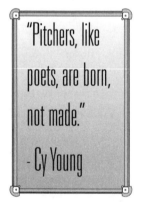

"Pitchers, like poets, are born, not made."
- Cy Young

Johnson knew that the Boston Somersets, named for owner Charles Somerset, had already signed Lou Criger, Young's favorite catcher, and convinced the pitcher to follow by finagling a $3,500 offer.

Signed just before the 1901 season started, Young got off to a great start, winning the Triple Crown of pitching (wins, strikeouts, and ERA) in his first season. He stayed eight seasons in Boston, where the team was also called the Americans, Puritans, and Pilgrims before becoming the Red Sox in 1907. While the team was changing names, their star pitcher was gaining in years and weight, convincing the club to ship him home to Cleveland, by then an American League club. On February 10, 1909, Young went to the Indians for Jack Ryan, Charlie Chech, and $12,500 – a considerable sum at the time.

Young had a single solid season left, winning 19 in 1909. Two years later, he completed his career as a member of the Boston Braves (then called Rustlers), adding four wins to his career total but losing a 1-0 verdict to Phillies rookie Grover Cleveland Alexander, a future 300-game winner, on September 7, 1911. It was the only year that baseball's four biggest winners – Young, Johnson, Alexander, and Christy Mathewson – were active at the same time. Young, who last pitched in an official game that October 6, went to spring training with the Braves in 1912 but was too fat to field the flurry of bunts that hitters were dumping in front of him.

Although he played against Ty Cobb, Napoleon Lajoie, and other Hall of Fame hitters, Young identified Wee Willie Keeler as his toughest out. "With that little bat and choppy swing, he could hit anything," he said. "You couldn't fool him with a curve, either. I always tried to keep the ball low and worked on him with my change-of-pace: fast, faster, and fastest."

Never paid more than $5,000 a season, Young was glad he traded his plow for a baseball.

"I had the benefit of a larger strike zone – from the top of the shoulders to the bottom of the knees – and I admit some of my cut-plug tobacco juice would get on the ball," he said long after he left the game. "And the ball wasn't so lively."

Hitters were effusive in their praise for the pitcher. Honus Wagner said Young had the best fastball he'd ever seen. Cap Anson, the Chicago White Stockings player-manager who tried to purchase his contract from Cleveland, said of Young, "The ball looks like it's shooting down from the hands of a giant."

A gentleman in an era known for rowdyism, Young was so well-liked that even the umpires gave him a gift – a leather travel bag – on "Cy Young Day" at the old Huntington Grounds ballpark in Boston on August 14, 1908. Young received a silver cup from the players, various floral tributes, and $7,500 in cash – more than double his annual salary. He even got an offer to coach the Harvard baseball team.

Young's records for wins, losses, starts, complete games, and innings pitched remain untouchable. The first pitcher to work well past his 40th birthday, Young was also the only one to star in both the 19th and 20th centuries. He finished with a .620 winning percentage.

Counting his three wins over Baltimore in the 1895 Temple Cup, a playoff between the NL's top teams, and the two he later won in the first World Series, Young actually had 516 victories.

Honored with election to the Baseball Hall of Fame in 1937 and the erection of a statue on the site of the old Huntington Avenue Grounds, now occupied by Northeastern University, Young received a posthumous honor in 1956 when Commissioner Ford Frick created the Cy Young Award, given annually to the best pitcher in the major leagues. The award was split in two, with one presented in each league, 11 years later.

After winning the award with a 31-6 record in 1968, Denny McLain wanted to know if he compared with Cy Young. "You've had one 30-win season," a writer said. "Cy Young did it five times."

Box Score of 300th Win

Young Baseball Almanac Box Score
Boston Pilgrims 5, Philadelphia Athletics 3
Game played on Friday, July 5, 1901

Philadelphia	ab	h	po	a	e		Boston	ab	h	po	a	e
Fultz cf	4	1	1	1	0		Dowd lf	4	1	1	0	0
Davis 1b	4	0	10	1	1		Stahl cf	2	1	0	0	1
Cross 3b	4	1	2	1	0		Collins 3b	3	3	2	5	1
Lajoie 2b	4	2	2	2	0		Freeman 1b	2	1	11	0	0
Seybold rf	4	1	1	0	0		Hemphill rf	4	1	3	0	0
McIntyre lf	4	0	1	2	0		Parent ss	4	3	1	4	0
Powers c	4	1	4	2	2		Ferris 2b	3	0	4	4	0
Dolan ss	4	0	2	6	0		Schreck c	3	0	5	0	1
McPherson p	1	0	0	2	1		Young p	2	1	0	0	0
a-Smith ph	1	1	0	2	1		Bernhard p	1	0	1	2	0
Totals	35	7	24	18	4		Totals	27	11	27	13	3

Philadelphia	2	0	0		0	0	0		0	0	1	–	3
Boston	0	2	2		1	0	0		0	0	x	–	5

a-Batted for McPherson in 9th.
DP-Philadelphia 2, Boston 2. **2B**–Collins, Seybold. **3B**–Cross, Stahl, Collins. **SB**–Lajoie 2, Freeman, Ferris. **SF**-Freeman, Ferris. **Earned Runs-** Philadelphia 2, Boston 1. **Base on Balls**-McPherson 3, Bernhard 1. **Strikeouts**-Young 5. **HBP**-Freeman (by McPherson. **Winning Pitcher**-Young. **Losing Pitcher**-McPherson. **T**–1:45.

Career Statistics

	YOUNG, Cy	Denton True Young; B: 3/29/1867, Gilmore, OH; D: 11/4/1955, Newcomerstown, OH; BR/TR, 6'2"/210 lbs.; Debut: 8/6/1890; HOF 1937

YEAR	TM-L	W	L	PCT	G	GS	CG	SH	SV	IP	H	R	HR	SO	ERA
1890	Cle-N	9	7	0.563	17	16	16	0	0	147	145	87	6	39	3.47
1891	Cle-N	27	22	0.551	55	46	43	0	2	423	431	244	4	147	2.85
1892	Cle-N	36	12	0.750	53	49	48	9	0	453	363	158	8	168	1.93
1893	Cle-N	34	16	0.680	53	46	42	1	1	422	442	230	10	102	3.36
1894	Cle-N	26	21	0.553	52	47	44	2	1	408	488	265	19	108	3.94
1895	Cle-N	35	10	0.778	47	40	36	4	0	369	363	177	10	121	3.26
1896	Cle-N	28	15	0.651	51	46	42	5	3	414	477	214	7	140	3.24
1897	Cle-N	21	19	0.525	46	38	35	2	0	335	391	189	7	88	3.78
1898	Cle-N	25	13	0.658	46	41	40	1	0	377	387	167	6	101	2.53
1899	StL-N	26	16	0.619	44	42	40	4	1	369	368	173	10	111	2.58
1900	StL-N	19	19	0.500	41	35	32	4	0	321	337	144	7	115	3.00
1901	Bos-A	33	10	0.767	43	41	38	5	0	371	324	112	6	158	1.62
1902	Bos-A	32	11	0.744	45	43	41	3	0	384	350	136	6	160	2.15
1903	Bos-A	28	9	0.757	40	35	34	7	2	341	294	115	6	176	2.08
1904	Bos-A	26	16	0.619	43	41	40	10	1	380	327	104	6	200	1.97
1905	Bos-A	18	19	0.486	38	33	31	4	0	320	248	99	3	210	1.82
1906	Bos-A	13	21	0.382	39	34	28	0	2	287	288	137	3	140	3.19
1907	Bos-A	21	15	0.583	43	37	33	6	2	343	286	101	3	147	1.99
1908	Bos-A	21	11	0.656	36	33	30	3	2	299	230	68	1	150	1.26
1909	Cle-A	19	15	0.559	35	34	30	3	0	294	267	110	4	109	2.26
1910	Cle-A	7	10	0.412	21	20	14	1	0	163	149	62	0	58	2.53
1911	Cle-A	3	4	0.429	7	7	4	0	0	46	54	28	2	20	3.88
	Bos-N	4	5	0.444	11	11	8	2	0	80	83	47	4	35	3.71
TOTAL	22	511	316	0.618	906	815	749	76	17	7356	7092	3167	138	2803	2.63

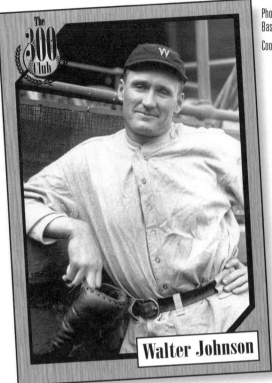

Photo courtesy of National Baseball Hall of Fame Library Cooperstown, N.Y.

Walter Johnson

Like Cy Young, **Walter Johnson** was a mild-mannered farm product who threw right-handed and relied on velocity as well as control. Armed with a fearsome fastball that he delivered with a sweeping sidearm motion, Johnson was variously called "Barney," after auto racer Barney Oldfield, or "the Big Train," because his heater had more speed than the best express train of his day. Grantland Rice, dean of the nation's sportswriters at the time, gave him the railroad moniker.

That heater helped him pitch 110 shutouts, a major-league record, and win 417 games – no mean feat for a pitcher who spent his entire 21-year career with a Washington Senators ballclub that often finished in or near the league basement. Because the team wound up in the second division for nearly half of his stellar career, the Humboldt, Kansas, native had to make do with a single run of support. He won more 1-0 games (38) than any other pitcher, but also lost 28 others.

Including those 1-0 games, his team was shut out 65 times — a big chunk of his 279 career losses.

During a four-day span late in the 1908 season, the righthanded flamethrower bailed out an injury-riddled Washington pitching staff by blanking the New York Highlanders (now called Yankees) three straight times: on Friday, Saturday, and Monday (Sunday ball was prohibited in New York at the time). "I must have been a green pea of a country boy or I never would have tried it," he said years later. "But at the time, it didn't seem extraordinary. A pitcher is supposed to pitch, isn't he?"

The Senators held their breath when a Jack Chesbro pitch hit Johnson on the arm during the Saturday game, but he dusted himself off and stayed in the game.

The 1909 season, the pitcher's third, epitomized Johnson's lack of support. Appearing in 40 games, he posted a solid 2.20 earned run average. But his won-lost record was 13-25 because the Senators suffered 10 shutout losses in games Johnson started. A persistent fever also hampered his performance.

Three years later, Johnson was so dominating that he lifted his ballclub by its bootstraps. His 33-12 record pushed the Senators into the first division for the first time — all the way up to second place — but still left them 14 games behind Joe Wood's Boston Red Sox. All Wood did was win 34 of 39 decisions in 1912, the only year in American League history when two pitchers topped 30 wins, and he beat Johnson 1-0 in a specially arranged duel on September 1.

Johnson started throwing shutouts as a rookie — two of his five wins were whitewashes — and never stopped. To most hitters, the Johnson fastball was a blur, something they could sense but not time.

"You can't hit what you can't see," whined Yankees outfielder Ping Bodie, a contact hitter who couldn't make contact.

A workhorse who routinely topped 350 innings per season, Johnson led the American League in strikeouts 12 times, wins six times, earned run average four times, and winning percentage twice. In 1913, he won the Triple Crown of pitching with a 36-7 record, 243 strikeouts, 11 shutouts, and a 1.14 ERA that remains the best single-season mark ever recorded in the American League. That was also the year he pitched 56 consecutive scoreless innings, a mark that stood for 55 years before Don Drysdale erased it. He also won the pitcher's Triple Crown in 1918 and 1924.

Illness and injury stopped Johnson's streak of 10 straight 20-win seasons in 1920, the same year he won his 300th game and pitched his only no-hitter, a 1-0 win over Boston. Only an error by Bucky Harris prevented a perfect game.

Walter Johnson was the only 300-game winner to spend his entire career with one team.

Although the no-hitter was arguably his best individual performance, there were plenty of other candidates. In 1912, a year he won 16 games in a row, he pitched 22 consecutive scoreless innings against the Philadelphia Athletics on consecutive days. In 1913, he pitched five one-hitters. On August 6, 1917, he needed his usual single run to top Eddie Plank, already a 300-game winner, in the legendary lefty's last appearance, as a member of the St. Louis Browns. In 1918, Johnson outlasted Lefty Williams of the White Sox, 1-0 in 18 innings. And in 1926, he topped Eddie Rommel of the A's in a 15-inning, 1-0 duel.

Although he had a 2-6 record against an opposing pitcher named Babe Ruth, allowed Ty Cobb to hit him at a .335 clip, and once made 21 wild pitches in a season, Johnson inspired shock and awe from opponents.

Ray Chapman, who later suffered a fatal beaning from Yankees pitcher Carl Mays, once walked away from the plate with only two strikes, telling umpire Billy Evans that he didn't want to delay the inevitable.

"He had only one pitch," said Cleveland shortstop Roger Peckinpaugh. "You knew what was coming, but so what?"

Too polite to brush back opposing hitters, Johnson was also worried about hurting someone seriously; batting helmets did not become standard until years after his retirement.

"If he had been willing to throw a few dusters and keep the batters on edge worrying about that cannonball he threw," said Cobb, who admitted hogging the plate against the pitcher, "nobody knows how many more games he might have won. But he was afraid of his own speed and what he might do to a batter."

A true gentleman, Johnson never smoked, drank, or swore. He didn't even play cards until late in his career. He was even known to slow himself down when winning lopsided games, pitching to young batters, or facing friends. Years later, when he managed Washington and Cleveland, his style was criticized as too easy-going. He still did well, finishing in the first division in three of his four years at the helm of the Senators and posting a managerial winning percentage of .550 – good, but not anywhere near his pitching winning percentage of .599.

"Johnson was the most amazing pitcher in the American League," said Casey Stengel, a rookie in 1912. "You knew what was coming but you couldn't hit it. And he had perfect control."

Johnson lost 28 games by a 1-0 score.

Photo courtesy of National Baseball Hall of Fame Library, Cooperstown, N.Y.

Most of all, he was blessed with blinding speed. Johnson's record of 3,509 strikeouts – achieved at a time when few hitters fanned 100 times per season – stood for 62 years. The ability to strike out any hitter at any time allowed the Washington wizard to complete 531 of 666 starts and post a lifetime earned run average of 2.17.

Pestered with questions about his fastball, Johnson had a response that suggested Yogi Berra was his speechwriter: "I throw as hard as I can when I think I have to throw as hard as I can."

Just as Cy Young made a smooth transition when the rules of pitching changed, Johnson continued to prosper after the advent of the lively ball in 1920. His last two 20-win seasons, in 1924 and 1925, not only helped Washington win its first pennant, but also to win two in a row.

Finally in the World Series at age 37, Johnson made a valiant effort in the 1924 opener, throwing 165 pitches as the Senators lost to John McGraw's Giants, 4-3 in 12 innings at Griffith Stadium. When he also lost the fifth game, 6-2, it seemed that Johnson's years of loyalty to the wallowing Washington franchise would not be rewarded with a World Series win. But fate had other ideas.

In the decisive seventh game, the Giants took a 3-1 lead into the eighth, but fell into a tie after a Bucky Harris grounder to third struck a pebble and bounded high over Freddie Lindstrom's head, allowing two runs to score. Harris, the team's youthful player-manager, called Johnson out of the bullpen in the ninth to preserve the deadlock.

Working out of jams for four straight innings, Johnson seemed gassed when the Senators came to bat in the bottom of the 12th. With one man out, catcher Hank Gowdy tripped over his own mask while chasing a pop foul by Muddy Ruel. Given another chance, Ruel doubled. Johnson followed with a grounder to short that Travis Young couldn't handle. Then Earl McNeely hit a grounder to third that seemed like a double-play that would end the inning.

But a pebble – maybe even the same one – deflected the ball, again sending it over Lindstrom and into left field. Ruel scored the run that gave Washington its only world championship and made Johnson a winner for the first time.

A year later, against the Pittsburgh Pirates, Johnson's luck changed: He won his first two World Series starts, 4-1 and 4-0, but lost his last, a rain-soaked 9-7 debacle in which he went all the way but yielded 15 hits. A leg injury, suffered while running the bases in the fourth game, proved almost as detrimental as the dreary weather. When American League president Ban Johnson angrily demanded to know why Harris didn't change pitchers, the manager said, "I went down with my best."

Johnson was the best of his generation. He not only won nine of the 14 Opening Day games he started, but pitched shutouts in seven of them, all while making sure to have visiting presidents sign base-balls for his collection. He missed another opener while staging a rare holdout, hoping to double his $4,500 salary after winning 25 games in 1911.

The consecutive 30-win seasons helped him climb toward the 300-win plateau. He needed eight years to reach 200 and 14 for 300, getting there on May 14, 1920, when he beat the Detroit Tigers, 9-8. Six years later, with a 7-4 win over the St. Louis Browns on May 12, 1926, he joined Cy Young as the only 400-game winners in baseball history. But he began to sense the beginning of the end when Lou Gehrig became the first player to hit two home runs against him in a single game on August 13 of that same year.

Had he not broken his leg during 1927 spring training, when roommate Joe Judge ripped a line drive off his right leg, Johnson's career could have continued. Able to win only five of the 18 games in which he appeared that season, Johnson accepted an offer to manage Newark of the International League. He later returned to the dugout as a manager, first with the Senators (1929-32) and then with the Indians (1933-35).

He might have graced Chicago with his presence, but Senators owner Clark Griffith persuaded White Sox counterpart Charles Comiskey to cover a rare two-year contract that kept the pitcher from joining the Federal League in 1914. Griffith, who couldn't match the

Federal League's offer, persuaded Comiskey that it would be bad publicity for the White Sox if Johnson became the star pitcher for the Chicago Whales.

Never paid more than $10,000 by the tight-fisted Griffith, Johnson also suffered several losses off the field. In 1921 alone, his father died of a stroke while flu killed his 2-year-old daughter. Nine years later, his 36-year-old wife lost her life to heat exhaustion. Those memories clouded his retirement years on Mountain View Farm, the 552-acre Maryland property he owned, though he did return to his first love – baseball – by spending a year in the Washington broadcast booth (1939) and staging wartime fund-raising exhibitions with Babe Ruth. He never sacrificed his principles, even rejecting a $10,000 offer to endorse a cigarette.

No one who ever played baseball was more of a natural. Capable of saving games as well as starting them, he went 40-30 in relief roles and, applying today's rules to yesterday's results, saved 34 more. Johnson could hit, too, as evidenced by the .433 batting average, a record for a pitcher, that he compiled at age 37 in 1925. He once hit more home runs in a season (one) than he gave up.

"From the first time I held a ball," said the blue-eyed, sandy-haired pitcher, "it settled in the palm of my right hand as though it belonged there. When I threw it, ball, hand, wrist, arm, shoulder, and back all seemed to work together."

His legs were not part of the equation. Johnson had a buggy-whip motion devoid of any follow-through.

The second of six children who grew up on a 160-acre Kansas farm, Johnson moved to California in 1902 after his father landed a job as a teamster in the newly-discovered oil fields. At 16, two years after he arrived, the angular right-hander with the long arms and strong back started playing for a sandlot team. He started as a catcher, but switched to pitching because he threw harder than anyone else.

Johnson soon progressed to semi-pro ball, eventually landing with a telephone company team in Weiser, Idaho. Paid $90 a month to throw fastballs and dig holes for poles, Johnson generated excitement with consecutive no-hitters and 77 consecutive scoreless innings – a harbinger of things to come.

When a traveling liquor salesman sent laudatory descriptions of Johnson to several professional clubs, most thought he'd been drinking too much of his own product. But one club – the Washington Senators – didn't.

With no scouts in his employ, quick-thinking manager Joe Cantillon sent injured catcher Cliff Blankenship to investigate. Johnson, who had been averaging 15 strikeouts a game, quickly caught the catcher's fancy and signed for a $100 bonus, $350 monthly, and return train fare in case he didn't stick with the Senators. Getting Johnson's signature on a contract on June 29, 1907, was the best decision in club history.

Brought east from Idaho, Johnson followed the prevailing tradition of pitching batting practice the day before his debut. "Walter Johnson pitched from the rubber before the game yesterday," *Washington Post* sports editor Ed Grillo wrote, "but he afforded little batting practice for the players of both teams, as his fastball seemed unhittable."

Johnson worked the first eight innings of a 3-2 defeat, yielding a Ty Cobb bunt single as the first hit against him in the majors, but impressed Cobb so much that the Detroit legend begged the Tiger front office to purchase the pitcher without regard to cost. His plea fell upon deaf ears.

Equally impressed by Johnson's debut was his own manager. "His absolute control was the best part of his work," Joe Cantillon said. "He has a great shoot to his fastball and, to tell the truth, he's the best raw pitcher I've ever seen. If nothing happens, that fellow will be a greater pitcher in two years than (Christy) Mathewson ever dared to be."

The manager must have been a prophet: when the Hall of Fame conducted its first election in 1936, Johnson and Mathewson were the only pitchers chosen, joining Cobb, Babe Ruth, and Honus Wagner in the inaugural Cooperstown class.

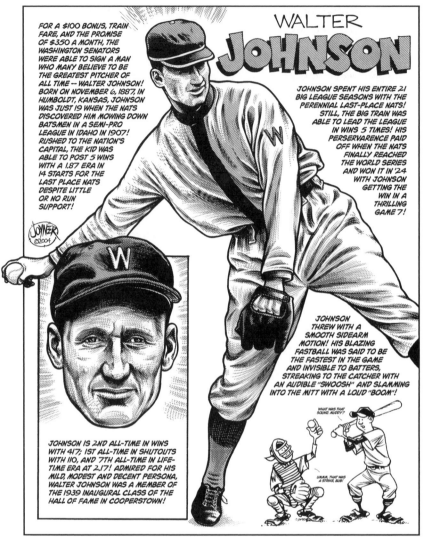

Courtesy of Ronnie Joyner

En route to the Hall of Fame, Johnson had more wins, complete games, shutouts, and strikeouts than any American League pitcher. Among pitchers who worked exclusively in the 20th century, nobody won more often. Nor was any athlete as highly respected: Johnson's grandchildren attended Walter Johnson High School in Bethesda, Maryland.

Johnson was such an icon in Washington that he was asked to replicate George Washington's feat of throwing a silver dollar across the Rappahannock River in Fredericksburg, a Maryland suburb. Not worried about injuring his retired right arm on that frosty day of February 22, 1936, Johnson succeeded on his second try.

"Christy Mathewson was the only fellow I knew who was even like Walter," Clark Griffith once told a reporter. "But he wasn't the pitcher Johnson was. Matty was an artist, but Johnson was a power-house."

Box Score of 300th Win

W. Johnson Box Score Washington Senators 9, Detroit Tigers 8							
Game played on Friday, May 14, 1920							
Detroit	ab	r	h	**Washington**	ab	r	h
Young 2b	4	1	1	Judge 1b	5	0	1
Bush ss	2	1	0	Milan lf	4	0	1
Cobb cf	5	0	1	Rice cf	4	2	2
Veach lf	4	0	3	Roth rf	1	3	0
Heilmann 1b	3	1	1	Harris 2b	5	2	1
Flagstead rf	4	2	1	Ellerbe 3b	4	1	3
Hale 3b	4	1	1	Shannon ss	4	1	3
Jones 3b	1	0	0	Garrity c	2	0	0
Stranage c	2	0	1	Zachary p	2	0	0
b-Pinelli pr	0	1	0	Erickson p	1	0	0
Ainsmith c	1	0	0	Johnson p	2	0	2
Glaisier p	2	0	0	Totals	34	9	13
a-Shorten ph	0	1	0				
Oldham p	0	0	0				
Dauss p	1	0	0				
Totals	33	8	9				

Detroit	0	1	0		2	0	5		0	0	0	–	8
Washington	3	0	0		0	3	0		2	0	1	–	9

a-Batted for Glaisier in 6th.
b-Ran for Stanage in 6th.
DP-Detroit 1. **LOB**-Detroit 8, Washington 12. **E**-Young, Rice, Garrity 2. **2B**-Veach 2, Harris, Stanage. **SB**-Judge, Harris 2, Ellerbe, Heilmann, Flagstead. **SF**-Roth, Heilmann 2, Garrity 2, Bush, Rice. **Base on Balls**-Glaisier 5, Zachary 2, Erickson 4, Oldham 2, Dauss 1. **Strikeouts**-Glaisier 2, Zachary 2, Erickson 1, Oldham 1. **Hits off** Zachary 5 in 4 IP, Erickson 1 in 1-1/3 IP, Johnson 3 in 3-2/3 IP, Glaisier 7 in 5 IP, Oldham 2 in 2/3 IP, Dauss 4 in 2-1/3 IP. **Winning Pitcher**-Johnson. **Losing Pitcher**-Dauss. T-2:35.

Career Statistics

JOHNSON, Walter			Walter Perry "Barney, The Big Train" Johnson; B: 11/6/1887, Humboldt, KS; D: 12/10/1946, Washington, DC; BR/TR, 6'1"/200 lbs.; Debut: 8/2/1907; HOF 1936											
YEAR	TM-L	W	L	PCT	G	GS	CG	SH	SV	IP	H	R	HR	SO	ERA
1907	Was-A	5	9	0.357	14	12	11	2	0	110	100	35	1	71	1.88
1908	Was-A	14	14	0.500	36	30	23	6	1	256	194	75	0	160	1.65
1909	Was-A	13	25	0.342	40	36	27	4	1	296	247	112	1	164	2.22
1910	Was-A	25	17	0.595	45	42	38	8	1	370	262	92	1	313	1.36
1911	Was-A	25	13	0.658	40	37	36	6	1	322	292	119	8	207	1.90
1912	Was-A	33	12	0.733	50	37	34	7	2	369	259	89	2	303	1.39
1913	Was-A	36	7	0.837	48	36	29	11	2	346	232	56	9	243	1.14
1914	Was-A	28	18	0.609	51	40	33	9	1	371	287	88	3	225	1.72
1915	Was-A	27	13	0.675	47	39	35	7	4	336	258	83	1	203	1.55
1916	Was-A	25	20	0.556	48	38	36	3	1	369	290	105	0	228	1.90
1917	Was-A	23	16	0.590	47	34	30	8	3	326	248	105	3	188	2.21
1918	Was-A	23	13	0.639	39	29	29	8	3	326	241	71	2	162	1.27
1919	Was-A	20	14	0.588	39	29	27	7	2	290	235	73	0	147	1.49
1920	Was-A	8	10	0.444	21	15	12	4	3	143	135	68	5	78	3.13
1921	Was-A	17	14	0.548	35	32	25	1	1	264	265	122	7	143	3.51
1922	Was-A	15	16	0.484	41	31	23	4	4	280	283	115	8	105	2.99
1923	Was-A	17	12	0.586	42	34	18	3	4	261	263	112	9	130	3.48
1924	Was-A	23	7	0.767	38	38	20	6	0	277	233	97	10	158	2.72
1925	Was-A	20	7	0.741	30	29	16	3	0	229	217	95	7	108	3.07
1926	Was-A	15	16	0.484	33	33	22	2	0	260	259	120	13	125	3.63
1927	Was-A	5	6	0.455	18	15	7	1	0	107	113	70	7	48	5.10
TOTAL	21	417	279	0.599	802	666	531	110	34	5914	4913	1902	97	3509	2.17

Dead-Ball Aces

Christy Mathewson – 373 Wins

Grover Cleveland Alexander – 373 Wins

Although their careers coincided and their victory totals were identical, Christy Mathewson and Grover Cleveland Alexander were polar opposites.

The former was a college star who leaped from the Bucknell campus to the majors with only a short sojourn in the minor leagues, while the latter was a Nebraska farm boy whose battles with the bottle and bouts with epilepsy cost him the confidence of teams and managers.

Christy Mathewson, whose father was a farmer in Factoryville, Pennsylvania, started playing ball at age 11, evolving into a pitcher because he threw harder than boys several years older. By the time he got to Bucknell, where he was a three-sport star, he was earning $200 a month, plus room and board, for pitching semi-pro ball in the summer.

His college resume included membership in the Glee Club and two literary societies, plus a stint as class president. But Mathewson created a bigger impression with his arm. Offered $90 a week to pitch for Taunton, Massachusetts, in the New England League, Mathewson learned a new pitch from one of his teammates, an obscure left-hander who couldn't control it.

Photo courtesy of National
Baseball Hall of Fame Library
Cooperstown, N.Y.

Christy Mathewson

"It was a freak delivery and I was fascinated," Mathewson said years later. "This kid Williams pitched the ball with the same motion that he used for his out-curve, but turned his hand over and snapped his wrist as he let the ball go."

This "fadeaway," the parent pitch of today's screwball, proved a valuable secret weapon for a young right-hander already turning heads with his fastball, curve, and uncanny control.

With Norfolk of the Virginia League in 1900, Mathewson won 20 of his first 22 and attracted offers from the New York Giants and Philadelphia Athletics. He picked the Giants, figuring they needed pitching help more desperately. The only problem was that Mathewson muffed his chance, going 0-3 with a 5.08 ERA.

The Giants were so disappointed in him they cancelled the deal, returning the pitcher and demanding that Norfolk return the $1,500 purchase price. But New York reversed course after the Cincinnati Reds drafted Mathewson from Norfolk for $100 that winter. The Giants arranged to reacquire the Bucknell product for aging veteran Amos Rusie.

Christy Mathewson was a collegiate checkers champion.

As baseball trades go, that one was a no-brainer: Mathewson won all but the last of his 373 career wins for the Giants, while Rusie went winless for the Reds.

Although Mathewson won 20 games as a rookie for the 1901 Giants, the team finished seventh. A year later, when he compiled a 14-17 mark, the team finished last, 53 games behind Pittsburgh. But a midseason managerial change gave Mathewson the lift he needed.

The minute that new manager John McGraw arrived, he ended the team's experiments with Mathewson at first base and shortstop, making the right-hander a full-time pitcher.

"That kid has as fine a pitching motion as I ever saw and as much stuff as any young fellow to come up in years," McGraw said. "He'll pitch from now on."

Responding to his new responsibility in 1903, Mathewson won 30 games, eight of them against pennant-winning Pittsburgh. That year, he launched a string of three straight 30-win seasons – a league record he would later share with Alexander. When he won 30 games for the fourth time in 1908, Mathewson not only became the first National Leaguer to do that, but the only one to win as many as 37 in a single season.

He was 32 and at the peak of his game when he earned his 300th win in 1912, a year better known for the sinking of the Titanic, the opening of Fenway Park, and the election of Woodrow Wilson as president.

After winning No. 300 in June of 1912, Mathewson looked like a good bet to reach 400, joining Cy Young and Walter Johnson in a highly exclusive fraternity.

Honus Wagner certainly thought so. "Mathewson knew more about batters in five minutes than the modern pitcher does in a whole season," Wagner said in 1929. "He had a fastball, slowball, a great curve, a drop, the fadeaway, and the best control I ever saw. Neither Mathewson nor Grover Cleveland Alexander ever let you have a ball in a spot where they knew you could hit it."

According to Giants catcher Roger Bresnahan, "Matty was the greatest pitcher of all time. He always pitched to the batter's weakness. He had all kinds of stuff and knew just when to use it."

Mathewson won 20 games in 13 different seasons, a National League record later tied by Warren Spahn, and got a dozen of those in succession, from 1903-14. He led the league in victories and shutouts four times, and strikeouts and earned run average (though not yet an official statistic) five times each. His career ERA of 2.13 trails only Mordecai Brown's 2.06 on the National League list.

"Next to control, the whole secret of big-league pitching is mixing 'em up," Mathewson said. "It means inducing a batter to believe that another kind of ball is coming from the one that is really to be delivered and thus preventing him from getting set to hit it."

A master at his craft, Mathewson specialized in economy of pitches. He often needed only 80 pitches, rarely reaching 100, even in pitching complete games.

His biggest wins came in the 1905 World Series against the powerful Philadelphia Athletics. He shut out the A's three times in six days, yielding 14 hits and one walk in 27 innings.

Although he threw 12 of his 79 lifetime shutouts in 1908, Mathewson missed another shot at a world championship because of a late-season base-running blunder instantly named "Merkle's boner" because it involved 19-year-old first baseman Fred Merkle.

It happened on September 23, when the Giants and Cubs were tied atop the standings, with the Pittsburgh Pirates a game-and-a-half back. Mathewson and Jack Pfeister, a lefty known as "Jack the Giant-Killer," dueled to a 1-1 tie as the two first-place teams headed into the last of the ninth inning at the Polo Grounds.

With one out, the Giants' Art Devlin singled, then was forced at second by Moose McCormick. Merkle singled to right, sending McCormick to third, and Al Bridwell followed with a single to center. McCormick scored what seemed to be the winning run, but Merkle, in his excitement, never touched second base. With jubilant fans pouring onto the field, the Cubs called for the ball and relayed it to second baseman Johnny Evers. After some deliberation, umpire Hank O'Day – involved in a similar play 19 days earlier – called Merkle out, creating a tie and depriving Mathewson of a certain win.

After hearing appeals from both sides, National League president Harry Pulliam sided with the umpire, ruling the game would have to be replayed if it impacted the pennant race. On October 3, Pittsburgh won its eighth straight, taking first place by one-half game over the Cubs and one-and-a-half over the Giants. With a three-way pennant playoff still possible, Chicago beat Pittsburgh and finished with a 98-55 record – the same mark New York had after sweeping a season-ending, three-game series from the Boston Doves. The Pirates, at 98-56, were a half-game behind and would lose another half-game to the winner of the makeup game.

Even the rubber-armed Mathewson, who would work 101 innings in 15 September appearances, wasn't up to the task. He yielded four runs in the third and lost, 4-2, to long-time rival Mordecai (Three-Finger) Brown, who relieved for the Cubs in the first inning.

"My arm was so sore and stiff I needed an hour to warm up," he admitted afterward. "I could barely lift it."

The loss was hard to take, not only because of the Merkle game, but also because the Giants outscored the Cubs, 652-624, and allowed opponents five fewer runs than the Cubs' total of 461.

Mathewson would play for pennant-winning teams three more times, but won only one world title during his 16-year career. Another misplay by Merkle was partly responsible.

In the seventh game of the 1912 World Series against the Boston Red Sox, Mathewson took a 2-1 lead into the bottom of the 10th inning. Boston's Clyde Engle led off with an easy fly ball to center fielder Fred Snodgrass, who dropped it, allowing Engle to reach second. Harry Hooper lined out to Snodgrass, then Steve Yerkes walked. When Tris Speaker popped up wide of first, Merkle failed to move from his position at first base and catcher Chief Meyers could not get to the ball on time. It dropped as a harmless foul ball. Given new life, Speaker singled, sending Yerkes to third. Larry Gardner then hit the game-winning sacrifice fly.

Snodgrass' error was called "the $30,000 Muff" because he denied his teammates, including the star-crossed Mathewson, the difference between the winners' share of $4,025 and the losers' share of $2,566 (17 players per team were eligible for the World Series).

Mathewson just rolled with the punches, as he always did.

"He never tried to be different," said long-time teammate Rube Marquard. "He never thought he was better than anybody else. That was just the way he carried himself and the way we saw him. What the hell, when you came down to it, he *was* different and on the mound he *was* better."

For much of his tenure with the Giants, Mathewson had a partner – a rarity in days before teams decided to try pitching rotations. He and southpaw George (Hooks) Wiltse combined for a record 463 wins while winning five pennants during their 11 seasons together, but he produced the combined single-season mark of 68 wins with Joe (Iron Man) McGinnity. It happened in 1904, the second straight season both pitchers topped 30 wins, when Mathewson went 33-12 and McGinnity was 35-8. One year earlier, when they became the first pair of teammates to post 30-win seasons, Mathewson was 30-13 and McGinnity 31-20.

In 1908, Mathewson (37-11) teamed with Wiltse (23-14) for 60 wins, only the fourth time that any 20th century tandem won that many. That was the same year McGraw rode Mathewson like a rusty lawn-mower in the waning days of summer. The pitcher reached career highs with 56 appearances and 390 innings pitched – 110 of them in

September alone. After Mathewson finally proved mortal in the makeup game against the Cubs, McGraw became the first manager to rotate his starters and rely on a regular relief pitcher, Otis (Doc) Crandall.

Called "Big Six" because he looked more imposing on the mound than his 6'1", 195-pound size suggested, Mathewson had no hard feelings toward his manager. In fact, they became friends and even roommates for a year – unlikely developments for such mismatched personalities. But the rabble-rousing McGraw, whose vocabulary was invariably profane, regarded the pitcher as the son he never had. Together with their wives, the Mathewsons and McGraws were a frequent foursome on the social circuit.

A voracious reader whose mom wanted him to be a preacher, Mathewson was described in 1909 as someone who "talks like a Harvard graduate, looks like an actor, acts like a businessman, and impresses you as an all-around gentleman."

His lone weakness was letting up with a big lead – a tendency that frustrated his manager.

"Matty was a great one for loafing when the pressure was off," said Larry Doyle, his teammate with the Giants. "He was only great when he had to be. In tight ballgames, he was impossible to hit. But when the score was lopsided, Matty didn't seem to care a whit about his reputation. He'd toss in plenty of fat ones."

Working exclusively in the Dead Ball Era, Mathewson didn't worry about home runs – even the cozy dimensions of the Polo Grounds were too much for the hitters of the time – and was equally stingy with bases on balls, once throwing 68 straight innings without walking a batter. He had a lifetime average of 1.59 walks per nine innings, but yielded more than 300 hits in five different seasons. Getting on base against him was a lot easier than scoring.

A mix-and-match master, Mathewson once said, "Anybody's best pitch is the one the batters aren't hitting that day. And it didn't take long to find out. If they started hitting my fastball, they didn't see it anymore that afternoon. If they started getting hold of my curveball,

I just put it away for the day. If they started hitting both of them on the same day, that's when they put me away."

Although he pitched no-hitters in 1901 and 1905, Mathewson always maintained that the highlight of his career was his three-shutout performance in the 1905 World Series. The marquee matchup might have come in the opener of that Series, when the Philadelphia Athletics started Eddie Plank, another future 300-game winner.

The Giants won, 3-0, on Matty's four-hitter as he started a streak of 28 scoreless innings in World Series play. Though later surpassed by both Babe Ruth and Whitey Ford, that mark is still the standard for both right-handers and National Leaguers.

Mathewson produced a record fourth World Series shutout in 1913, beating Plank and the A's in the second game, but otherwise lost five of his other six Series decisions after 1905. As a result, the Giants lost potential world titles three times in a row (1911-13), an ignominious mark no National League team has duplicated.

Proving that all good things must come to an end, Mathewson began to fade in 1914, when the Cubs finally knocked the Giants from the top rung in the National League standings. He lost more than he won in 1915, and was demoted to the bullpen a year later. When offered a chance to manage at Cincinnati, Mathewson requested a trade.

McGraw obliged, dealing three future Hall of Famers – Mathewson, Edd Roush, and Bill McKechnie – for Buck Herzog and Red Killefer. Cincinnati fans, tired of watching Mathewson beat their team (68-14 lifetime), got to see the pitcher post the last win of his illustrious career.

In a specially-arranged farewell duel set for the second game of a Labor Day doubleheader between the Reds and Cubs, Mathewson beat Brown, 10-8, evening their lifetime records as rivals at 13-13.

The man whose mother hoped he would be a minister instead became a baseball legend, praised in print and by preachers. The soft-spoken pitcher was the subject of songs, sonnets, and books, even writing *Pitching in a Pinch* himself – without the services of a ghostwriter. He also was an early advocate of a union for baseball players, whom he thought were poorly treated by club owners.

Modest to a fault, Mathewson avoided attention, creating the impression he was aloof. He even pulled down the shades of railroad cars so that crowds couldn't see him.

"He could walk past admirers like he was striding alone on an empty beach," Chief Meyers remembered. Only once, when National League president Harry Pulliam upheld the ruling that the Merkle game was a tie, did the pitcher display a temper, threatening to retire unless the game was given to the Giants. He later softened those remarks, saying, "We'll just have to beat them again."

Though few people beat Mathewson, the trenches of World War I proved too potent. A captain with the American Expeditionary Forces, he contracted tuberculosis after inhaling poison gas. Against the orders of doctors who mandated complete rest, Mathewson left his Saranac Lake, New York, sanitarium to take a job as president of the Boston Braves. After collapsing, he returned to Saranac Lake, where he died on the first day of the 1925 World Series at the age of 47. Eleven years later, he and Walter Johnson were the first pitchers admitted to the newly-created Baseball Hall of Fame.

"Christy Mathewson was the greatest pitcher who ever lived," said Connie Mack, who saw all of the game's biggest winners during his 50-year tenure as manager of the Philadelphia A's. "He had knowledge, judgment, perfect control, and form."

Mathewson actually agreed to Mack's offer to join the A's in 1901, the debut year of the American League, but didn't realize his contract had already been acquired by the Giants. Warned that the new league would fail, and that the Giants would sue to keep him, Mathewson went to New York instead of Philadelphia. The rest of his story made baseball history.

Box Score of 300th Win

Mathewson Box Score
New York Giants 3, Chicago Cubs 2

Game played on Thursday, June 13, 1912

Chicago	ab	r	h	New York	ab	r	h
Sheckard lf	3	0	1	Devore lf	4	0	0
Schulte rf	4	0	0	Doyle 2b	4	1	3
Downs ss	4	0	0	Snodgrass 1b	3	0	1
Leach 3b	4	0	1	Murray rf	3	0	1
Miller df	4	0	1	Becker cf	3	0	1
Saier 1b	4	0	1	Herzog 3b	3	1	1
Evers 2b	4	1	1	Myers c	2	1	2
Archer c	3	1	1	Fletcher ss	2	0	0
Cheney p	3	0	0	Mathewson p	3	0	1
Totals	33	2	6	Totals	27	3	10

Chicago	0	0	0	0	1	0	1	0	0	–	2
New York	0	0	0	0	2	1	0	0	x	–	3

DP-Chicago 1. **E**-Devore, Schulte. **LOB**-Chicago 5, New York 4. **2B**-Myers, Mathewson. **3B**-Leach. **HR**-Archer. **SB**-Becker, Doyle. **SF**-Snodgrass. **SFF**-Fletcher, Murray. **Base on Balls**-Cheney 1, Mathewson 1. **Strikeouts**-Cheney 5, Mathewson 8. T-1:45

Career Statistics

MATHEWSON, Christy — Christopher "Big Six, Matty" Mathewson; B: 8/12/1878, Factoryville, PA; D: 10/7/1925, Saranac Lake, NY; BR/TR, 6'1.5"/195 lbs.; Debut: 7/17/1900; HOF 1936

YEAR	TM-L	W	L	PCT	G	GS	CG	SH	SV	IP	H	R	HR	SO	ERA
1900	NY-N	0	3	0.000	6	1	1	0	0	33	37	32	1	15	5.08
1901	NY-N	20	17	0.541	40	38	36	5	0	336	288	131	3	221	2.41
1902	NY-N	14	17	0.452	35	33	30	8	0	284	246	118	3	164	2.06
1903	NY-N	30	13	0.698	45	42	37	3	2	366	321	136	4	267	2.26
1904	NY-N	33	12	0.733	48	46	33	4	1	367	306	120	7	212	2.03
1905	NY-N	31	9	0.775	43	37	32	8	2	338	252	85	4	206	1.28
1906	NY-N	22	12	0.647	38	35	22	6	1	266	262	100	3	128	2.97
1907	NY-N	24	12	0.667	41	36	31	8	2	315	250	88	5	178	2.00
1908	NY-N	37	11	0.771	56	44	34	11	5	390	285	86	5	259	1.43
1909	NY-N	25	6	0.806	37	33	26	8	2	275	192	57	2	149	1.14
1910	NY-N	27	9	0.750	38	35	27	2	0	318	292	100	5	184	1.89
1911	NY-N	26	13	0.667	45	37	29	5	3	307	303	102	5	141	1.99
1912	NY-N	23	12	0.657	43	34	27	0	4	310	311	107	5	134	2.12
1913	NY-N	25	11	0.694	40	35	25	4	2	306	291	94	8	93	2.06
1914	NY-N	24	13	0.649	41	35	29	5	2	312	314	133	16	80	3.00
1915	NY-N	8	14	0.364	27	24	11	1	0	186	199	97	9	57	3.58
1916	NY-N	3	4	0.429	12	6	4	1	2	65	59	27	3	16	2.33
	Cin-N	1	0	1.000	1	1	1	0	0	9	15	8	1	3	8.00
	Year	4	4	0.500	13	7	5	1	2	74	74	35	4	19	3.01
TOTAL	17	373	188	0.665	636	552	435	79	28	4788	4223	1621	89	2507	2.13

Like Christy Mathewson, **Grover Cleveland Alexander** used three straight 30-win seasons as a springboard to 373 lifetime victories, tops on the National League list.

Named for a president, he pitched like royalty. Alexander won the Triple Crown of pitching a record four times (1915-17 and 1920), set National League records for shutouts in a season (16) and career (90), and brought the St. Louis Cardinals their first world title with a heroic relief stint in the 1926 World Series finale.

His best years came with the Phillies. In 1915, when he pitched the Phillies to the National League pennant, he had 36 complete games and four one-hitters, including one spoiled with two outs in the ninth. The 16-shutout season followed. Proving he was durable as well as talented, he pitched and won both ends of doubleheaders in both 1916 and 1917.

Alexander, who pitched in at least 45 games in each of his seven seasons with the Phillies, credited his endurance to farm chores he performed as a kid. "A pitcher may have a great arm," he said, "but if his legs don't hold up under him, he's a dead duck."

His upper body was almost as powerful as his throwing arm, which seldom was sore.

Although the lively ball came into baseball in 1920, the 6'1", 185-pound right-hander kept winning. He was 37 when he won his 300th game on September 20, 1924, beating the New York Giants for the Chicago Cubs. He won 73 more times in his war-interrupted career – an amazing achievement at an advanced athletic age for a pitcher with personal demons.

He might have been even better had he stayed sober, but he resorted to drinking binges that left him with a hangover on days he was scheduled to pitch. Married twice to the same woman, the pitcher promised he'd stop drinking but was unable to keep his word.

Alexander also overcame a broken wrist, a broken ankle, and epileptic fits that increased in intensity after his combat duty in World War I. He carried spirits of ammonia with him in case he needed to be

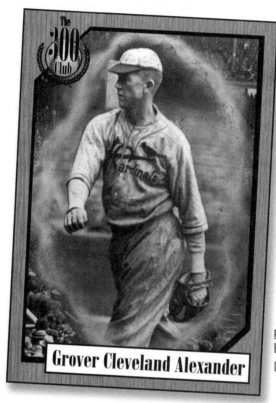

Grover Cleveland Alexander

Photo courtesy of National
Baseball Hall of Fame Library
Cooperstown, N.Y.

revived. To compound his problems, a wartime shrapnel injury to his right ear caused hearing loss.

Alexander never worried about his physical problems while pitching. He liked to get his job done quickly. He and Bill Killefer, his favorite catcher, knew each other so well they didn't need signs. "You throw 'em, I'll catch 'em, and we'll get out of the park early today," said Killefer. Alexander's games sometimes took an hour-and-a-half or less. He finished one game in 58 minutes.

Eight-time batting champion Honus Wagner was one of many admirers.

"He has more different kinds of pitches than any man I ever faced," said the legendary shortstop of the Pittsburgh Pirates. "Alex has a fast ball, medium ball, slow ball, drop ball, and an assortment of curves, all of which he can throw sidearm or overhand. Plus he has perfect control and knows how to mix them up so well that there's no chance to out-guess him."

Another opponent who reached the Hall of Fame, outfielder Max Carey, raved about Alexander's ability to place any pitch exactly where he wanted it. "Alex had the most perfect control of any pitcher I ever saw," Carey said of Alexander, who walked 1.65 batters per nine innings during his 20-year career.

Pat Moran, who eventually lost his job as manager of the Phillies because he complained about the trade of Alexander, praised the pitcher's personality. "There is nothing swell-headed about (Alexander), as there is with some stars," he said. "He is an equal with the other players and always pulling for the team to win, whether he is pitching or not. Off the diamond, he is just as friendly and sociable as he is during the game. His popularity as a player does not out-weigh his popularity as a man."

Moran was popular with the pitcher, too. The former catcher once gave the young Alexander invaluable advice that helped him con-serve his energy and pile up huge win totals.

"Don't try to strike 'em all out," Moran told him. "Use the men behind you. Be smart – save that arm."

Alexander listened. One of his first wins was a 1-0, 12-inning marathon against 44-year-old Cy Young, who was finishing his career the same season that Alexander was starting. Young worked 11 scoreless innings before the Phillies pushed across a run to deny him win No. 512. Alexander was just getting started: the six-time strikeout king would average more than 27 wins per year over his first seven seasons.

He was a man of multiple pitches, motions, and nicknames. Fellow pitcher Jesse Haines, his teammate with the Cardinals, said, "I called him 'Old Low & Away,' because that's the way he pitched everybody: down at the knees and nicking the outside corner with his good fastball or his short, sharp curve."

Killefer called the pitcher Alkali Pete (later shortened to just Pete) after Alexander slipped and fell into a pool of alkali and mud while on a hunting trip in Texas. When he wasn't just "Old Pete," he was variously known as "Alec," "Alex," or "Alexander the Great."

Opponents had nastier names for the pitcher, who won 94 games from 1915-17 and openly admitted he wanted to challenge Cy Young's record of 511 victories. When the war halted his streak of 30-win seasons at three, leaving him tied for that record with Christy Mathewson, he admitted disappointment that he couldn't go for four in a row.

"I consider my curve my main strong point," the pitcher said when asked to describe his repertoire. "I have pretty good speed and a good change-of-pace, which is important, but the main thing with me is curves."

He had several different varieties, thrown from different angles at different speeds, but all designed to freeze the hitter.

Utilizing a short stride and minimal windup, Alexander had an easy motion that put little strain on his arm, allowing him to finish what he started and work often. There were no doctors, trainers, or pitching coaches to dictate otherwise.

In his first year, Alexander threw seven shutouts and struck out 227 batters, a rookie record that survived until Dwight Gooden topped it in 1984. Even Nolan Ryan, a future 300-game winner who became the single-season and career leader in strikeouts, might not have fanned that many in an era that emphasized contact over clout.

Alexander realized control was more vital than velocity. "Every kid pitcher wants to set a batter's shirt on fire with every pitch, just to make an impression," he wrote in 1939. "They want to flash into the Hall of Fame by pitching a no-hit game. But I got myself into the Hall without a no-hitter."

One of 13 children born to his farmer parents in rural Nebraska, Alexander learned control by throwing rocks at chickens who didn't want to be served for dinner.

Like Walter Johnson, he played semipro ball for a telephone company team and attracted the attention of independent professional clubs. In 1909, his first pro season, Alexander was pitching well for

Galesburg, Illinois, of the Central Association when he was almost killed running the bases. A shortstop's throw struck his head, knocking him out for two days and leaving him with a case of double vision that persisted for months.

The problem disappeared during the winter, allowing the right-hander to resume his career. He went 29-14 for the Syracuse Stars of the New York State League, convincing the Philadelphia Phillies to buy his services for the sum of $750. No club has ever made a better purchase, as the Phillies found when they gave Alexander baptism by fire that fall.

Pitted in a City Series exhibition game against the cross-town Philadelphia Athletics, who had just won the World Series, Alexander pitched five hitless innings, earning a rotation spot for 1911.

Had there been a Rookie of the Year Award at that time, Alexander would have won it. Even though his home park was the hitter-friendly Baker Bowl, he went 28-13 with seven shutouts, completed 31 of 37 starts, fanned 227, and worked 11 games in relief. He led the league in wins, innings, complete games, and shutouts, including a 1-0 September win over Cy Young in one of the old veteran's last games. Alexander finished the year with more wins than Christy Mathewson (26) or Rube Marquard (24).

Why Alexander thrived in Baker Bowl, a ballpark better sized for goldfish than ballplayers, remains a mystery. The distance down the right field line was only 272 feet, and the power alley in right-center was 320 at its deepest. It was 341 feet from home to left, a decent distance, and 408 to dead center. Perhaps it was a good thing the Phillies traded him before the lively ball changed the complexion of the game.

It isn't every day that a team dumps a pitcher who keeps leading his league in wins, strikeouts, and earned run average, but that's exactly what happened to Alexander.

Still the only right-hander to win the pitching Triple Crown three straight seasons, he won 190 games – one-third of all the Phillies' wins – during his seven-year tenure with the team. But he got his 300th win while wearing the uniform of the Chicago Cubs.

With America about to enter World War I, the Phillies decided it would be best to deal their star pitcher rather than risk the chance he might not return from the war in one piece – if at all. So they sent him to the Cubs, along with Bill Killefer, for pitcher Mike Prendergast, catcher William Dilhoefer, and $55,000 – a considerable sum in 1917.

For the Phillies, the deal triggered a tumble so steep that the franchise later became the first in any sport to lose 10,000 games. In all but one of the next 31 seasons, the team finished in the second division, emboldening writers to dub them "the futile Phils."

Alexander, on the other hand, still had great moments up his sleeve – after a one-year interval for wartime service that almost certainly deprived him of the chance to win 400 games.

An artillery sergeant on the French front lines with the American Expeditionary Force in 1918, the pitcher suffered shell shock, seizures, and hearing loss. Always quiet, he became reclusive and reflective after his return. But he could still pitch.

To prove the point, he won his fourth pitching Triple Crown in 1920, leading the league with 27 wins, 173 strikeouts, and a 1.91 earned run average. He had two more 20-game seasons left in that aging right arm – one for the Cubs in 1922 and one for the St. Louis Cardinals in 1927. That made him the first pitcher to win 20 for three different teams.

He reached the World Series with two of them, the 1915 Phillies and the 1926 and 1928 Cardinals. After Alexander, the Phillies did not win the pennant again until 1950 and did not have a pitcher with a 20-win season until Robin Roberts did it that same year.

Although he enjoyed his best years with the Phillies, Alexander won his only World Series ring with the Cards. It happened in 1926, after the pitcher's penchant for partying and unpredictable behavior had eroded the patience of Joe McCarthy, the no-nonsense manager promoted to run the Cubs that spring.

"Alex could still pitch, but he insisted on going by his own rules and that wasn't good for the rest of the team," said McCarthy, "I had to let him go."

On June 22, 1926, the Cubs let the Cards claim Alexander in a $6,000 waiver deal they would soon regret. In his first game as a Cardinal, Alexander beat McCarthy's Cubs, 3-2, and won eight more games, including a shutout against Chicago. That effort helped the Cardinals win their first pennant with a two-game margin over the runner-up Cincinnati Reds. Their World Series opponents, the New York Yankees, were heavy favorites because of their 1-2 punch of Babe Ruth and Lou Gehrig, but the oddsmakers hadn't considered Alexander.

The crafty veteran started and won the second and sixth games, then watched from the bullpen while the teams met for Game 7 on October 10, a cold, dreary day that cut down the size of the Yankee Stadium crowd to 38,093. Jesse (Pop) Haines, the Cardinal starter, had a 3-2 lead when a blister forced his exit with the bases full, two outs in the seventh, and heavy-hitting rookie Tony Lazzeri due to bat. Rogers Hornsby, the St. Louis player-manager, had told Alexander to stay ready and not to celebrate his Game 6 win – just in case.

Even though he had pitched a complete game the previous day and was not warming up in the bullpen, Alexander got the call when Haines couldn't continue. He'd held Lazzeri hitless in four at-bats during Game 6 and Hornsby needed him to get the rookie one last time.

"I figured the young fellow was more nervous than I was," said Alexander, who deliberately took his time strolling in from the bullpen. "If I were the worrying kind, I wouldn't have pitched that many years in the big leagues."

Always confident when it came to his pitching, Alexander had already led the National League in shutouts seven times, and in wins and complete games six times each. He didn't need much warm-up time.

"The umpire let me throw eight warm-up pitches, but I just lobbed the last two," the pitcher said later. "I knew how to pitch to Lazzeri and he knew I did. He knew I wasn't going to throw a fastball by him. I wasn't crazy. He murdered fastball pitching."

Alexander needed only four pitches to strike out the Yankee rookie. He then pitched two more scoreless innings to nail down the win. The only man to reach base was Ruth, who walked on a border-line 3-2 pitch, but was thrown out trying to steal in the ninth inning. "I wasn't going to let that big monkey beat me," said the pitcher, who nailed down winners' checks worth $5,584.51.

The first world championship for the city of St. Louis in baseball's modern era was also the only one of Alexander's career. He had pitched and won the 1915 Phillies-Red Sox opener, but his team lost the next four. In 1928, when the Yankees swept the Cardinals, Alexander was the losing pitcher in Game 2.

Showing signs of age in 1929, Alexander spent part of the season in what would now be called an alcohol detox center. He returned in July, just after Bill McKechnie became the St. Louis manager for the second time.

"We were in Pittsburgh and Alec said, 'I'd like to pitch here,'" the manager remembered. "I was a little skeptical because he hadn't pitched in weeks, but I agreed and he pitched a shutout. Our next stop was Philadelphia, where he had been so great and had many friends. We were tied after nine innings and I sent Alec in, saying 'Hold 'em until we can get that winning run for you.' He pitched five scoreless innings, we won in the 14th, and he had No. 373."

That 11-9 win at Philadelphia would be his last, as his sobriety ended so stunningly that St. Louis shipped him home for the final six weeks of the season. Alexander believed he had broken a tie with Christy Mathewson for tops on the National League victory list, but later learned that Mathewson had been charged with a 1902 defeat that should have been a win. The official decision left the two pitchers tied.

Because of his career achievements, the hapless Phillies decided to give the old man one more chance. On December 11, 1929, they traded Homer Peel and Bob McGraw to the Cards for Alexander and Harry McCurdy. But Alexander did no better than the crumbling stock market, going 0-3 in nine games and leaving the majors for good.

Although his dad wanted him to become a lawyer, Alexander knew no profession beyond baseball. He might have made more money in law: his peak as a player was $17,500 in 1927.

After the Phillies cut him for the final time, Alexander pitched briefly in the minors and then spent years with the House of David, a barnstorming team, before hanging up his spikes. Seeking to make ends meet, he even joined a flea circus where he recounted tales of his 1926 World Series exploits. Unlike fellow war veteran Christy Mathewson, whom he beat in two of their three confrontations, Alexander lived to attend his induction ceremonies at the Baseball Hall of Fame.

Career Statistics

ALEXANDER,Grover							Grover Cleveland "Old Pete" Alexander; B: 2/26/1887, Elba, NE; D:11/4/1950 St. Paul, NE; BR/TR, 6'1"/185; Debut: 4/15/1911; HOF 1938						
YEAR	TM-L	W	L	PCT	G	GS	CG-SHO	SV-BS	IP	H	R	HR	SO	ERA
1911	Phi-N	28	13	0.683	48	37	31-7	3	367	285	133	5	227	2.57
1912	Phi-N	19	17	0.528	46	34	25-3	3	310	289	133	11	195	2.81
1913	Phi-N	22	8	0.733	47	36	23-9	2	306	288	106	9	159	2.79
1914	Phi-N	27	15	0.643	46	39	32-6	1	355	327	133	8	214	2.38
1915	Phi-N	31	10	0.756	49	42	36-12	3	376	253	86	3	241	1.22
1916	Phi-N	33	12	0.733	48	45	38-16	3	389	323	90	6	167	1.55
1917	Phi-N	30	13	0.698	45	44	34-8	0	388	336	107	4	200	1.83
1918	Chi-N	2	1	0.667	3	3	3	0	26	19	7	0	15	1.73
1919	Chi-N	16	11	0.593	30	27	20-9	1	235	180	51	3	121	1.72
1920	Chi-N	27	14	0.659	46	40	33-7	5	363	335	96	8	173	1.91
1921	Chi-N	15	13	0.536	31	30	21-3	1	252	286	110	10	77	3.39
1922	Chi-N	16	13	0.552	33	31	20-1	1	245	283	111	8	48	3.63
1923	Chi-N	22	12	0.647	39	36	26-3	2	305	308	128	17	72	3.19
1924	Chi-N	12	5	0.706	21	20	12	0	169	183	82	9	33	3.03
1925	Chi-N	15	11	0.577	32	30	20-1	0	236	270	106	14	63	3.39
1926	Chi-N	3	3	0.500	7	7	4	0	52	55	26	0	12	3.46
	StL-N	9	7	0.563	23	16	11-12	2	148	136	57	8	35	2.91
	Year	12	10	0.545	30	23	15-2	2	200	191	83	8	47	3.05
1927	StL-N	21	10	0.677	37	30	22-2	3	268	261	94	11	48	2.52
1928	StL-N	16	9	0.640	34	31	18-1	2	243	262	107	15	59	3.36
1929	StL-N	9	8	0.529	22	19	8	0	132	149	65	10	33	3.89
1930	Phi-N	0	3	0.000	9	3	0	0	21	40	24	5	6	9.14
TOTAL	20	373	208	0.642	696	600	437-90	32	5190	4868	1852	164	2198	2.56

Box Score of 300th Win

Alexander Box Score			
Chicago Cubs 7, New York Giants 3			

Game played on Saturday, September 20, 1924			

Chicago	ab	r	h	New York	ab	r	h
Adams ss	7	1	1	Lindstrom 3b	4	0	1
Heathcote cf	4	1	2	O'Connell 3b	2	1	0
Grantham 2b	5	0	1	Fisch 2b	6	1	2
Fitzgerald c	6	1	1	Nehf rf	0	0	0
Fribert 3b	5	1	3	Youngs rf	5	0	3
Grigsby lf	5	3	1	Kelly cf	6	0	3
Hartnett c	6	0	4	Terry 1b	6	1	0
Cotter 1b	6	0	2	Wilson lf	6	0	2
Alexander p	6	0	1	Jackson ss	6	0	3
Totals	50	7	16	Gowdy c	5	0	0
				Barnes p	2	0	0
				a-Southworth ph	1	0	0
				Jonnard p	0	0	0
				b-Bentley ph	1	0	1
				c-McQuillan pr	0	0	0
				Ryan p	0	0	0
				d-Snyder ph	1	0	0
				Maun p	0	0	0
				Baldwin p	0	0	0
				Totals	51	3	15

Chicago	0	1	0	0	0	1	1	0	0	0	0	4	7
New York	0	0	1	0	0	0	0	1	1	0	0	0	3

a-Batted for Barns in 7th.
b-Batted for Jonnard in 9th
c-Ran for Bentley in 9th.
d-Batted for Ryan in 11th..
DP-Chicago 1, New York 1. **LOB-**Chicago 12, New York 13. **E-**Adams, Heathcote, Grantham, Friberg Hartnett, O'Connell, Kelly, Jackson. **2B-**Wilson. 3B-Hrtnett. **SB-**Frisch. **SF-**Heathcote, Granthanm. **Base on Balls-**Barnes 1, Ryan 2, Alexander 1. **Strikeouts-**Jonnard 2, Barnes 1, Ryan 2, Alexander 5. **Hits off** Alexander 15 in 12 IP, Barnes 10 in 7 IP, Jonnard 0 in 2 IP, Ryan 1 in 2 IP, Maun 3 in 1/3 IP, Baldwin 1 in 2/3 IP. **Winning Pitcher-**Alexander. **Losing Pitcher-**Maun. T-2:30.

The Winningest Southpaw

Warren Spahn – 363 Wins

Had wartime military service not interfered, Warren Spahn could have won 400 games. In fact, he might have challenged Walter Johnson for second place on the career victory list.

Although he made his major-league debut in 1942, Spahn soon swapped his Boston Braves jersey for army fatigues – and became the only ballplayer to win a battlefield commission during World War II. He also won a Bronze Star, a Purple Heart, and the confidence that he could overcome insurmountable odds.

With his military discharge delayed by his commission, Spahn was still in Germany while most of his baseball teammates were assembling for spring training in 1946. But he returned in time to post an 8-5 record as a 25-year-old rookie and launch a career marked by remarkable consistency.

By the time he was finished in 1965, Warren Edward Spahn not only had more wins than any left-handed pitcher, but more wins than any pitcher who played in the postwar era. Only two National Leaguers, Christy Mathewson and Grover Cleveland Alexander, ever won more.

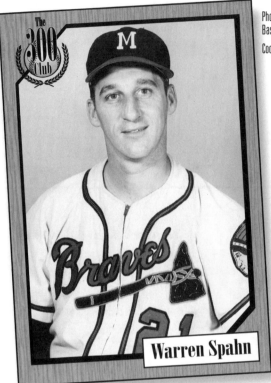

Like both of those legends, who were still active the year he was born, Spahn cranked out 20-win seasons with the regularity of the Old Faithful geyser. Once the season started, the high-kicking southpaw baffled batters with pinpoint control and an assortment of pitches that kept them guessing. When his fastball faded in mid-career, the pitcher reinvented himself, switching to sliders and screwballs without missing a beat.

He was 39 when he pitched his first no-hitter, winning 4-0 against the Philadelphia Phillies on September 16, 1960, and five days past his 40th birthday when he bagged another no-hitter, blanking the heavy-hitting San Francisco Giants on April 28, 1961. Spahn's barehanded grab and backhanded flip of a Matty Alou bunt in the ninth inning kept that hitless game intact, giving Spahn his 290th win and 52nd shutout.

"This is ridiculous," he said during the clubhouse celebration. "A fellow my age shouldn't be pitching no-hitters." At the time, only Cy Young had pitched a no-hitter at such an advanced athletic age. Nolan Ryan and Randy Johnson, also 300-game winners, have done it since.

When he won his 300th game with a 2-1, six-hit victory over the Chicago Cubs at Milwaukee County Stadium on August 11, 1961, Spahn gave no thought to retirement. His miraculous left arm contained 63 more victories, 23 of them during a last-hurrah 1963 campaign that could only be described as a pitcher's magical mystery tour.

Had Bobby Bragan, the new manager of the Milwaukee Braves, not allowed him to pitch all 16 innings at windy Candlestick Park on July 2, 1963, Spahn might have prolonged his career even more. He never confirmed it, but he may have over-extended himself in that 200-pitch performance, a 1-0 loss to San Francisco's young ace, Juan Marichal.

Why else would Spahn succumb to advancing age so suddenly? Just a year after posting a 23-7 record for the second time in his career, the lefty lost his edge, finishing with a 6-13 record that ended his 21-year tenure with the Braves. Sold to the pitching-poor New York Mets for $1, Spahn was supposed to serve as both pitcher and coach. He won four of his first five decisions, then lost 11 straight, but refused to remove himself from the pitching rotation. Casey Stengel let him go for the second time, but Spahn wouldn't quit. He hooked on with San Francisco, a pennant contender, and went 3-4, which was not good enough to save his career.

Adamant about not wanting to retire, Spahn had no choice, finishing 10 wins behind Mathewson and Alexander on the lifetime victory chart. But pitching exclusively in the lively ball era made Spahn's achievements all the more remarkable.

He had 363 wins, the exact same number of hits as a batter, and 63 shutouts, one short of Eddie Plank's major-league record for lefties. He led the National League in complete games nine times, seven of them in succession from 1957-63, and won at least 20 games 13 times, a record shared by Mathewson during the "modern era" that started in 1901.

The only pitcher to start All-Star Games in three different decades, Spahn was an All-Star 17 times, five more times than any other pitcher (runner-up was Tom Seaver, another 300-game winner). He helped himself with his bat, his glove, and a prolific pickoff move that was anathema to the few runners who reached base against him. Although he worked in a four-man rotation most of his career, he'd pitch on shorter rest if needed and would work in relief between starts. He was such a good hitter (35 home runs, the record for NL pitchers) that he once pinch-hit for future MVP Joe Torre, a rookie catcher with the 1960 Braves who would catch Spahn's 300th win a year later.

"No pitcher has ever made such magnificent use of his God-given equipment," Branch Rickey once said of Spahn. "He has no equal. He knows how to pitch, when to pitch, what to pitch. Others may not agree with me, but my honest opinion is that there never has been a better pitcher in the history of baseball."

During the decade of the 1950s, when the National League's eight teams played a 154-game schedule, teams played rivals 22 times each. As a result, Spahn had frequent head-to-head confrontations with Willie Mays, Stan Musial, Ernie Banks, Jackie Robinson, Frank Robinson and other future Hall of Famers. Still, the crafty left-hander won 202 times, more than any other pitcher, during the decade. A master of consistency, Warren won 101 games from 1950-54 and another 101 games from 1955-59.

After an 0-for-12 start to his career, Mays got his first hit on May 28, 1951, with a home run against Spahn. Mays connected again in 1963 to win the 16-inning game. Those two, plus 15 more, gave him more career home runs against Spahn than anyone else.

"He was something like 0-for-21 (actually 0-for-12) the first time I saw him," Spahn said of Mays years later. "His first major-league hit was a home run off me – and I'll never forgive myself. We might have gotten rid of Willie forever if I'd only struck him out."

Musial, a seven-time batting champion, hit .314 with 14 homers against Spahn – even though both were left-handed. It was little consolation to the pitcher that he held Musial to a lower batting average than the rest of the National League's pitchers.

"He had great confidence in himself and nothing could shake that confidence," said Del Crandall, Spahn's primary catcher during his heyday in Milwaukee. "He just went out and did

After losing on a Willie Mays home run, Spahn said: "For the first 60 feet, it was a helluva pitch."

his job and there is no question he was the best left-hander who ever lived."

Although fans of Sandy Koufax and Lefty Grove might disagree, Spahn did things neither they nor any other pitcher could top. He led his league in complete games nine times and in victories eight times. He not only led in ERA three times, but also was the only pitcher to do it in three different decades. He also led his league in innings pitched, strikeouts, and shutouts four times each, pitched more innings (5,243) than any left-hander, and finished more games (382 complete games in 665 starts), indicating that many of his 245 losses were close games.

"Spahn hated to miss a turn," remembered Gene Conley, who also pitched for the Braves in Milwaukee. "If your turn was rained out and he was due the next day, then you sat out and he pitched. I remember one time they started me and held Spahn back a day. He didn't like that at all. He went up to the front office and got it squared away. He didn't want to miss a turn. He loved baseball and loved to pitch so much you got the feeling that pitching was his whole life."

It didn't start that way. He played first base in a semi-pro league with his dad, a wallpaper salesman, and wanted to keep that position at South Park High School. But a talented incumbent blocked his path, forcing Spahn to try pitching.

His father, Ed Spahn, built a mound in his backyard and worked hard with young Warren, one of six children. "He insisted I throw with a fluid motion and the high leg kick was part of deception to the hitter," Spahn said of his dad. "Hitters said the ball seemed to come out of my uniform."

At 15, he was playing six days a week for three different teams: South Park High School, the American Legion, and the Buffalo Municipal League. Father and son even played together, manning opposite infield corners, for one team. Within three years, Spahn had attracted the eye of a Boston Braves scout who offered a $150 bonus and a minor-league contract for $80 a month.

He accepted, launching his professional career in 1940.

America was already at war by the time Spahn reached the Braves, then managed by Casey Stengel, after a 19-6 season at Evansville of the Three-I League. He went north with the 1942 Braves, but was optioned to Hartford after refusing to knock down Dodger shortstop Pee Wee Reese with a pitch. Stengel later called it the biggest mistake he ever made.

Spahn went 17-12 in the Eastern League, returning to the Braves in time to start a game on September 26 against the New York Giants at the Polo Grounds. Spahn was behind, 5-2, in the eighth when fans rushed the field, forcing a forfeit to the Braves. The game went into the books as a 9-0 win, and a complete game for Spahn, but he received no credit for the win because he trailed at the time of the forfeit. His big-league record that year shows four games, two of them starts, and one complete game, but a 0-0 record.

Had Spahn spent 1942 in Boston rather than Hartford, he might have produced the 10 wins that separate him from Alexander and Mathewson on the lifetime victory list. But the pitcher, who marched off to war that fall, never regretted his date with destiny.

Assigned to the Army's combat engineers, Spahn came within a whisker of losing his life when the Rhine River bridge at Remagen, Germany, collapsed, killing dozens of comrades, just minutes after he was standing next to it. Losing baseball games hardly compared.

"It was a great learning experience," admitted Spahn, who later played a German sergeant on a television episode of *Combat*. "I didn't want to be a serviceman, but my country was in trouble. I spent three-and-a-half years away, but I grew up. I think it made me a better pitcher. I was able to perform better under stress than before I went into the service because of the training I had gotten. I never once felt I was deprived."

In 1946, the year Spahn became a civilian again, the Braves had a new manager, with Billy Southworth succeeding Stengel. But the careers of Spahn and Stengel would intersect again.

After a long and prosperous career with the Braves in both Boston and Milwaukee, Spahn found Stengel his manager again with the 1965 New York Mets – and Yogi Berra, lured out of retirement, as a battery mate. Noting that Stengel had sandwiched tenures with bad teams around a Yankees stint that produced 10 pennants in 12 years, Spahn said, "I played for Casey before and after he was a genius." When asked if he and Berra would form baseball's oldest pitcher-catcher tandem, he said, "I don't know if we'll be the oldest, but we'll certainly be the ugliest."

The hook-nosed pitcher had already developed a reputation as a practical joker, often in tandem with fellow pitcher Lew Burdette. They delighted in torturing diminutive Donald Davidson, a dwarf who rose from batboy to traveling secretary during his long career with the Braves in three different cities, and tested the limits of several managers and coaches. But none could argue with their record: 201 wins from 1956-60 and more than twice that many, 443, during the decade they were teammates in Milwaukee (1953-63).

One of the best left-right tandems in baseball history, Spahn and Burdette were at their best with the game on the line. In the 1957 World Series, when a case of the flu kept Spahn from making his scheduled start in Game 7, Burdette took over on two days' rest and pitched his third complete game and second shutout of the Series. Spahn won the other game as the Milwaukee Braves won their only world championship.

A year later, Spahn won two games, one of them a two-hit shutout, in a seven-game rematch with the Yankees, but Burdette didn't duplicate his magical October of 1957. Including his 1-1 mark in the 1948 World Series between the Boston Braves and Cleveland Indians, Spahn was 4-3 in Series play with a 3.05 ERA, just four points above his regular-season mark. He also had a 1-0 All-Star record, winning the 1953 game in relief of starter Robin Roberts.

Had the Cy Young Award been created before 1956, or given to pitchers in both leagues before 1967, Spahn would have won a handful. He finished first only in 1957, when he went 21-11 with a 2.69 ERA, but was second in 1958, 1960, and 1961. Editors of *The ESPN Baseball Encyclopedia* agreed, awarding imaginary National League "Cys" to Spahn in 1949, 1953, 1958, and 1961.

He could have won the trophy in either of his two 23-7 seasons, especially while posting a career-best 2.10 ERA in 1953, the first year the Braves played in Milwaukee after leaving Boston. Ten years later, with the same record, the balding left-hander had 22 complete games, seven of them shutouts, at the ripe old age of 42. Given any support in the 16-inning game, Spahn would have been 24-6.

The 1963 campaign was an "I'll show them" season for the legendary left-hander. In 1962, Milwaukee manager Birdie Tebbetts decided to try a five-man rotation, and Spahn bristled. Appearing in four fewer games than he did the year before, Spahn dropped to 18 wins, interrupting a six-year string of 20-win seasons. One of his 14 losses came at the Polo Grounds when Hobie Landrith, a light-hitting catcher, hit a pop fly down the right-field line at the horseshoe-shaped Polo Grounds. Little more than a 250-foot fly ball, it narrowly cleared the wall, scoring a runner who had reached on an error. The Mets, who would win only 39 other games that season, beat the Braves and their ace, 3-2. It was the only home run Landrith hit for the Mets.

Given the chance to pitch more frequently under Bobby Bragan, who replaced Tebbetts after 1962, Spahn responded. He liked the heavy workload, appearing at least 40 times in five different seasons and twice making at least 38 starts. In Spahn's mind, more games meant more wins – for himself and for his team.

Although he had three knee surgeries during his career, Spahn never had arm problems. "I never put too much strain on my arm," said the pitcher, who stayed in shape each winter by swimming and working on his Oklahoma cattle ranch. "Mechanics are so important. You've got to be a student of pitching."

A great learner, Spahn picked up the curveball from his dad Ed, the slider from long-time Braves pitching coach Whitlow Wyatt, and the pickoff move from Willard Donovan, a lefty nobody remembers. "Every one of his pitches had an idea behind it," Wyatt once said.

The idea, from Spahn's perspective, was to keep hitters guessing. "You have to be able to throw strikes," he said, "but you try not to whenever possible."

His game kept getting better as he aged. After the age of 30, he won 276 games – a total exceeded only by Cy Young (316) and Phil Niekro (287).

"I never threw a ball down the middle of the plate," Spahn said. "The plate is 17 inches wide. I always figured the middle 12 belonged to the hitter. I concentrated on hitting the corners or the two-and-a-half inches on each side."

Named after President Warren G. Harding, Spahn was born in 1921. He not only wore his birth year on his uniform, but also won exactly 21 games in seven different seasons. Numerologists also love the fact that he had 363 wins and 363 base hits.

Spahn's bat gave him a huge advantage over opponents. In an era without interleague play or the designated hitter, he was the only pitcher to homer in 10 different ballparks during the regular season. He also joined Hank Aaron, the career home run leader for 27 years, as the only Braves players to homer in more than 15 consecutive seasons (Spahn connected 17 years in a row).

That string overlapped the 1958 season, when Spahn performed the rare feat of hitting .300 and winning 20 games.

Spahn gave up more than his share of home runs: a total of 433, two of them to future Hall of Famers Willie Mays and Sandy Koufax.

"I hit him pretty well," Stan Musial once told St. Louis writer Bob Broeg, "but most of those hits came early in our careers when he could really throw hard and I had quicker reflexes. He'd try to buzz one by me. Over the years, I learned I had to give in, to go to the opposite field against him, to wait on the ball a split-second longer, or I wouldn't have a chance. Facing Warren was the greatest challenge I knew because the man was a pitching scientist, an artist with imagination."

Although he won four single-season strikeout titles, Spahn was one of three 300-game winners who never fanned 200 men in a season (along with Early Wynn and Tom Glavine). Although far from the form of Nolan Ryan, Roger Clemens, or Randy Johnson, who powered their way to 300 wins, Spahn did fan 18 men in a 15-inning game (losing, 3-1, to the Cubs on June 14, 1952, the same day the Braves signed Hank Aaron) and 15 in his first no-hitter, in 1960.

Spahn and Koufax had a relationship not unlike the tortoise and the hare. Spahn, steadily plodding along with his penchant for winning 20 every summer, eventually became the "winningest" southpaw, as the pitcher described himself, while Koufax streaked across the big-league firmament like a white-hot meteor, shining brightly for five seasons before disappearing. Spahn lasted much longer than the Dodger southpaw, who didn't come close to 300 wins, because he avoided injuries and was able to evolve into a different kind of pitcher.

According to former teammate Johnny Sain, who became a highly-respected pitching coach, "Warren was able to change over from being a power pitcher. He was one of the smartest men ever to play the game. He came up with a screwball to help when his fastball began to fade, and then added the slider. And consider the ability of a man to be able to pitch no-hit games and even jerk up big strikeout performances when he was 40 years old."

Sain knew Spahn well. In 1948, their ability to pitch well and pitch often helped the Boston Braves win their first pennant since 1914. Starting on September 6, they started 11 of the team's next 16 games, with Spahn going 4-1 and Sain posting a 5-1 mark. The key game, won by Spahn, was a 14-inning, 2-1 decision over the Brooklyn Dodgers, traditionally Spahn's nemesis because of their compact ballpark and collection of righthanded sluggers.

The work of the Spahn-Sain tandem, plus several weather postponements, inspired *Boston Post* sports editor Gerry Hern to write a poem on September 14 that urged Spahn and Sain to shoulder the workload for the Braves over the final few weeks. They did, starting three games each during a 12-game span, and reaping the benefit of a rainout and three off-days. It wasn't long before Braves fans started chanting, "Spahn and Sain and pray for rain."

Sain had only a few seasons left, but Spahn seemed destined to pitch forever. "He'll never get into Cooperstown," Musial said of Spahn, "because he'll still be pitching."

In 1973, Spahn did get into Cooperstown – in his first year of eligibility– with 83.2 percent of the vote. (The 16.8 percent of the electorate who failed to include him must have been smoking some potent stuff.)

Spahn's records and achievements are so monumental that there's not enough room on his plaque in the Hall of Fame gallery. He won the first home game for the Milwaukee Braves and holds a myriad of franchise marks. The oldest 20-game winner in baseball history (at age 42 in 1963), he twice won 20 after age 40 – a feat also accomplished only by Cy Young – with 177 wins after age 35 and 75 between the ages of 40 and 44. Spahn won his last game on September 12, 1965, beating Chicago, 9-2, for San Francisco in the second game of a doubleheader.

"People say my absence from the major leagues (because of military service) may have cost me a chance to win 400 games," Spahn once said, "but I don't know about that. I matured a lot in three years and think I was a lot better equipped to handle major-league hitters at 25 than I was at 22. And I pitched until I was 44. Maybe I wouldn't have been able to do that otherwise."

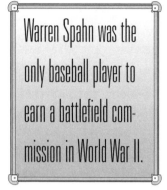

Warren Spahn was the only baseball player to earn a battlefield commission in World War II.

Warren Spahn was the only baseball player to earn a battlefield commission in World War II.

Like Greg Maddux, a later 300-game winner whose number was also retired by the Braves, Spahn won with guile and grace. "Hitting is timing," he said often during his career. "Pitching is upsetting timing."

Spahn did that, throwing five pitches for strikes (fastball, curve, screwball, slider, changeup), but disguising them with an overhand motion and a kick that resembled the Radio City Rockettes. He remembered what he threw to whom and when. And he prided himself on durability.

"One of the things I dislike about baseball today is we've made non-athletes out of pitchers," he said during the 1999 All-Star Game at Fenway Park. "They pitch once a week. They count pitches. They don't hit. They don't run. That's not my kind of baseball."

Spahn's 300th win *was* his kind of baseball. He went all the way on a six-hitter, walking one and fanning five, as the Milwaukee Braves edged the Chicago Cubs, 2-1, in two hours and twenty-five minutes. He drove in the first run of the game with a fifth-inning sacrifice fly, then watched Gino Cimoli hit a rare home run, his third of the season, in the eighth. Hank Aaron and Eddie Mathews, who would join Spahn in Cooperstown, collected two of the Braves' six hits while Joe Torre scored on Spahn's fly ball.

The largest Milwaukee crowd in three seasons (40,775) turned out to see Spahn become the first 300-game winner since Lefty Grove of the Boston Red Sox in 1941. Counting Grove, only 12 previous pitchers had won 300 games.

Two years later, when the Braves honored him at County Stadium, the visiting Los Angeles Dodgers presented him with a plaque that read, "You have our vote for the Hall of Fame – if you retire now."

Like George Burns, Spahn never wanted to retire. He always maintained that baseball retired him.

Even though he left the game the year before the Braves transferred to Atlanta, their third major-league home, Spahn is honored with a bronze statue in front of Turner Field. His No. 21 hangs in a place of honor inside the ballpark, along with the retired numbers of Aaron (44), Mathews (41), Phil Niekro (35), Greg Maddux (31), and Dale Murphy (3).

It's not surprising that three of those numbers belonged to 300-game winners. For pitchers, there is no higher standard.

Career Statistics

SPAHN, Warren				Warren Edward Spahn; B: 4/23/1921, Buffalo, NY; D: 11/24/2003, Broken Arrow, OK; BL/TL, 6'/175 lbs.; Debut: 4/19/1942; HOF 1973												
YEAR	**TM-L**	**W**	**L**	**PCT**	**G**	**GS**	**CG**	**SH**	**SV**	**IP**	**H**	**R**	**HR**	**SO**	**ERA**
1942	Bos-N	0	0	...	4	2	1	0	0	15	25	15	0	7	5.74
1946	Bos-N	8	5	0.615	24	16	8	0	1	125	107	46	6	67	2.94
1947	Bos-N	21	10	0.677	40	35	22	7	3	289	245	87	15	123	2.33
1948	Bos-N	15	12	0.556	36	35	16	3	1	257	237	115	19	114	3.71
1949	Bos-N	21	14	0.600	38	38	25	4	0	302	283	125	27	151	3.07
1950	Bos-N	21	17	0.553	41	39	25	1	1	293	248	123	22	191	3.16
1951	Bos-N	22	14	0.611	39	36	26	7	0	310	278	111	20	164	2.98
1952	Bos-N	14	19	0.424	40	35	19	5	3	290	263	109	19	183	2.98
1953	Mil-N	23	7	0.767	35	32	24	5	3	265	211	75	14	148	2.10
1954	Mil-N	21	12	0.636	39	34	23	1	3	283	262	107	24	136	3.14
1955	Mil-N	17	14	0.548	39	32	16	1	1	245	249	99	25	110	3.26
1956	Mil-N	20	11	0.645	39	35	20	3	3	281	249	92	25	128	2.78
1957	Mil-N	21	11	0.656	39	35	18	4	3	271	241	94	23	111	2.69
1958	Mil-N	22	11	0.667	38	36	23	2	1	290	257	106	29	150	3.07
1959	Mil-N	21	15	0.583	40	36	21	4	0	292	282	106	21	143	2.96
1960	Mil-N	21	10	0.677	40	33	18	4	2	267	254	114	24	154	3.50
1961	Mil-N	21	13	0.618	38	34	21	4	0	262	236	96	24	115	3.02
1962	Mil-N	18	14	0.563	34	34	22	0	0	269	248	97	25	118	3.04
1963	Mil-N	23	7	0.767	33	33	22	7	0	259	241	85	23	102	2.60
1964	Mil-N	6	13	0.316	38	25	4	1	4	173	204	110	23	78	5.29
1965	NY-N	4	12	0.250	20	19	5	0	0	126	140	70	18	56	4.36
	SF-N	3	4	0.429	16	11	3	0	0	71	70	34	8	34	3.39
	Year	7	16	0.304	36	30	8	0	0	197	210	104	26	90	4.01
TOTAL	21	363	245	0.597	750	665	382	63	29	5243	4830	2016	434	2583	3.09

Box Score of 300th Win

Spahn
Baseball Almanac Box Score
Chicago Cubs 1, Milwaukee Braves 2

Game played on Friday, August 11, 1961 at County Stadium

Chicago Cubs	ab	r	h	rbi	Milwaukee Braves	ab	r	h	rbi
Heist cf	4	0	0	0	Cimoli cf	4	1	2	1
Zimmer 2b	4	0	2	0	Bolling 2b	4	0	0	0
Santo 3b	3	1	0	0	Mathews 3b	4	0	1	0
Altman rf	4	0	1	0	Aaron rf	2	0	1	0
Williams lf	4	0	1	0	Adcock 1b	2	0	0	0
Rodgers 1b	4	0	1	1	Thomas lf	3	0	1	0
Kindall ss	4	0	1	0	Torre c	3	1	0	0
Bertell c	3	0	0	0	McMillan ss	3	0	1	0
Banks ph	1	0	0	0	Spahn p	2	0	0	1
Curtis p	2	0	0	0	Totals	27	2	6	2
McAnany ph	1	0	0	0					
Totals	34	1	6	1					

Chicago	0	0	0		0	0	1		0	0	0	–	1	6	1
Milwaukee	0	0	0		0	1	0		0	1	x	–	2	6	2

Chicago Cubs	IP	H	R	ER	BB	SO
Curtis L (7-7)	8.0	6	2	1	2	6
Totals	8.0	6	2	1	2	6

Milwaukee Braves	IP	H	R	ER	BB	SO
Spahn W (12-12)	9.0	6	1	1	1	5
Totals	9.0	6	1	1	1	5

E–Williams (9), Bolling (8), Mathews (10). DP–Chicago 2. **HR**–Milwaukee Cimoli (3,8th inning off Curtis 0 on, 1 out). **SH**–Santo (1,off Spahn). **Team LOB**–8. **SF**–Spahn (2,off Curtis). **Team**–4. **CS**–Heist (2,2nd base by Spahn/Torre). **SB**–Aaron (17,2nd base off Curtis/Bertell). **U-HP**–Shag Crawford, **1B**–Al Barlick, **2B**–Bill Jackowski, **3B**–Ed Vargo. **T**–2:25. **A**–40,775.

The Professor

Greg Maddux – 355 wins

Out of uniform, Greg Maddux didn't look like a pitcher. He favored casual clothes and glasses with black rims, suggesting a cross between a college professor and Clark Kent, mild-mannered reporter for *The Daily Planet*. On the pitcher's mound, however, Maddux was Superman, mightier than virtually all of his opponents.

He didn't have a fastball like a speeding bullet, or a slider more powerful than a locomotive, but he knew how to pitch by paying careful attention to batters' tendencies. Blessed with a photographic memory, Maddux never made the same mistake twice.

A master of mechanics, he won by outsmarting the opposition. "If you get a hit off him, he'll never throw you that pitch again," said Cincinnati catcher Eddie Taubensee, who faced Maddux several times. "He's not only the best pitcher – he's the smartest pitcher."

Maddux never kept written notes on hitters; he kept all the information in his head. "If you watch the game, and you throw certain pitches in certain locations, you know that hitters are likely to hit to certain places on the baseball field," he said. "It's pretty much common sense. If hitters did one thing against five other pitchers, they're probably going to do the same thing off you."

While with the Atlanta Braves, Maddux would often astound manager Bobby Cox and pitching coach Leo Mazzone by predicting where a ball would be hit. As a result, the Braves always seemed to have their defense positioned perfectly when he was on the mound.

Maddux had the National League's best ratio of walks-to-innings-pitched nine times. Knowing they weren't going to get many free passes, batters had to hit their way on base against him.

"You pitch to get hitters out," said Maddux, who once went 69 consecutive innings without issuing a walk, "and sometimes you walk some. I was in situations where we usually had leads, so I could be a little bit more aggressive in the strike zone."

He threw the ball down the middle and watched it wiggle.

"It's not how hard you throw but what your ball does in the last 10 feet," said Maddux, the only man to win at least 15 games in 17 consecutive seasons. "I always felt like I threw more balls down the middle of the plate than anybody, but was able to have the ball do a little something the last 10 feet that enabled me to get away from that. Because of that, my location looked better."

Before Maddux, no pitcher had ever won more than two consecutive Cy Young Awards. Maddux won four straight.

An eight-time All-Star, Maddux brought home the award for the first time in 1992, the last year of his first term with the Chicago Cubs, and won it for the last time by unanimous vote in 1995, when he helped the Atlanta Braves win their only world championship. Winning the award that year made Maddux only the second man, after Sandy Koufax, to win consecutive Cys by unanimous vote.

Maddux might have won two more – he was second in 1997 and third in 2000. "After I won my first one, I realized it was so much fun that I wanted to do it again," he said. "I didn't want to let my guard down, become complacent, and relax a little bit. Being able to win one and back it up with another one was something to be proud of. To me, that was pretty cool."

The only man in baseball history to post double-digit wins for 20 straight seasons, he won at least 15 games in 18 different seasons – helping him roar past 300 wins before retiring with 355. That was one more than Roger Clemens, but eight short of Warren Spahn's record for most wins of the postwar era. For a guy who never threw hard, that was a monumental achievement.

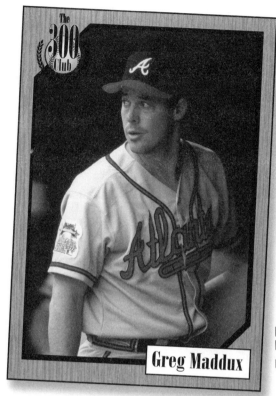

Greg Maddux

Photo courtesy of National Baseball Hall of Fame Library Cooperstown, N.Y.

His cut fastball couldn't break a pane of glass, but it broke plenty of hitters' hearts. He economized on pitches – preferring to go right after hitters with an 0-2 count – and had many games with ridiculously low pitch counts (69 in one game, 78 in another, for example). But he could get strikeouts when he needed them, once reaching a career high of 204 that trailed Lefty Grove's best by only five.

Maddux helped himself as a hitter who could lay down a bunt, and as a fielder who could pounce on a roller and turn it into a double play. He won 18 Gold Gloves, a record for a pitcher.

Maddux led National League pitchers in starts seven times, in innings and shutouts five times each, in wins and complete games three times each, and in winning percentage twice.

Some of his numbers were numbing – especially for hitters. After posting a 1.56 earned run average, he followed up with a 1.63, joining

Walter Johnson (1918-1919) as the last two pitchers to post successive seasons with such microscopic statistics. He also became the first National League right-hander with three straight ERA crowns since Grover Cleveland Alexander, another 300-game winner, did it from 1915-17.

Completing his four-year Cy Young run with a 19-2 record, Maddux teamed with Tom Glavine and John Smoltz to bring Atlanta its first world championship in any sport. "When you win a Cy Young," he said, "you go home and you're the only one who's happy. In 1995, it was much more special because everyone in the clubhouse, the front office, and the city of Atlanta got to share in it."

The Braves beat Colorado and Cincinnati in the playoffs before taking on the heavy-hitting Cleveland Indians in the World Series. Maddux, making his first World Series appearance in the opener, set the tone for the six-game Atlanta victory with a two-hit, 3-2 win. The Indians got only four balls out of the infield against him.

"I get asked by managers and media all the time: how good was he?" said Cox, the Atlanta manager. "Was he the best pitcher I ever saw? Was he the smartest pitcher I ever saw? Was he the best competitor I ever saw? Was he the best teammate I ever saw? The answer is yes to all of the above."

Don Sutton, an earlier 300-game winner, observed Maddux mostly from the broadcast booth. "I used to watch and think: 'That's not the best fastball, that's not the best curveball, that's not the best slider, and that's not even the best changeup. But that's the best pitcher.'"

The sinker and changeup were his best pitches, but he also got good mileage out of his cut fastball, with an occasional curve completing his repertoire. He worked both sides of the plate, especially against left-handed hitters. He went down and away against righties. And his pitches always had great movement. With control and command of his fastball, plus his ability to change speeds, Maddux didn't need much more.

"He set hitters up," Mazzone said. "He pitched them one way in order to set them up for later. He was like a poker player who never played his hand all at once."

The son of a fast-pitch softball star who also spent time as a poker dealer at the MGM Grand, Maddux knew the game well. He didn't worry about Tony Gwynn, who hit him well but mostly hit singles, or Barry Bonds, whose home runs against him usually came with no one on base or in the early innings.

"Barry was probably the best hitter I faced because he could take you deep and if you walked him, he could steal second and third," Maddux said. "He was so good the last 10 years I faced him that he turned into the easiest guy in the world to pitch against. All I had to do was throw four pitches 10 feet outside."

For nearly a decade, Maddux, Glavine, and Smoltz were like the pitching version of the Yankees' Murderers' Row. They combined for seven Cy Youngs over an eight-year stretch, including the season Maddux won it with the Cubs. "I learned a lot of things from him," Smoltz said of Maddux. "Not how to throw like him but the way he set up hitters and the way he looked for things. He had the ability to spot and initiate the contact he wanted to. It was just fun to watch."

Glavine seconded the thought: "He was really good at looking at a hitter, watching how he took a pitch, watching how he swung, and using that information to dictate what he was going to do with pitch selection and pitch location."

In one game, Maddux had a big enough lead to experiment late in the game. He threw Jeff Bagwell an eighth-inning fastball that the Houston slugger hit out of the park. The solo home run just happened to be the only hit of the night – ruining what would have been the only no-hitter for Maddux. But the pitcher didn't mind. He still managed to post a .688 winning percentage and 2.63 ERA during his Atlanta tenure.

"I have absolutely zero regrets about anything that has ever happened to me in baseball," said Maddux. "Everyone talks about hitting the Lotto, but I was lucky enough to hit it for 23 straight years."

The Texas native launched his pro career when the Chicago Cubs gave him an $85,000 bonus after drafting him in the second round of the amateur free agent draft in June 1984. Arriving in the National League in 1986, he went 8-18 over his first two seasons and even consulted a sports psychologist in desperation before pitching coach Dick Pole suggested he concentrate on making good pitches rather than getting outs. The advice worked.

"I'd rather make a good pitch and give up a bloop single than make a bad pitch and get an out," Maddux once said. "I only know one way to pitch. I can't get caught up in the artificial turf or grass or big fences or short fences. The individual stuff is great but I had more than my fair share. I wanted to help my team win."

An All-Star and 18-game winner in 1988, Maddux never looked back. When he opted for free agency after the 1992 season, he had many suitors, ranging from the pitching-rich Braves to the filthy-rich Yankees. He turned down $6 million more from New York, mainly because he preferred the familiar National League, but also because the Braves had just won consecutive pennants and had a reputation for treating pitchers well.

It was a marriage made in baseball heaven. "The bottom line was his heart," said Terry Pendleton, a previous free agent signee with the Braves. "He had the heart of a lion. He didn't care who you were, how big you were, what bat you used, or who you played for. He came at you the best way he knew how."

Even rivals admired him. "There are so many things you can pick up from him," said Randy Johnson, who joined Maddux in the 300 club. "He's what I call a true pitcher. He doesn't throw hard, but he's extremely smart."

After 11 stellar seasons in Atlanta, Maddux moved back to the Cubs (as a free agent) and lasted long enough to win his 300th game for Chicago. He spent his last three seasons with the Dodgers, who traded for him twice, and then with the San Diego Padres.

Maddux won his 300th while pitching for the Cubs on August 7, 2004, a sunny day in San Francisco. He worked the first five innings of an 8-4 victory, yielding all four Giants runs, before 42,578 fans at Pacific Bell Park. Barry Bonds had an RBI single against him.

"We were in the middle of the pennant race," Maddux said, "and it was something that was going to happen eventually. I just didn't want it to turn into a circus. I had witnessed (Roger) Clemens going through it the year before and saw where it could be a big distraction. That was the last thing I wanted. I just wanted to hurry up and get it so we could concentrate on winning the division."

Maddux, who got the milestone win on his second try, got good support from his teammates. "I didn't pitch very well," he admitted, "but the offense came through and the bullpen came through. We scored a lot and we scored early. I gave up some runs early and was kind of scuffling. I was trying to do whatever I could to keep the game close. I wanted to win the game more for a shot at the postseason than because it was my 300th win."

Kathy Maddux, his wife, was in charge of ticket and travel arrangements for a myriad of family and friends. "I didn't want it to drag on," said the pitcher, "and put my wife through another five days of hotel arrangements, tickets, and 15 phone calls for everybody who wants to come. That's the kind of inconvenience it puts on your family when you go through something like that. I know it's a big deal and I was thrilled to accomplish it, but it puts a lot of added burdens on the people around you."

Although Maddux never won more than 20 games in a season, reaching 300 was relatively easy for a man of such consistency. He avoided injury as easily as he avoided controversy. And he kept himself and teammates loose by being as silly off the field as he was serious on it.

"He doesn't take himself too seriously," Glavine once said of the man the Braves called Mad Dog.

Mazzone backed that up. "We were three months into the season and I hadn't been out to the mound to talk to him all year," the pitching coach wrote in his book. "Before the game, he asked me about that.

He said, 'It gets kind of lonely out there. I'll look in during the sixth inning so come out and pay me a visit.'

"Sure enough, in the sixth inning, he looked into the dugout and Bobby said, 'Hey, Mad Dog is looking in. Something must be wrong. Go check it out.' I ran out and said, 'Mad Dog, you're pitching a great game.' He said, 'Yeah, I feel good. Everything's going fine.' We shot the bull for a minute and he said, 'Okay, we've got our TV time now. Thanks for coming out. You know, sometimes it helps just to talk to somebody.'"

Maddux said the most influential people in his career were Cox, Mazzone, San Diego manager Bud Black, and a man few people know: Ralph Medar. "When I was 15 or 16 and just starting out, he taught me the importance of making each pitch do something for the last 10 feet," Maddux said. "He was a retired guy who knew a lot about movement on the baseball as opposed to velocity and I bought into it. He changed my arm angle and showed me how to make the ball sink."

Maddux related to Black because he had been a starting pitcher – and even a Maddux opponent late in his career. "The guy understood exactly what it was like to be a starting pitcher," he said of Black. "I really enjoyed playing for him my last couple of years."

When he retired after the 2008 season, Maddux was showered with honors. Both the Braves and Cubs retired his No. 31, a uniform number he shared with Hall of Famer Ferguson Jenkins in Chicago. In Atlanta, the number hangs in the outfield alongside other famous Braves, including Dale Murphy (3), Warren Spahn (21), Phil Niekro (35), Eddie Mathews (41), and Hank Aaron (44).

"That was special," said Maddux. "That was one of the coolest things that ever happened. You sit in the dugout all those years and look up at those numbers. And I got a double dose of it so I was twice as lucky. Ernie Banks, Ron Santo, and Ryne Sandberg are icons in Chicago. It was a privilege and an honor to be up there next to those guys."

Maddux might follow in the footsteps of older brother Mike and become a major-league pitching coach. Used mainly as a reliever, Mike won 39 games in a 15-year career that started in 1986, when Greg beat him in baseball's first match-up of rookie brothers. He later became one of the best-respected coaches in the business.

"I have a lot of interest in that but not right now," Greg Maddux told the Atlanta media when his number was retired. "I'm enjoying watching my kids grow up and I'm enjoying catching up on what I missed for the last 25 years."

In 2009, that meant plenty of golf, both as a player and a tournament organizer, and personal summer travel – something he and his wife could never do before. After a year away from baseball, however, Maddux accepted an offer to be assistant to the general manager of his original team, the Chicago Cubs. His duties include serving as a special spring training instructor.

He knows where he'll be during the last weekend of July in 2014: making a speech at the Baseball Hall of Fame in Cooperstown. Eligible together, Maddux and Glavine just might stroll down the aisle together – partners again in retirement.

One thing is certain: the Maddux plaque will be topped by the letter "A." It would stand for both Atlanta and the quality of the performance he delivered.

Box Score of 300th Win

Maddux Baseball Almanac Box Score
Chicago Cubs 8, San Francisco Giants 4

Game played on Saturday, August 7, 2004 at Pacific Bell Park

Chicago Cubs	ab	r	h	rbi	San Francisco Giants	ab	r	h	rbi
Patterson cf	5	1	1	2	Durham 2b	4	1	1	0
Garciaparra ss	5	2	3	0	Ledee rf	3	0	0	0
Alou lf	5	1	1	2	Mohr ph,rf	2	0	1	0
Sosa rf	4	0	0	0	Snow 1b	4	1	1	0
Ramirez 3b	5	2	2	1	Bonds lf	3	0	1	1
Lee 1b	5	1	2	1	Alfonzo 3b	5	2	3	1
Walker 2b	3	0	2	2	Pierzynski c	3	0	2	1
Bako c	3	1	1	0	Torrealba pr,c	1	0	0	0
Maddux p	2	0	0	0	Grissom cf	4	0	1	0
Leicester p	0	0	0	0	Cruz ss	3	0	1	1
Mercker p	0	0	0	0	Hennessey p	1	0	0	0
Remlinger p	0	0	0	0	Walker p	0	0	0	0
Macias ph	1	0	0	0	Tucker ph	0	0	0	0
Farnsworth p	0	0	0	0	Feliz ph	1	0	0	0
Hawkins p	0	0	0	0	Herges p	0	0	0	0
Totals	38	8	12	8	Perez ph	1	0	0	0
					Tomko p	0	0	0	0
					Totals	35	4	11	4

Chicago	0	0	0	2	2	2	0	0	2	–	8	12	0
San Francisco	1	0	2	0	0	1	0	0	0	–	4	11	3

Chicago Cubs	IP	H	R	ER	BB	SO
Maddux W (11-7)	5.0	7	4	4	3	3
Leicester	0.1	1	0	0	0	1
Mercker	0.2	0	0	0	0	0
Remlinger	1.0	1	0	0	0	0
Farnsworth	1.0	1	0	0	1	0
Hawkins	1.0	1	0	0	0	2
Totals	9.0	11	4	4	4	6
San Francisco Giants	**IP**	**H**	**R**	**ER**	**BB**	**SO**
Hennessey L (0-1)	4.2	7	4	4	1	5
Walker	1.1	2	2	2	0	2
Herges	2.0	1	0	0	0	3
Tomko	1.0	2	2	2	1	0
Totals	9.0	12	8	8	2	10

E–Ledee (1), Alfonzo (10), Cruz (6). **DP**–San Francisco 1. **2B**–Chicago Ramirez (29,off Hennessey); Walker (18,off Hennessey); Garciaparra (4,off Hennessey); Lee (33,off Hennessey); Bako (5,off T Walker), San Francisco Alfonzo (19,off Maddux); Pierzynski (21,off Maddux); Mohr (11,off Remlinger); Bonds (18,off Hawkins). **3B**–San Francisco Durham (6,off Maddux). **HR**–Chicago Patterson (13,6th inning off T Walker 1 on, 1 out); Alou (26,9th inning off Tomko 1 on, 0 out). **SH**–Maddux (8,off T Walker); Bako (1,off Herges); Cruz (4,off Farnsworth). **Team LOB**–7. **SF**–Bonds (2,off Maddux). **HBP**–Pierzynski (9,by Farnsworth). **Team**–11. **SB**–Garciaparra (2,2nd base off Hennessey/Pierzynski). **HBP**–Farnsworth (1,Pierzynski). **U-HP**–Ted Barrett, **1B**–Lance Barksdale, **2B**–Alfonso Marquez, **3B**–Ed Rapuano. **T**–3:11. **A**–42,578.

Career Statistics

MADDUX, Greg				Gregory Alan "Mad Dog" Maddux; B: 4/14/1966, San Angelo, TX; BR/TR, 6'0"/170; Debut: 9/3/1986; ALL STAR										
YEAR	TM-L	W	L	PCT	G	GS	CG	SHO	SV	IP	H	R	HR	SO	ERA
1986	Chi-N	2	4	0.333	6	5	1	0	0	31	44	20	3	20	5.52
1987	Chi-N	6	14	0.300	30	27	1	1	0	155	181	111	17	101	5.61
1988	Chi-N	18	8	0.692	34	34	9	3	0	249	230	97	13	140	3.18
1989	Chi-N	19	12	0.613	35	35	7	1	0	238	222	90	13	135	2.95
1990	Chi-N	15	15	0.500	35	35	8	2	0	237	242	116	11	144	3.46
1991	Chi-N	15	11	0.577	37	37	7	2	0	263	232	113	18	198	3.35
1992	Chi-N	20	11	0.645	35	35	9	4	0	268	201	68	7	199	2.18
1993	Atl-N	20	10	0.667	36	36	8	1	0	267	228	85	14	197	2.36
1994	Atl-N	16	6	0.727	25	25	10	3	0	202	150	44	4	156	1.56
1995	Atl-N	19	2	0.905	28	28	10	3	0	209	147	39	8	181	1.63
1996	Atl-N	15	11	0.577	35	35	5	1	0	245	225	85	11	172	2.72
1997	Atl-N	19	4	0.826	33	33	5	2	0	232	200	58	9	177	2.20
1998	Atl-N	18	9	0.667	34	34	9	5	0	251	201	75	13	204	2.22
1999	Atl-N	19	9	0.679	33	33	4	0	0	219	258	103	16	136	3.57
2000	Atl-N	19	9	0.679	35	35	6	3	0	249	225	91	19	190	3.00
2001	Atl-N	17	11	0.607	34	34	3	3	0	233	220	86	20	173	3.05
2002	Atl-N	16	6	0.727	34	34	0	0	0	199	194	67	14	118	2.62
2003	Atl-N	16	11	0.593	36	36	1	0	0	218	225	112	24	124	3.96
2004	Chi-N	16	11	0.593	33	33	2	1	0	212	218	103	35	151	4.02
2005	Chi-N	13	15	0.464	35	35	3	0	0	225	239	112	29	136	4.24
2006	Tot-N	15	14	0.517	34	34	0	0	0	210	219	109	20	117	4.20
	Chi-N	9	11	0.450	22	22	0	0	0	136	153	78	14	81	4.69
	LAD-N	6	3	0.667	12	12	0	0	0	73	66	31	6	36	3.30
2007	SDP-N	14	11	0.560	34	34	1	0	0	198	221	92	14	104	4.14
2008	Tot-n	8	13	0.381	33	33	0	0	0	194	204	105	21	98	4.22
	SDP-N	6	9	0.400	26	26	0	0	0	153	161	80	16	80	3.99
	LAD-N	2	4	0.333	7	7	0	0	0	40	43	25	5	18	5.09
TOTAL	23	355	227	0.610	744	740	109	35	0	5008	4726	1981	353	3371	3.16

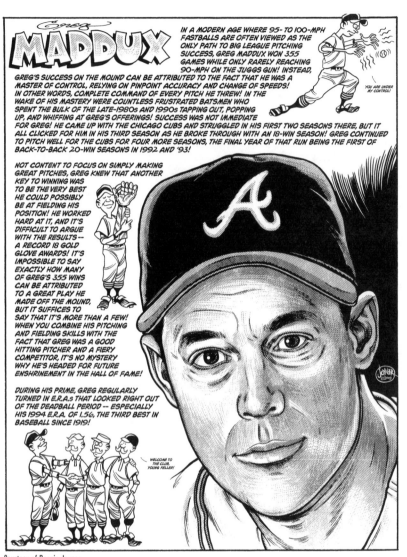

GREG MADDUX

IN A MODERN AGE WHERE 95- TO 100-MPH FASTBALLS ARE OFTEN VIEWED AS THE ONLY PATH TO BIG LEAGUE PITCHING SUCCESS, GREG MADDUX WON 355 GAMES WHILE ONLY RARELY REACHING 90-MPH ON THE JUGGS GUN! INSTEAD, GREG'S SUCCESS ON THE MOUND CAN BE ATTRIBUTED TO THE FACT THAT HE WAS A MASTER OF CONTROL, RELYING ON PINPOINT ACCURACY AND CHANGE OF SPEEDS! IN OTHER WORDS, COMPLETE COMMAND OF EVERY PITCH HE THREW! IN THE WAKE OF HIS MASTERY WERE COUNTLESS FRUSTRATED BATSMEN WHO SPENT THE BULK OF THE LATE-1980s AND 1990s TAPPING OUT, POPPING UP, AND WHIFFING AT GREG'S OFFERINGS! SUCCESS WAS NOT IMMEDIATE FOR GREG! HE CAME UP WITH THE CHICAGO CUBS AND STRUGGLED IN HIS FIRST TWO SEASONS THERE, BUT IT ALL CLICKED FOR HIM IN HIS THIRD SEASON AS HE BROKE THROUGH WITH AN 18-WIN SEASON! GREG CONTINUED TO PITCH WELL FOR THE CUBS FOR FOUR MORE SEASONS, THE FINAL YEAR OF THAT RUN BEING THE FIRST OF BACK-TO-BACK 20-WIN SEASONS IN 1992 AND '93!

YOU ARE UNDER MY CONTROL!

NOT CONTENT TO FOCUS ON SIMPLY MAKING GREAT PITCHES, GREG KNEW THAT ANOTHER KEY TO WINNING WAS TO BE THE VERY BEST HE COULD POSSIBLY BE AT FIELDING HIS POSITION! HE WORKED HARD AT IT, AND IT'S DIFFICULT TO ARGUE WITH THE RESULTS -- A RECORD 18 GOLD GLOVE AWARDS! IT'S IMPOSSIBLE TO SAY EXACTLY HOW MANY OF GREG'S 355 WINS CAN BE ATTRIBUTED TO A GREAT PLAY HE MADE OFF THE MOUND, BUT IT SUFFICES TO SAY THAT IT'S MORE THAN A FEW! WHEN YOU COMBINE HIS PITCHING AND FIELDING SKILLS WITH THE FACT THAT GREG WAS A GOOD HITTING PITCHER AND A FIERY COMPETITOR, IT'S NO MYSTERY WHY HE'S HEADED FOR FUTURE ENSHRINEMENT IN THE HALL OF FAME!

DURING HIS PRIME, GREG REGULARLY TURNED IN E.R.A.s THAT LOOKED RIGHT OUT OF THE DEADBALL PERIOD -- ESPECIALLY HIS 1994 E.R.A. OF 1.56, THE THIRD BEST IN BASEBALL SINCE 1919!

WELCOME TO THE CLUB, YOUNG FELLER!

Courtesy of Ronnie Joyner

The Rocket

Roger Clemens – the man known as "The Rocket" – blazed across the baseball universe for 24 seasons, winning the Cy Young Award a record seven times, blowing by opposing batters, and finally touching down with 354 wins.

The Rocket did everything but pitch a no-hitter. He won the Triple Crown of pitching twice, led his league in victories four times, and posted the best earned run average seven times. He also won five strikeout crowns and a pair of world championship rings. He is one of only four men to win a Cy Young Award in both leagues.

The first one meant the most to the 6'4" right-hander. "I was coming off shoulder surgery," Clemens recalled, "and any time a pitcher has surgery, it is major even when the doctor (James Andrews) says it is minor. I had played defensive end in high school football and led with my shoulder quite a bit so I knew I had a little bit of fraying cartilage. After Dr. Andrews cleaned it up, I came back and won my first 14 decisions. That set the stage for a fantastic season, not only for myself, but for the Red Sox."

En route to a regular-season record of 24-4 in 1986, Clemens became the first pitcher to strike out 20 batters in a nine-inning game, against the Seattle Mariners on April 29. He duplicated that feat 10 years later, on September 18, 1996, when he shut out the Detroit Tigers. He did not issue a walk in either game – an example of

By Bill Purdom,
courtesy of
GoodSportsArt.com

exquisite control that impressed Red Sox pitching coach Bill Fischer, who once went 84 innings without issuing a free pass.

"That 20-strikeout game changed my life because it changed what people expected from me," he said, "but the other Cy Young season that I remember most was 2001 just because of what our country had gone through (with the September 11 terrorist attacks)."

That was the year Clemens started the season 20-1, a baseball first, and finished 20-3. He was also the first 20-game winner to go a whole season without a complete game, the first starting pitcher to win the Cy Young without a complete game, and the first Yankee to win it in 23 years. His magic lasted into the seventh game of the World Series, which he left in a 1-1 tie against Arizona's Curt Schilling.

Clemens claimed his hardware in different uniforms, winning three Cy Young Awards with the Boston Red Sox, two with the

Toronto Blue Jays, one with the New York Yankees, and one with the Houston Astros.

He was almost unbeatable in 1986, winning 14 straight at one point, striking out 238, and posting a 2.48 earned run average. The starting and winning pitcher in the All-Star Game, with three perfect innings, Clemens pulled a rare trifecta, winning MVP honors in both the Midsummer Classic and the regular season, as well as the Cy Young Award.

He also soaked in pitching suggestions offered by Tom Seaver, a Boston teammate in 1986 who had won his 300th game the previous season.

On April 29, 1986, in Boston's Fenway Park, 23-year-old Roger Clemens struck out a single-game record 20 batters.

By Bill Purdom, Courtesy of GoodSportsArt.com

"Tom was in Boston for a short period of time, but I got to listen to what he had to say and I got to see him pitch," said Clemens. "He was only in the 87-88 (mph) range, but when he got himself into a little trouble, the next thing you knew, he would strike somebody out to get out of it. He was a power pitcher who knew what he was doing out there."

Clemens, who grew up in Texas and attended college there, idolized native Texan Nolan Ryan and faced him a few times in Ryan's final years. He also picked up pitching tidbits from Don Drysdale, another righthanded power pitcher, during spring training encounters.

"I got to spend some quality time with Don when he had his radio show," Clemens said. "He wasn't in a hurry to go anywhere after his show, so he turned off his tape recorder and spent some quality time with me talking about pitching. He's the one who told me the most important pitch of the game was the second knockdown pitch because that's when the hitter knows the first one was a mistake."

Like Drysdale, Clemens was feared by batters because he often pitched inside. He once gave Mike Piazza a concussion when he hit the catcher with a pitch. He later drew a $50,000 fine for allegedly throwing the jagged piece of a broken bat at Piazza during the 2000 "Subway Series" between the Yankees and the Mets.

Intimidating batters must have helped; Clemens led the American League in wins four times, in 1986, 1987, 1997, and 1998, and finished second in 2001, his sixth and final 20-win season.

He spent 13 years with Boston, two with Toronto, and five with the Yankees before crossing league lines and pitching in Houston for three seasons. A fitness fanatic famous for running miles along the Charles River during his time in Boston, Clemens actually got better as he got older. He was 37 when he pitched the fourth and final game of the 1999 World Series for the Yankees, cementing a sweep of the Atlanta Braves. He was 39 in 2001 when he became the oldest man to start the seventh game of the World Series, and he was 45 when he signed a one-year Yankee contract for $28,000,022 on May 6, 2007 (the extra $22 signified his uniform number).

There were many memorable moments along the way.

He won his first game, a 5-4 win over the Minnesota Twins, on May 20, 1984, and struck out 15 Kansas City Royals in a game two months later. He was American League Pitcher of the Month – the first of many awards he would win.

"He seemed to be unflappable," said two-time MVP Cal Ripken, Jr., of the rookie Clemens. "He was composed and under control all the time. Certain pitchers are their own worst enemy, but he was a rock of stability on the mound. I don't know how he figured it out so quickly."

Clemens was only in his 40th major-league game when he struck out eight men in succession, tying an American League record, during his 20-strikeout game against Seattle in 1986.

"The thing that amazed me," catcher Rich Gedman said later, "was that they had so many swings and weren't even able to hit a foul ball. It wasn't like he was trying to paint the corners or anything. He was challenging them and they weren't able to get a bat on the ball."

Manager John McNamara was amazed, too. "I've never seen a pitching performance as awesome as that – and I've seen perfect games by Catfish Hunter and Mike Witt."

Ten years later, Clemens fanned 20 again. After that game, he received an autographed ball from the Detroit Tigers that listed each "victim's" name and how many times he had struck out in the game.

In 1997, his first year in Canada after signing with the Blue Jays as a free agent, Clemens became the first American Leaguer since Hal Newhouser in 1945 to win the Triple Crown of pitching. He had 21 wins, 292 strikeouts, and a 2.05 earned run average.

"When you're with a new team, there is obviously a little more energy," he said, "and a little more excitement. I didn't even think about the Triple Crown until Mel Queen, our pitching coach, mentioned it coming down the stretch, when I had four or five starts left."

Clemens won another Triple Crown in 1998, becoming the first American League pitcher to win two straight since Lefty Gomez in 1937.

Over the years, his repertoire changed. "The first time I struck out 20 in a game, I threw mainly a fastball and a curveball, with maybe a little bit of a changeup and one or two sliders," he said. "Then in 1996, it was fastball, slider, and split-fingered fastball."

Clemens got into the record book again with multiple achievements on June 13, 2003. He not only won his 300th game with a 5-2 win over the St. Louis Cardinals, but also became the first Yankee to reach that plateau in Yankee Stadium (Tom Seaver had done it as a visiting player in 1985).

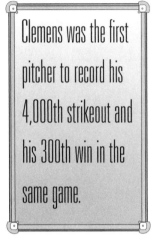

Clemens was the first pitcher to record his 4,000th strikeout and his 300th win in the same game.

At the advanced baseball age of 40 years, 10 months, and 9 days, Clemens also became the first pitcher to notch No. 300 in an interleague game, the first to win it on Friday the 13th, and the first to notch his 4,000th strikeout during his 300th win. He fanned 10 Cardinals while yielding six hits and two walks in 6 2/3 innings, leaving with a 3-2 lead. The Yankees padded the lead with a two-run seventh, and solid bullpen work from Chris Hammond, Pablo Osuna, and Mariano Rivera.

"I started thinking about 300 when I got past 250 wins," Clemens said. "Media people kept asking me about it and suggesting that I might be the last 300-game winner. That inspired me a little bit. Until then, it was just a number. And it looked like a number that was fairly far away."

Clemens didn't get it on his first try. He lost his first attempt, against the Red Sox at Yankee Stadium, and got a no-decision against the Reds a week later in Cincinnati. Then the Chicago Cubs beat him at Wrigley Field. That set the stage for the June 13 contest with the Cardinals. When he struck out the side in the first inning, he knew it would be his night.

With 55,214 fans howling between raindrops, Clemens made Edgar Renteria his 4,000th strikeout victim in the second, when he registered three strikeouts after a leadoff double. By the time he left the game in the seventh inning, he'd reached double digits in strikeouts for the 103rd time.

Born in Ohio, but raised in Texas, Clemens jumped at the chance to join his hometown Houston Astros in 2004. After signing as a free

agent in January, he went 18-4 to post the best winning percentage
(.818) in the National League. Though he was embarrassed to yield
six runs in the first inning of the All-Star Game that year, Clemens

Courtesy of Ronnie Joyner

deserved recognition as the league's best pitcher. Giving him the Cy Young Award was a no-brainer for the voters, who named him on 88 percent of their ballots and made him, at 42, the oldest man ever to win it.

He was even better a year later with a career-best 1.87 ERA, and an opponents' batting average of .198 – the third time in his career he held hitters under the "Mendoza Line" (.200).

Together with Andy Pettitte, who also left the Yankees to pitch for his hometown Astros, Clemens helped pitch Houston to its first World Series. His most significant outing occurred in the fourth game of the National League Division Series against the favored Atlanta Braves. With the Astros almost out of players in the 15th inning, Clemens made the first pinch-hitting appearance of his career, then took the mound in his first relief outing since 1984. Though troubled by back and hamstring problems, he worked three scoreless innings, prolonging a tie that Chris Burke eventually broke with a solo homer in the 18th.

"I was having some small back issues and some leg problems," said Clemens. "I noticed before the game that the starter for Game 5 in Atlanta was not there. I asked Jim Hickey, the pitching coach, what was going on. He said that pitcher was ill and I'd probably have to pitch that game. Then, when the fourth game went into extra innings, (manager) Phil Garner looked at me and told me to put my spikes on. I thought I might be going in to drop a sacrifice bunt but he said, 'How's your arm?' I said, 'You've got to be kidding me.' I hadn't even thrown yet. So I called my oldest son, Koby, who was up in the press box, and had him come down and meet me in the batting cage. I ended up throwing and getting loose so I told Phil I was fine. He was already through (Brad) Lidge and working on (Chad) Qualls and (Dan) Wheeler.

"If you asked our bullpen catcher or bullpen coach, they probably thought the game was going to end pretty quick if I got the call because I didn't have much in the pen. But once I got the call to get into the game, my adrenalin jumped. My emotions kicked in and I had pretty good stuff for three innings."

Clemens credited Jimy Williams, who preceded Garner as Astros manager, for helping him learn to handle a bat.

"Jimy grabbed me in spring training and offered to show me a few things if I could meet him at the park at 7:00 every morning," said the 11-time All-Star. "We bonded for 45 minutes every morning and he was dead on. He said if I could handle the bat, he could keep me in the game longer and it would add up to five more wins per year."

Although the Astros lost the World Series to the Chicago White Sox, they wouldn't have gotten there without Clemens. He produced another 13-win season in 2005, then slipped to just seven in the injury-riddled summer of 2006.

Retirement seemed likely, but the competitive bug bit Clemens again. On May 6, 2007, he shocked the baseball world by signing with the Yankees again. When he started on Old Timers Day at Yankee Stadium, the 44-year-old pitcher was older than five of the "old timers" being honored.

With age and injuries hampering his performance, Clemens split 12 decisions, ending the season with 354 wins, one fewer than Greg Maddux on the lifetime list.

"I felt I won 200 games because of my stuff but 300 because of my will and desire to get through those games," Clemens said. "You have to will yourself through a lot of games if you're going to get those.

"When I had all my pitches working and my control was on, I was supposed to win. Those are the 2-1 or 2-0 games with 10 or more strikeouts. But the games that gave me the most satisfaction were the ones where I had very average stuff and my control was off so I had to rely on pitching. I had to concentrate extremely hard and get out of a bases-loaded situation or maybe men on second and third a couple of times to get out of the game and still win, 4-3. Then there were times when I was on the ropes for six or seven innings but still won. On the way home, my phone would ring and my catcher and I would share a laugh over what happened."

Clemens didn't have too many laughs during his childhood. His parents separated during his infancy and he suffered a second loss when his stepfather died before Clemens turned 10.

"The biggest influences on me were my mother and grand-mother," he said. "I watched how they worked, how they went about their lives. My mom worked three jobs so she could provide for the six of us. We weren't desperately poor, but we were poor. I have photos of myself as a youngster where I didn't have baseball pants; I had the game shirt, but I played in my jeans. I had a cool red glove with stars on it but that's all we could afford."

Clemens helped his mom clean warehouses and worked in his grandmother's garden, planting corn and vegetables.

"I admired how hard she worked," he said, "just to make things happen. One of my best moments happened in Cleveland, when I won my 20th game of the season and my grandmother was feeling well enough to be at that game. When it ended, I went over and gave her the game ball. That's a memory I will always have."

As a youth, Clemens pitched and played first base. But he didn't throw hard until he got to college and gained both size and strength.

"My brothers, sisters, and my wife – my whole family – were out there pushing me in the beginning of my career. My mother said that if I was going to play baseball, I should do it well. She told me to love what I do and do it well."

Clemens was devoted to his mom, Bess, who died in 2005, his wife, Debbie, and sons Koby, Kory, Kacy, and Kody – all given names starting with the letter "K," the scoring symbol for a strikeout. Koby, a third baseman in the Houston organization who once homered against his dad in an exhibition game, was California League Player of the Year in 2009.

"There was pressure pitching at home (in Houston) because I had family and friends who were watching me as I grew up," he said. "There was big-time pressure in Boston and New York, too – either you thrive on it or you don't. But I lived in Houston since the eighth grade, after my dad passed away up north, and lived most of my life in Texas. My foundation is there. I remember going to the Astrodome as a kid to watch Nolan Ryan pitch."

A three-sport star at Spring Woods High School, Clemens also starred for his American Legion team. He later became a college All-America at both San Jacinto junior college and the University of Texas, pitching the Longhorns to victory in the 1983 College World Series and convincing the Red Sox to take him in the first round of the amateur draft.

"I got something like $121,000 to sign," he said. "We split it up into two payments for tax purposes. I paid off my mom's condominium, got a new car, and put the rest in the bank. I never had aspirations of being a 300-game winner or getting into the Hall of Fame. I just played to take care of my family and, once I did that, to help people in the community who were less fortunate than I was. I also wanted to help young children because I was one of those kids once."

After a whirlwind tour of the Boston minor league system, Clemens reached the majors less than a year later.

"My first year in Boston, I knew I needed to get stronger, to build up a lot of innings. I watched Bob Gibson, Don Drysdale, and Nolan Ryan and saw how they incorporated their legs into their deliveries. I always felt that when my elbow was on fire and when my shoulder was killing me, I could still go out there and have quality starts. It was when I had issues with the lower half of my legs that I was in trouble. Once your legs lock up or you have a groin pull, it's difficult to continue."

Both early and late in his career, Clemens was on a careful pitch count.

"They were very protective of me," he recalled. "I had to rely on my managers to trust me on how I felt, how my body felt, how I was feeling between starts. My first four or five years, they were very cautious with me. But in the middle of my career, I had a lot of games with high pitch counts, maybe 130 or 150 pitches, one with 162. I just ended up not throwing so many side sessions. Thank goodness I didn't have to rely on fine-tuning a breaking ball or a control problem.

"My last five years, I was treated like I was 21 again. They were worried about my age and wanted to have me ready in September and October."

Even when treated with tender loving care by his teams, Clemens did have injuries. They included a 1984 muscle strain in his right forearm, a groin strain that sent him to the disabled list in 1993, shoulder surgery in 1985, a hamstring pull that knocked him out in Game 2 of the 2005 World Series after two innings, and another hamstring problem that curtailed his second stint with the Yankees two years later.

The outspoken pitcher also had conflicts, including complaints against Red Sox teammates who smoked on the team bus and arguments with both management and officials. He missed most of spring training in 1987 because of a salary dispute eventually resolved by Commissioner Peter Ueberroth, and the first five days of the 1991 season after criticizing umpire Terry Cooney during the final game of the American League Championship Series between Boston and Oakland the previous fall. That incident also resulted in a $10,000 fine.

As he developed into a Boston icon, the pitcher pestered Red Sox ownership to improve facilities for family and friends of players at Fenway Park and even criticized the legendary facility itself. Clemens was gone before stadium upgrades were made, but he had made his point.

He also made his point with Toronto ownership by demanding a trade to a contending team before his three-year, $24.75 million contract expired. The Blue Jays obliged by swapping the big right-hander to the Yankees for David Wells, Graeme Lloyd, and Homer Bush on February 18, 1999. It was the only time in his career that Clemens was traded, though he traded his own services on the free-agent market seven times.

Some of the contracts he signed, especially late in his career, raised eyebrows – even in his own clubhouse. He was granted special arrangements that allowed him to come out of retirement in June, join his team for the stretch drive, and stay home when not scheduled to pitch on the road.

He finished his Red Sox career with 192 wins and 38 shutouts, tying Cy Young for the team lead in both categories, had his best years with the Blue Jays (41-13 in two seasons), and then went 77-36 in his first tour with the Yankees.

Clemens came within a whisker of joining Don Larsen as the only man to pitch a postseason no-hitter. It happened in the fourth game of the 2000 American League Championship Series against Seattle, when Al Martin's leadoff double in the seventh was the only blemish in a 5-0 Clemens win.

In his career, he went 14-10 in 34 postseason starts, but never lost a World Series game. He was 3-0 in the Fall Classic, but his early dis-

Roger Clemens won a record seven Cy Young Awards during a career that started in Boston but also included stops in Toronto, New York, and Houston. He finished with 354 wins, one behind Greg Maddux on the lifetime list.

Photo courtesy of Bill Menzel

appearance from the sixth game of the 1986 series between the Red Sox and Mets created considerable controversy. Lifted with a 3-2 lead after seven innings at Shea Stadium, Clemens watched a series of Sox relievers blow the game in the 10th inning.

Clemens never struck out 300 men in a season. But he came close, with 292 for the 1997 Blue Jays and 291 for the 1988 Red Sox. Both were club records, though Pedro Martinez later knocked Clemens into second place on the Boston list.

Clemens pitched his final game with the Yankees on September 16, 2007, then retired, ranking only behind Ryan on the career strikeout list. Randy Johnson, who joined the 300 Club in 2009, eventually passed him.

Conditioning was the key to his longevity.

Throughout his career, Clemens could be found running in local neighborhoods, including the streets of Toronto and the neighborhoods of New York. "It kept my mind clear and got all the negative energy out of my body," Clemens said. "In Houston, there was a two-and-a-half mile track to (highway) I-10 and back. If I didn't pitch well or felt I didn't get my cardio done that day, I was able to get out and start getting ready for my next start. When teammates couldn't find me, I told them I only sat at my locker to put my uniform on."

Stunned fans sometimes encountered him during his runs, and called disbelieving friends on their mobile phones. They also joined in, trying to keep up with the finely-tuned athlete.

Even in retirement, Clemens keeps in shape by pitching batting practice to minor-leaguers or neighborhood kids. "You can't just throw to one group because everyone wants to take their swings against you," he laughed. "So I throw from 55 feet for an hour or more, still getting the ball in there at about 85 miles an hour. It's good practice for the kids and a great workout for me, but my arm is pretty sore for the next day or so."

His lone regret was not throwing a hitless game, Clemens said. "I know I took a handful of potential no-hitters very late into a game. I know I came close a couple of times. I remember when Dave Stieb pitched for Toronto and had two games in a row where he lost no-hitters in the ninth inning. Then he finally got one. You have to be lucky to pitch one.

"For me, it goes back to being a power pitcher. I attacked the strike zone. So I gave up some hits. But other than that, there are no regrets. I was fortunate to keep my health and had a dream job that provided a wonderful life for my family."

Career Statistics

CLEMENS, Roger				William Roger "Rocket" Clemens; B: 8/4/1962, Dayton, OH; BR/TR, 6'4"/220; Debut: 5/15/1984; ALL STAR											
YEAR	TM-L	W	L	PCT	G	GS	CG	SHO	SV	IP	H	R	HR	SO	ERA
1984	Bos-N	9	4	0.692	21	20	5	1	0	133	146	67	13	126	4.32
1985	Bos-N	7	5	0.583	15	15	3	1	0	98	83	38	5	74	3.29
1986	Bos-N	24	4	0.857	33	33	10	1	0	254	179	77	21	238	2.48
1987	Bos-N	20	9	0.690	36	36	18	7	0	281	248	100	19	256	2.97
1988	Bos-N	18	12	0.600	35	35	14	8	0	264	217	93	17	291	2.93
1989	Bos-N	17	11	0.607	35	35	8	3	0	253	215	101	20	230	3.13
1990	Bos-N	21	6	0.778	31	31	7	4	0	228	193	59	7	209	1.93
1991	Bos-N	18	10	0.643	35	35	13	4	0	271	219	93	15	241	2.62
1992	Bos-N	18	11	0.621	32	32	11	5	0	246	203	80	11	208	2.41
1993	Bos-N	11	14	0.440	29	29	2	1	0	191	175	99	17	160	4.46
1994	Bos-N	9	7	0.563	24	24	3	1	0	170	124	62	15	168	2.85
1995	Bos-N	10	5	0.667	23	23	0	0	0	140	141	70	15	132	4.18
1996	Bos-N	10	13	0.435	34	34	6	2	0	242	216	106	19	257	3.63
1997	Tor-A	21	7	0.750	34	34	9	3	0	264	204	65	9	292	2.05
1998	Tor-A	20	6	0.769	33	33	5	3	0	234	169	78	11	271	2.65
1999	NYY-A	14	10	0.583	30	30	1	1	0	187	185	101	20	163	4.60
2000	NYY-A	13	8	0.619	32	32	1	0	0	204	184	96	26	188	3.70
2001	NYY-A	20	3	0.870	33	33	0	0	0	220	205	94	19	213	3.51
2002	NYY-A	13	6	0.684	29	29	0	0	0	180	172	94	18	192	4.35
2003	NYY-A	17	9	0.654	33	33	1	1	0	211	199	99	24	190	3.91
2004	Hou-N	18	4	0.818	33	33	0	0	0	214	169	76	15	218	2.98
2005	Hou-N	13	8	0.619	32	32	1	0	0	211	151	51	11	185	1.87
2006	Hou-N	7	6	0.538	19	19	0	0	0	113	89	34	7	102	2.30
2007	NYY-A	6	6	0.500	18	17	0	0	0	99	99	52	9	68	4.18
TOTAL	24	354	184	0.658	709	707	118	46	0	4916	4185	1885	363	4672	3.12

Box Score of 300th Win

Clemens Baseball Almanac Box Score
St. Louis Cardinals 2, New York Yankees 5

Game played on Friday, June 13, 2003, at Yankee Stadium

St. Louis Cardinals	ab	r	h	rbi	New York Yankees	ab	r	h	rbi
Cairo 2b	5	0	1	0	Soriano 2b	4	0	0	0
Drew rf	3	0	1	0	Jeter ss	4	1	1	0
Pujols 1b	3	0	2	0	Giambi 1b	3	0	0	0
Edmonds cf	4	1	1	1	Posada c	3	0	1	1
Rolen 3b	4	1	2	0	Ventura 3b	4	0	1	0
Renteria ss	4	0	1	0	Matsui cf	4	1	2	1
Martinez dh	3	0	0	1	Sierra dh	4	2	2	1
Matheny c	3	0	0	0	Mondesi rf	4	1	1	2
Palmeiro ph	1	0	0	0	Rivera J. lf	3	0	2	0
Robinson lf	4	0	0	0	Clemens p	0	0	0	0
Simontacchi p	0	0	0	0	Hammond p	0	0	0	0
Yan p	0	0	0	0	Osuna p	0	0	0	0
Kline p	0	0	0	0	Rivera M. p	0	0	0	0
Totals	34	2	8	2	Totals	33	5	10	5

St. Louis	0	1	0		1	0	0		0	0	0	–	2	8	0
New York	1	1	0		1	0	0		2	0	x	–	5	10	0

St. Louis Cardinals	IP	H	R	ER	BB	SO
Simontacchi L (4-4)	6.0	8	5	5	2	5
Yan	1.0	0	0	0	1	0
Kline	1.0	2	0	0	0	0
Totals	8.0	10	5	5	3	5

New York Yankees	IP	H	R	ER	BB	SO
Clemens W (7-4)	6.2	6	2	2	2	10
Hammond	0.1	2	0	0	0	0
Osuna	1.0	0	0	0	0	0
Rivera SV (8)	1.0	0	0	0	0	1
Totals	9.0	8	2	2	2	11

E–None. DP–St. Louis 1. **2B**–St. Louis Rolen (23,off Clemens), New York Posada (11,off Simontacchi); J Rivera (6,off Simontacchi). **HR**–St. Louis Edmonds (18,2nd inning off Clemens 0 on, 0 out), New York Matsui (6,2nd inning off Simontacchi 0 on, 0 out); Sierra (4,4th inning off Simontacchi 0 on, 2 out); Mondesi (12,7th inning off Simontacchi 1 on, 0 out). **SF**–Martinez (3,off Clemens). **U-HP**–Gary Darling, **1B**–Chris Guccione, **2B**–Larry Vanover, **3B**–Jerry Meals. **T**–3:03. **A**–55,214.

Connie's Curvers

Eddie Plank – 326 Wins

Lefty Grove – 300 Wins

The first left-handed members of the 300 Club both started their careers with Connie Mack's Philadelphia Athletics. Eddie Plank spent his first 14 seasons with the club, while Lefty Grove spent his first nine years with Mack. Both were eventually traded to raise revenue for a franchise stricken first by the Federal League challenge and later by the Great Depression.

Eddie Plank was the only 300-game winner who reached the milestone outside the two traditional leagues. He was with the St. Louis Terriers of the Federal League on August 28, 1915, when he won his 300th with a 3-2 win over the Kansas City Packers.

A left-hander who said little, Plank won his first 285 games for the Philadelphia Athletics after Mack plucked him off the Gettysburg College campus on the recommendation of former big-league pitcher Frank Foreman, who was the coach of the college club.

Plank, a late starter, was 21 when he enrolled at the school and 25 when he got his first win (both Grove and Warren Spahn, a later 300-game winner, were the same age when they notched their first victories).

Plank, who often talked to himself on the mound, had eight 20-win seasons – seven with the A's and one in his only Federal League

Photo courtesy of National
Baseball Hall of Fame Library
Cooperstown, N.Y.

Eddie Plank

season. He also kept his earned run average under 2.90 for 15 straight seasons – a difficult feat even during the Dead Ball Era.

Plank perplexed opposing hitters, teammates, umpires, and spectators by pitching so deliberately that he could have been called "The Human Rain Delay." Plank had a routine that slowed the pace of the game so much that fans dependent on train schedules deliberately avoided his starts. Umpires had to order him to throw the ball.

His pitching arsenal included a fastball, curve, and control (he walked fewer than two men per nine innings). Although he never led his league in any of the pitching Triple Crown categories, he did finish first in starts and shutouts twice each, and appearances, complete games, saves, and winning percentage once apiece.

Never the ace of the A's, Plank was always a perfect partner. He and Rube Waddell were together for six years (1902-07), all but one in concert with Chief Bender, who joined the team in 1903. Plank and Bender combined for 458 wins, second on the lifetime list for pitching tandems, during their 12 seasons together. Not surprisingly, the A's won five pennants during that timeframe – and six total during Plank's time with the team. In three of those seasons, they went on to win the World Series.

Plank and the A's missed another pennant in 1907, when they finished a game-and-a-half behind the Tigers even though they were a game ahead in the loss column. Rainouts were treated as cancellations rather than postponements until 1908, when the top two teams were separated by only one-half game in the standings.

Although he had a fine career winning percentage of .627, Plank only led the American League in that department one time. It happened in 1906. Slowed by a sore arm that allowed him to work just once in the last 50 games, Plank went 19-6 – interrupting a string of 20-win seasons – but finished 21 of 25 starts. His percentage that year was .760. After a winter of rest, Plank was potent again in 1907, winning 24 games and topping the American League with eight shutouts.

"Plank was not the fastest, not the trickiest, and not the possessor of the most stuff," said Hall of Fame second baseman Eddie Collins. "He was just the greatest."

The developer of a sidearm "crossfire" pitch that overpowered left-handed batters, Plank won more games than any left-hander until Spahn passed him in 1963, almost a half-century later. No American League left-hander has ever won more.

"Never did he pitch the ball over the center of the plate unless he absolutely had to," said fellow A's pitcher Jack Coombs.

Critics called him a nibbler, but Plank didn't care. Nor did he care when teammates complained they could hear him talking to himself – he was concentrating so hard that he didn't realize his little sermons on the mound could be heard.

"He pitched to spots," said Smoky Joe Wood, one of the best pitchers of the day. "They didn't do that much in his day, but he did it. He was very studious out there."

Perhaps the college background helped. A farm boy who was the fourth of seven children, Plank was 17 before he started playing baseball with a loosely organized neighborhood team. Already a master of control, thanks to years of aiming rocks at fence-sitting birds, he caught the eye of the Gettysburg College coach. Plank's professional career was curtailed before it started when the Virginia League folded, canceling his 1901 contract with Richmond before he ever threw a pitch. That's when Mack stepped into the picture, snapping up the pitcher with no minor-league experience.

It was a decision Mack would never regret.

Although he frequently complained about a sore arm, Plank pitched like a veteran at the top of his game. Unafraid to pitch inside, he peaked in 1904 with 26 wins, one of them a 13-inning, 1-0 shutout of Cy Young.

Plank's duels with Christy Mathewson were legendary, dating back to their college days when Gettysburg faced Bucknell. Long before the days of interleague play, Plank and Mathewson met on the grand stage of the World Series several times.

In 1905, when Mathewson pitched three complete-game shutouts for the Giants against the A's, Plank was 0-2 despite a 1.59 earned run average. He lost a 3-0 verdict to Mathewson in the opener and a 1-0 game to Joe McGinnity in Game 4.

In the second game of the 1913 classic, both Plank and Mathewson threw blanks for nine innings before the Giants broke through with three in the 10th. Mack was blamed for the Game 2 loss because he let Plank hit with the bases loaded and nobody out in the bottom of the ninth. He hit into a force at home, the A's never scored, and Mathewson himself collected the game-winning hit against the tiring Plank in the 10th.

Plank redeemed himself – and his manager – with a two-hitter that gave the A's a 3-1 win over Mathewson in the decisive fifth game.

According to the game report in the *Washington Evening Star*, "There really never was a time when Plank was in danger. He went through the nine innings without once faltering and displayed even better form than in his previous contest with the master of them all, Mathewson."

Plank's other World Series win came in 1911, when his five-hitter against the Giants in Game 2 gave the A's a 3-1 win and tied a Series that Philadelphia would eventually win in six games. Often the victim of non-support in October (i.e. his 1-0 loss to Bill James of the Boston Braves in 1914), Plank lost five of seven Series decisions with an excellent earned run average of 1.32.

Without Plank, the Athletics might not have won pennants in 1902, 1905, 1910, 1911, 1913, and 1914. There was no World Series in 1902 (the feuding American and National Leagues would start the classic a year later), and arm problems kept Plank sidelined when the A's beat the Cubs in 1910.

Plank began his career in 1901, the year of the American League's initial season. He won 17 as a rookie, then topped 20 in five of the next six seasons. A stalwart with the A's for 14 seasons, Plank gave Philadelphia 285 wins – 23 percent of the team's total.

After a lackluster relief appearance in his big-league debut on May 13, 1901, Plank won his first start five days later, when he beat the Washington Nationals, 11-6. The first of his 69 career shutouts was a 6-0 win over the Milwaukee Brewers, soon to become the St. Louis Browns.

"Gettysburg Eddie," as his teammates called him, played second fiddle to Rube Waddell early in his career, but he never complained, maintaining Mack's confidence in him for any assignment.

"The better the hitter, the better he liked it," said Eddie Collins of Plank. "If the man had a reputation to uphold, the fans would urge him on and he would be aching to hit. Eddie would fuss and fiddle with the ball, his shirt, and his shoes, then maybe talk to the umpire. He would try to pick off the base runners. Then he would finally turn his attention to the fretting batter, who would probably pop up in disgust."

Called "the king of dawdlers" in one biographical sketch, Plank had other quirks. In addition to being a hypochondriac, he hated having his picture taken before a start. Plank also believed his arm contained a certain number of pitches per day and that a pitcher would be finished when the "supply" was exhausted.

It was a wonder, in retrospect, that he managed to complete 410 of his 529 starts. He worked at least 300 innings five times, four of them in succession from 1902-05. Although he drove his teammates crazy as an off-the-field introvert, Plank earned their praise with his poise on the pitcher's mound.

"Waddell may have had a sharper-breaking curve and more speed," said Coombs, "but when it comes down to a question of brains combined with ability and real worth to a team, there never was a pitcher the superior of Ed Plank."

Mack, the man whose opinion mattered most, also had high praise for the 5'11", 175-pound lefty. "When there was a game I absolutely had to win," Mack said late in his career, "Edward was the man I would send out there."

Mack hated to let Plank pursue greener pastures, but he had no choice when the well-financed Federal League challenged the existing majors in 1914. Mack managed to keep Plank for that season, but released him, along with Bender and Coombs, so that they could sign with teams in the new league. Mack simply couldn't match the Federal's funds. In fact, he stayed afloat by selling off his stars.

At age 40, Plank performed well for St. Louis, posting a 21-11 record. But it was the last time he would win 20 games.

When the Federal League folded after two years, players were sold to established clubs, including the St. Louis Browns. That's where Plank completed his career; he went 21-21 over two seasons before vetoing a trade to the Yankees after the 1917 season. He finished with a flourish at age 41, posting a 1.79 earned run average that was his second-best, and pitching 10 innings of shutout ball against old nemesis Walter Johnson (who beat him seven times) before losing, 1-0, in 11 innings.

"I am through with baseball," Plank said when he retired. "I have my farm and my home and enough to take care of me, so why should I work and worry any longer?"

Even an unprecedented three-year contract offer from Miller Huggins, manager of the Yankees, couldn't dissuade him.

Back in Gettysburg, where he once worked as a tour guide of the famous battlefield, Plank resumed his former life as a farmer. He also operated an automobile agency and pitched in a six-team industrial league owned by Bethlehem Steel. But he didn't have much time to enjoy his golden years, suffering a fatal stroke at age 50 in 1926. Plank earned posthumous election to the Baseball Hall of Fame in 1946, the same year the Veterans Committee picked Rube Waddell – his partner in pitching and perpetuity.

Box Score of 300th Win

Plank Box Score St. Louis Terriers 3, Kansas City Packers 2							
Game played on Saturday, August 28, 1915							
Kansas City	**ab**	**r**	**h**	**St. Louis**	**ab**	**r**	**h**
Chadbourne cf	4	0	0	Tobin cf	4	0	2
Kenworthy 2b	4	0	1	Vaughn 2b	4	1	1
Kruger lf	3	0	0	W. Miller lf	4	1	1
Perring 1b	4	0	0	Borton 1b	4	0	0
Bradley 3b	4	1	1	Hartley c	4	0	0
Gilmore rf	2	0	0	Drake rf	3	0	1
Hawlings ss	4	1	1	E. Johnson ss	3	1	1
Easterly c	3	0	1	Bridwell cf	1	0	0
Henning p	3	0	1	Plank p	2	0	0
a-Brown ph	1	0	0	Totals	29	3	6
b-Enzenroth ph	0	0	0				
Totals	32	2	5				

Kansas City	0	0	0	0	0	0	2	0	0	–	2
St. Louis	0	0	1	2	0	0	0	0	x	–	3

a-Batted for Easterly in 9th
b-Batted for Henning in 9th
DP-St. Louis 2. **E**-Bradley, Rawlings, Easterly, Hartley, E.Johnson, Bridwell. **2B**-Kenworthy, Vaughn, Henning. **SB**-Vaughn, W. Miller, E. Johnson. **SF**-Bridwell, Kruger, Plank. **Base on Balls**-Henning 1, Plank 4. **Strikeouts**-Henning 2, Plank 2. T-1:54

Career Statistics

PLANK, Eddie	Edward Stewart "Gettysburg Eddie" Plank; B: 8/31/1875, Gettysburg, PA; D: 2/24/1926, Gettysburg, PA; BL/TL, 5'11.5"/175 lbs.; Debut: 5/13/1901; HOF 1946

YEAR	TM-L	W	L	PCT	G	GS	CG	SH	SV	IP	H	R	HR	SO	ERA
1901	Phi-N	17	13	0.567	33	32	28	1	0	260	254	133	2	90	3.31
1902	Phi-N	20	15	0.571	36	32	31	1	0	300	319	140	5	107	3.30
1903	Phi-N	23	16	0.590	43	40	33	3	0	336	317	128	5	176	2.38
1904	Phi-N	26	17	0.605	44	43	37	7	0	357	311	111	2	201	2.17
1905	Phi-N	24	12	0.667	41	41	35	4	0	346	287	113	3	210	2.26
1906	Phi-N	19	6	0.760	26	25	21	5	0	211	173	70	1	108	2.25
1907	Phi-N	24	16	0.600	43	40	33	8	0	343	282	115	5	183	2.20
1908	Phi-N	14	16	0.467	34	28	21	4	1	244	202	71	1	135	2.17
1909	Phi-N	19	10	0.655	34	33	24	3	0	265	215	74	1	132	1.76
1910	Phi-N	16	10	0.615	38	32	22	1	2	250	218	89	3	123	2.01
1911	Phi-N	23	8	0.742	40	30	24	6	4	256	237	85	2	149	2.10
1912	Phi-N	26	6	0.813	37	30	23	5	2	259	234	90	1	110	2.22
1913	Phi-N	18	10	0.643	41	30	18	7	4	242	211	87	3	151	2.60
1914	Phi-N	15	7	0.682	34	22	12	4	3	185	178	68	2	110	2.87
1915	StL-F	21	11	0.656	42	31	23	6	3	268	212	75	1	147	2.08
1916	StL-A	16	15	0.516	37	26	17	3	3	235	203	78	2	88	2.33
1917	StL-A	5	6	0.455	20	14	8	1	1	131	105	39	2	26	1.79
TOTAL	17	326	194	0.627	623	529	410	69	23	4495	3958	1566	41	2246	2.35

Photo courtesy of National Baseball Hall of Fame Library Cooperstown, N.Y.

Lefty Grove

Lefty Grove's route to Cooperstown was more direct. Only six years after becoming the second left-hander with 300 wins, he was awarded a spot in the Hall of Fame.

His selection was a no-brainer. Like Warren Spahn, a fellow lefty whose career started the year after Grove's ended, he didn't win his first game until he was 25. But he proceeded to win so often that his .680 percentage ranks first among all 300-game winners and fifth among all pitchers.

Grove had two separate careers: one with the Philadelphia Athletics, where he filled the pitching slot vacated by Eddie Plank, and one with the Boston Red Sox, who were able to acquire him after Depression-era financial problems forced Philadelphia's Connie Mack to sell his stars.

The son of a Maryland coal miner, Grove worked in the mines, too, along with his three brothers, before deciding he liked daylight and fresh air better than peering into mine shafts for 50 cents a day. "I didn't put the coal in the ground and don't see why I should have to dig it out," he said.

That terse statement was a long declaration from a temperamental soul with little use for teammates who made errors when he pitched, managers who tried to calm him, or fans who tried to get his autograph. He often directed outbursts against locker-room equipment and even had words with Mack, the highly-respected A's manager who also owned the team.

Like Steve Carlton, a future 300-game winner who also spent his best years in Philadelphia, Grove grimaced whenever a reporter approached. He refused all interview requests after one writer produced an article the pitcher considered inaccurate and unfair.

Teammates also suffered the wrath of Grove. In pursuit of his 17th straight win during the dog days of August in 1931, the pitcher reacted to a 1-0 loss by pouncing on Jimmy Moore, the player whose error cost him the game – plus the regular (Al Simmons) who sat out with a minor illness. He was also upset about losing a game to a pitcher with a losing record (Dick Coffman) and being the first A's pitcher to finish on the wrong end of a shutout that season.

Another time, during a relief appearance, Grove yielded two runs on an error by Mule Haas, came off the field, and fired his glove into the dugout wall. "That's the last relief pitching I'll ever do for this ballclub!" he screamed.

Rattled by consecutive errors by Max Bishop and Jimmie Dykes in a 1929 game, Grove got even more perturbed when Mack said, "That will be all for you today, Robert." Grove, seated halfway down the bench, replied, "To hell with you, Mr. Mack." The soft-spoken manager responded by rising, walking down to where the pitcher was sitting, and pointing. "And the hell with you, too, Robert," he said. The whole bench – even Grove – laughed. The pitcher departed peacefully, laughing all the way to the clubhouse.

On other days, Grove was beyond consolation. He'd barricade himself behind locked hotel room doors and refuse to meet with

Mack. He rejected the manager's lessons on how to hold runners on base, and often refused managerial orders for an intentional walk.

"I was a tough loser," Grove said years after he retired. "It burned me up worse than a fever to get beat. I considered it my fault when I lost."

During his tenure with Philadelphia, when he relied almost entirely on a red-hot fastball, he didn't have to worry much about runners: the 6'3", 190-pounder won seven straight league strikeout titles. In fact, Grove and Sandy Koufax were the only pitchers who twice performed the rare feat of striking out the side on nine pitches.

Grove struck out more than 200 in a season just once, and never topped 209, but won seven straight strikeout crowns because most hitters of the day – with the notable exceptions of Babe Ruth and Lou Gehrig – emphasized contact over clout.

"We did not have speed clocks during my playing days," said Hall of Fame second baseman Charlie Gehringer, "but I know I never hit against anyone who threw the ball with more speed than Lefty Grove. He rarely threw curves or changes of pace, especially in his early years."

Writer Arthur Baer was even more descriptive. "Grove could throw a lamb chop past a wolf," he noted.

Robert Moses Grove – called Lefty by most, but Old Moses by friends – started his strange path to the majors as an amateur first baseman on a Maryland mining company team. One day while taking a relay throw from right field, he turned and fired a quick and perfect strike to the plate. His coach noticed and made him a pitcher.

Signed by Martinsburg, West Virginia, in the Blue Ridge League, Grove attracted the attention of Jack Dunn, owner of the minor-league Baltimore Orioles. Martinsburg needed a new fence and was willing to swap Grove for a check that would cover the cost: $3,500.

Dunn, the same man who had signed an earlier left-handed pitcher named Babe Ruth, reaped the rewards of signing Grove immediately. Grove won at least 25 games in three of his four full seasons in Baltimore and rang up four strikeout crowns. Dunn, whose star pitcher helped produce four pennants, inadvertently cost Grove many more major-league wins when he turned down several offers, including a $75,000 bid from John McGraw of the New York Giants.

Only when Mack agreed to pay $600 above the $100,000 sale price the Yankees paid the Boston Red Sox for Ruth did Dunn sell Grove.

The pitcher didn't complain. "Dunn treated us okay," he said years later of the minor-league owner who paid him $7,500 per season, plus a share of the profits the team produced. "We were getting bigger salaries in Baltimore than lots of big-league clubs were paying. We couldn't make $750-$1,000 a month in the big leagues in those days."

As a rookie with the A's, Grove had more walks than strikeouts – and a losing record. Still plagued by wildness the next year, he split 26 decisions. But then Mack discovered that slowing Grove down on the mound worked wonders for his control. He made the pitcher count to himself – a tactic that almost backfired when opponents saw his lips move and realized what he was doing.

Something must have worked, since Grove's walk totals dipped for the fourth straight year in 1928 and he soared to a 24-8 record. It was the second of seven straight 20-win seasons.

When the A's won three straight pennants from 1929-31, Grove was the anchor of the pitching staff. He improved each year, going from 20-6 to 28-5 to 31-4.

Grove saved the second and fourth games of the 1929 World Series, which Philadelphia won in five. On October 12, he fanned four of the six Cubs he faced while working two scoreless innings to complete a 10-8 win. That game featured the greatest comeback in World Series history, as Philadelphia scored all of its runs in the bottom of the seventh as the Cubs blew an 8-0 lead. In the 1930 World Series against the St. Louis Cardinals, Grove won the first game as a starter and the fifth game as a reliever – one day after losing the fourth game when an error allowed two unearned runs to score.

In his career, Grove won four of his six World Series decisions, helping the A's win world titles in 1929 and 1930, and then enjoyed the last 30-win season until Denny McLain duplicated the feat in 1968 for the Detroit Tigers.

During that 1931 season, the left-hander's four losses were all so close that he might have gone undefeated with better support (he finished on the wrong side of 2-1, 7-5, 1-0, and 4-3 scores).

Winning his second straight Triple Crown of pitching in 1931 helped Grove win the first American League Most Valuable Player Award, chosen by members of the Baseball Writers Association of America. Babe Ruth, a close competitor for MVP honors, hit nine career home runs against Grove. But it took him 10 years to do it. "What's he got up his arm, a machine gun?" the slugger blurted after a game against Grove.

Bill Dickey, another Yankee slugger and future Hall of Famer, shared those sentiments.

"One day we were playing the Athletics in Yankee Stadium," he said. "We were behind by one run in the last of the ninth. We loaded the bases with nobody out. Connie Mack signaled his pitcher off the mound and we all looked toward the bullpen to see who was coming in. But nobody was coming in from the bullpen. Grove walked out of the dugout, threw five warmup pitches, and proceeded to strike out the side on 10 pitches."

Grove, George Earnshaw, and Rube Walberg won 72 of Philadelphia's 107 victories in 1931 and were the major reason the team led the league with a 3.47 earned run average, helping the A's finish ahead of the second-place Yankees.

Although the A's fell from their perch atop the league in 1932, Grove couldn't be faulted. He went 25-10 that year and 24-8 in 1933 before moving on, a victim of Mack's financial crunch. It was during the 1933 season, on July 3, that Grove stopped a Yankees' streak of 308 consecutive games without being shut out. In that game at Yankee Stadium, he fanned Ruth three times and Gehrig twice. Grove also pitched in the first All-Star Game, working three innings of relief and saving the 4-2 victory for the American League. He would be an All-Star five more times, but not all of them as a representative of the A's.

With the Depression wreaking economic havoc both in and out-side of baseball, Mack had to make drastic moves to stay afloat – just as he did 19 years earlier during the Federal League challenge. Like Eddie Plank, Mack's previous prized southpaw, Lefty Grove was sold.

He was an attractive prize: in Philadelphia, he crafted a .712 win-ning percentage on a 195-79 record with a 2.88 earned run average, 51 saves, and 20 shutouts. His average of 25 wins per year convinced the Boston Red Sox to pay heavily for his services.

On December 12, 1933, the A's sent Grove, Max Bishop, and Walberg to the Red Sox for Harold Warstler, Bob Kline, and $125,000.

That deal, and others, brought Mack more than $900,000 but plunged his franchise into oblivion. The A's would not recover until they moved to Oakland (from Kansas City) in 1968.

Grove, who avoided personal financial loss by investing in government bonds, also had a change of fortune on the field. He hurt his arm during 1934 spring training and talked of retiring – but not until Boston owner Tom Yawkey talked him out of it. Finding that his arm hurt less when he threw his curve, the pitcher reinvented him-self, morphing from a power pitcher into a finesse artist. Throwing curveballs, sinkers, and occasional forkballs, Grove still managed to win four more ERA titles, but won 20 games only once in eight seasons with the Red Sox. In fact, he averaged only 13 wins per season with Boston.

"Groves was a thrower until after we sold him to Boston and he hurt his arm," Mack said of the man who dropped the "s" from his surname years earlier. "Then he learned to pitch."

His titanic temper accompanied him to Boston. After losing a 4-2 verdict to the White Sox, he stormed into the clubhouse and yelled, "You think Grove is going to pitch his arm off for you hitless wonders?" For the rest of that series, the still-pouting pitcher walked five miles each way between the hotel and the ballpark.

Most of the time, the pitcher had plenty of support. Like Shibe Park, where Grove spent his early years, Fenway Park was a paradise for hitters, as Jimmie Foxx, Joe Cronin, and Ted Williams proved. The park was often a graveyard for left-handed pitchers because of the proximity to the plate of the Green Monster, the left field wall that rose 37 feet from field level.

Grove was an exception to that rule.

"He had the most beautifully coordinated motion I ever saw," Williams said.

Had he pitched during the Dead Ball Era, like Plank, or in home ballparks that were little more than bandboxes, Grove might have won 500 games – or so he suggested several times. Instead, he had to settle for the bottom rung in the 300 Club, tied at exactly 300 wins with Early Wynn.

Grove was wearing Red Sox red when he won his 300th game on July 24, 1941, after failing in two previous tries. Although he yielded 12 hits, Grove beat the Cleveland Indians, 10-6, at Fenway Park. Only 10,000 paid to see him become the first 300-game winner since Grover Cleveland Alexander, with 6,000 women watching for free in a Ladies Day promotion.

Winning 300 meant the world to the pitcher, who kept inscribed balls from each of his major-league wins.

"When I got to 275," Grove admitted, "I said, 'by gosh, I'm gonna win 300 or bust.' And when I got No. 300 in Boston, that was all. Never won another game. I knew it was time to go. You know how old your body feels. I just couldn't do it anymore."

On December 7, 1941, the day of the bombing of Pearl Harbor, Grove informed Yawkey of his decision to retire while they were hunting turkeys in South Carolina. The owner didn't argue.

Grove was going out just as Ted Williams was coming in. "He was a moody guy, a tantrum thrower like me," said Williams. "But when he punched a locker, he always did it with his right hand. He was a careful tantrum thrower."

By the time he retired after the 1941 season, Grove had won 300 games and lost 141 in 17 seasons. He led the American League in earned run average nine times – four more than anyone else – and in winning percentage five times. On a yearly basis, he ranked first in percentage five times, wins four times, complete games and shutouts three times each, and saves once (during his 28-5 season in 1930, he made 32 starts but also had a career-best nine saves).

Grove seldom helped himself at the plate – he fanned 593 times, a record for a pitcher – but was close to perfection on the mound. A fiery but focused competitor, he often pitched inside, but never threw at a man's head.

"It never bothered me who was up there with the bat," said Grove. "I'd hit 'em in the middle of the back or hit 'em in the foot, it didn't make any difference to me. But I never threw at a man's head. Never believed in it."

Once he took off his uniform for the last time, Grove's anger also dissipated. He was a genial host at the bowling alley he owned and operated, even smiling when reminded of his outbursts on the diamond. He even spent some of his retirement years coaching in Little League.

"If I owned a ballclub," he once said, "I'd want one that had 25 guys as eager to win as I was."

Box Score of 300th Win

Grove Baseball Almanac Box Score
Boston Red Sox 10, Cleveland Indians 6

Game played on Thursday, July 24, 1941

Cleveland	ab	r	h	rbi		Boston	ab	r	h	rbi
Boudreau ss	5	2	3	1		DiMaggio cf	4	1	0	0
Rosenthal cf	4	1	1	0		Finney rf	4	1	1	0
Walker lf	4	1	2	1		Cronin ss	4	2	0	0
Heath rf	4	2	2	1		Newsome ss	0	0	0	0
Keltner 3b	4	0	2	1		Williams lf	3	3	2	2
Trosky 1b	2	0	1	0		Spence lf	0	0	0	0
Mack 2b	1	0	0	0		Foxx 1b	3	1	1	2
Grimes 2b, 1b	4	0	0	1		Tabor 3b	4	2	3	4
Desautels c	3	0	1	0		Doerr 2b	5	0	0	0
a-Hemsley ph	1	0	0	0		Peacock c	3	0	2	1
Krakauskas p	2	0	0	0		Grove p	4	0	1	0
Harder p	1	0	0	0		Totals	34	10	10	9
Milnar p	0	0	0	0						
b-Bell ph	1	0	0	0						
Totals	36	6	12	5						

Cleveland	0	1	3	0	0	0	2	0	0	–	6
Boston	0	0	0	2	2	0	2	4	X	–	10

a-Batted for Desautels in 9th.
b-Batted for Milnar in 9th.
LOB-Cleveland 4, Boston 9. **E**–Trosky, Mack, Brimes, Williams. **2B**–Keltner 2, Boudreau, Grove. **3B**–Walker, Foxx. **HR**–Boudreau, Tabor 2, Williams. **SB**–Boudreau, Heath. **SF**-Finney. **Base on Balls**-Krakauskas 4, Harder 2, Milnar 2, Grove 1. **Strikeouts**-Krakauskas 3, Harder 1, Milnar 1, Grove 6. **Hits off** Krakauskas 1 in 3 IP, Harder 6 in 3-2/3 IP, Milnar 3 in 1-1/2 IP. **Winning Pitcher**-Grove. **Losing Pitcher**-Milnar. **T**–2:27.

Career Statistics

GROVE, Lefty				Robert Moses Grove; B: 3/6/1900, Lonaconing, MD; D: 5/22/1975, Norwalk, OH; BL/TL, 6'3"/190 lbs.; Debut: 4/14/1925; HOF 1947											
YEAR	**TM-L**	**W**	**L**	**PCT**	**G**	**GS**	**CG**	**SH**	**SV**	**IP**	**H**	**R**	**HR**	**SO**	**ERA**
1925	Phi-A	10	12	0.455	45	18	5	0	1	197	207	120	11	116	4.75
1926	Phi-A	13	13	0.500	45	33	20	1	6	258	227	97	6	194	2.51
1927	Phi-A	20	13	0.606	51	28	14	1	9	262	251	116	6	174	3.19
1928	Phi-A	24	8	0.750	39	31	24	4	4	261	228	93	10	183	2.58
1929	Phi-A	20	6	0.769	42	37	19	2	4	275	278	104	8	170	2.81
1930	Phi-A	28	5	0.848	50	32	22	2	9	291	273	101	8	209	2.54
1931	Phi-A	31	4	0.886	41	30	27	4	5	288	249	84	10	175	2.06
1932	Phi-A	25	10	0.714	44	30	27	4	7	291	269	101	13	188	2.84
1933	Phi-A	24	8	0.750	45	28	21	2	6	275	280	113	12	114	3.20
1934	Bos-A	8	8	0.500	22	12	5	0	0	109	149	84	5	43	6.50
1935	Bos-A	20	12	0.625	35	30	23	2	1	273	269	105	6	121	2.70
1936	Bos-A	17	12	0.586	35	30	22	6	2	253	237	90	14	130	2.81
1937	Bos-A	17	9	0.654	32	32	21	3	0	262	269	101	9	153	3.02
1938	Bos-A	14	4	0.778	24	21	12	1	1	163	169	65	8	99	3.08
1939	Bos-A	15	4	0.789	23	23	17	2	0	191	180	63	8	81	2.54
1940	Bos-A	7	6	0.538	22	21	9	1	0	153	159	73	20	62	3.99
1941	Bos-A	7	7	0.500	21	21	10	0	0	134	155	84	8	54	4.37
TOTAL	17	300	141	0.680	616	457	298	35	55	3940	3849	1594	162	2266	3.06

Lefty

Steve Carlton – 329 Wins

Steve Carlton was different. A left-handed pitcher who parlayed unorthodox philosophies into a Hall of Fame career, he never hesitated to share them with managers, trainers, teammates, or ownership – or to deny them to a press corps hungry for information about an intensely private person.

Even after he retired, Carlton remained a paradox, serving as spokesman for FanFest at the All-Star Game and delighting audiences as an after-dinner speaker who often exceeded his allotted time, but still turning down requests from media members.

During a 24-year career concentrated in St. Louis and Philadelphia, Carlton won 329 games, four Cy Young Awards, two World Series rings, and a place in the Hall of Fame.

He would have won more had he played for better Philadelphia teams or perfected his slider earlier in his career.

"He painted a ballgame," said Rich Ashburn during his days in the Philadelphia broadcast booth. "Stroke, stroke, stroke. And when he got through, it was a masterpiece."

Carlton never pitched a no-hitter, but he won often enough to pitch his teams into postseason play seven times. He was 4-2 in the National League Championship Series and 2-2 in World Series games. When he retired in the spring of 1989, his resume included six 20-win seasons, five strikeout crowns, and a 19-strikeout game. He also led

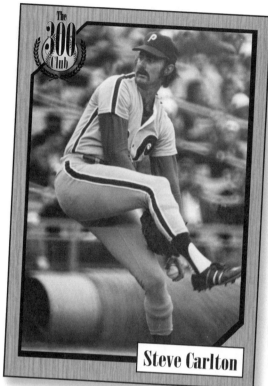

Steve Carlton

Photo courtesy of National
Baseball Hall of Fame Library
Cooperstown, N.Y.

his league in innings pitched five times, though he knew the value of conserving his strength by taking himself out of games – especially later in his career.

According to Dallas Green, who managed Carlton to a 24-9 season with the 1980 Phillies team that won the World Series, "Steve was a manager's dream. All he did was go out there and perform every time he walked out on the mound. He was capable of pitching any baseball game he wanted to pitch. I loved the guy. I loved his competitiveness. I loved the way he approached his work.

"He was an easy guy to manage in that he was a no-B.S. guy. Complete games weren't a big deal to him. Winning the ballgame was. If we had a big lead in the seventh or eighth inning, he'd walk down to me and say, 'If you got anybody who needs any work, go ahead (and use him).' A lot of pitchers would bitch and moan until they got the complete game. But he had faith in our judgment. He also knew that if he could save some pitches for the next time, he would. He knew it was going to catch up with him, so he conserved whatever he could conserve."

That approach, coupled with Carlton's dedication to a fitness regimen that ranged from reaching into a barrel of rice to silent meditation, kept the pitcher free of any disabling injury until late in his career.

Running was *not* part of the program.

"Lefty (Carlton's nickname) preferred not to run," Green said. "I'm kind of an old-school pitching guy and felt we were pretty lax in our running and preparation programs for pitchers. I knew Lefty worked with Gus Hoefling, our trainer, so before my first spring training as manager, I went down to Florida and said, 'Gus, I want to learn what you do with Steve and understand why you do it and what it does for him.' We worked all winter, with him putting me through the different exercises, including flexibility and stretching. When we got to spring training, I told the pitchers, 'You can do my program, which is based on running, or you can do Steve's. But you can't do both. And you can't use one to get out of the other.'

"A couple of guys tried to keep up with Steve, but there was no way. He was so determined in his work ethic and the way he approached his work with Gus that guys could not duplicate what he was capable of doing. Eventually they came back to the running program."

That season marked the first world championship season in Phillies history.

"Gus always maintained that he worked as much with Steve's mind as he did with his body," Green said. "That's what you saw when Steve took the mound. There was total dedication to his chore that day, which was winning the game.

"But Lefty never thought about personal goals. His goal was to be successful every time out there. I don't think he ever looked into the future and said, 'I'm going to be a 300-game winner' or 'I'm going to have 3,000 strikeouts.' He had a desire to be a great pitcher but never exuded that to me, his teammates, or anybody else."

Chris Wheeler, who broadcast Carlton's 300th win in 1983, agreed.

"Personal stuff didn't mean a thing to him," said Wheeler, still a part of the Philadelphia broadcast team. "Was he happy when it was over and he won his 300th game? Sure he was. But we were on the road, in St. Louis, and it was just another road game to him. He didn't have the crowd behind him. It wasn't the same as the night he got his 3,000th strikeout in Philadelphia. The crowd at Veterans Stadium was roaring on every out.

"When he finally got it, the catcher rolled the ball back to the dugout so that Steve could keep it as a souvenir. But he didn't like that because it interrupted the game and took him out of his routine. That wasn't the way he liked to do things."

Fellow Phillies broadcaster Gary Matthews, who played left field and batted fifth in Carlton's 300th win, also remembered Carlton as a pitcher who cared only about team goals.

"The milestones weren't as important to him as winning a championship," said Matthews, who also batted against Carlton while playing for the Giants, Braves, and Cubs. "It seemed like every time Steve pitched, it was 'win' day. He was a no-nonsense kind of guy who gave 100 percent. As a batter, you knew that when Steve was out on the mound, you had to buckle up. It was going to be a long day."

Matthews said Carlton would pitch inside if he had to. "If you were on his team and somebody got hit, he would hit two of their guys," he said. "Steve had the ability to strike guys out after hitting a guy so he didn't worry about it. I can't say enough about him."

Matthews got three hits, scored two runs, and knocked in another during Carlton's 300th win, on September 23, 1983. The Phillies also got help from leadoff man Joe Morgan, who went 1-for-4 and scored a run in the 6-2 victory.

"We knew at the time he was one of the best pitchers of all time and was going to the Hall of Fame," Morgan said of Carlton. "He already had 290 wins when I signed with the Phillies – I contributed to some of those. Facing him was like facing Sandy Koufax or Bob Gibson. You had to have the same intensity in the batter's box they had out there on the mound – or they were going to embarrass you. I relished that challenge."

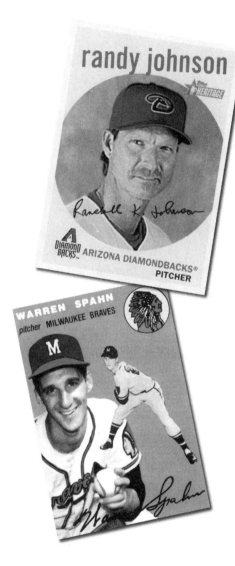

Randy Johnson, Warren Spahn, Steve Carlton, and Sandy Koufax were arguably the best left-handed pitchers of all time.

Courtesy of Topps

On the night he joined the 300 club, Carlton struck out 12 Cardinals in eight innings, yielded seven hits, and walked one. Al Holland pitched the ninth.

Pitching coach Claude Osteen was surprised. "Warming up, he didn't have very good stuff," Osteen said.

Although Carlton preferred Tim McCarver as his personal catcher in both St. Louis and Philadelphia, McCarver had retired to the broadcast booth before Carlton sought his 300th win. That night's assignment went to Bo Diaz.

"Timmy had been retired for three years," Wheeler said, "so Lefty had to get used to other guys. Bo was a good defensive catcher and Steve liked the way he called the game."

During their time as teammates, Carlton and McCarver were as close as Johnny Carson and Ed McMahon. They hunted for fine wine during the season and deer during the winter, always talking pitching in the process. McCarver even joked that they would be buried 60 feet, 6 inches apart (the distance from the pitching rubber to home plate).

It was Carlton who rescued McCarver's career after the Boston Red Sox released the catcher during the 1975 season. At Carlton's urging, the Phillies signed him, prompting Carlton to respond with consecutive 20-win seasons in 1976-77. The Phillies won the National League East both years, but lost to the Reds and Dodgers, respectively, in the National League Championship Series. Philadelphia fell again in 1978, losing to the Dodgers in the championship series, before finally reaching the World Series two years later.

McCarver and Carlton teamed in St. Louis from 1965-69, and in Philadelphia from 1975-80 plus a portion of the 1972 campaign. A two-time All-Star himself, McCarver helped Carlton with his mechanics, changing his position on the pitching rubber, as well as his confidence. He also helped relax the pitcher, who was a rookie when he brashly told McCarver to call for more breaking pitches when they were behind in the count.

Carlton relaxed so well in 1972 that he stood the baseball world on its ear. Although the Phillies won only 59 games, Carlton won 27 of them – a whopping 45.8 percent. He won 15 games in a row, completed 30 of his 41 starts, and struck out 310 in 346 innings pitched. He led the league in wins, starts, complete games, innings, strikeouts, and earned run average (1.97), giving him both the Triple Crown of pitching and a unanimous Cy Young Award – the first trophy ever given to a Phillies pitcher.

Even though writers who had been spurned by Carlton were voting for the award, there was no other choice. No other Phillies starter won more than four games that season.

"What he did on a losing team before 1980 was really fabulous," said Green. "If you look at Steve and (Tom) Seaver, who were compatriots, during the 10 years they went almost head-to-head, Lefty brought some unbelievable statistics to the party."

Green, a former pitcher who later became director of scouting and minor-league operations for the Phillies, saw most of the home games Carlton pitched during the team's down years. As manager of the 1980 team, he was also the direct beneficiary.

"Bob Boone and Keith Moreland were Lefty's catchers that year," he said. "It took awhile for Booney to gain his confidence and have Steve trust him and work with him. But he was very intelligent, an intellectual type of catcher. He studied the game plan and gave Steve a lot of stuff to work with. Steve came to count on him a good bit.

"But in 1980, Booney was having an off-year offensively and Keith was our backup guy. I didn't know whether Steve was going to be able to work with Keith or not. But he was willing to do it. It helped the team because Keith had a very good year offensively for us and helped us win a lot of ballgames."

Counting his two wins against the Kansas City Royals in the 1980 World Series, plus his 7-1 victory over the Houston Astros in the National League Championship Series, Carlton actually won 27 games that season – matching his effort of 1972.

A year later, Lefty wasn't so lucky; he lost both of his starts in a special Division Series, created in haste when owners reacted to a player strike that had split the season in half. He compensated in 1983, winning the first and fourth games of the NLCS against the

Los Angeles Dodgers – a Carlton nemesis – before losing Game 3 of the World Series to the Baltimore Orioles.

The Dodgers seemed to have his number. In the first game of the 1977 NLCS, he couldn't hold a 5-1 lead in the seventh. After two walks and a single filled the bases with two outs, Ron Cey tied the score with a grand slam. Carlton couldn't win the fourth game either, falling to Tommy John.

In 1978, Carlton repaid the favor in Game 3 with a complete game, 9-4 win over Don Sutton, a future 300-game winner, and hit a three-run homer in the process. But the Phillies again failed to win the playoffs – for the third consecutive season.

Carlton had experienced postseason defeat earlier in his life. As a schoolboy standout for North Miami High, Carlton's team went to the state finals but lost. Scouts from the St. Louis Cardinals, Pittsburgh Pirates, and Kansas City Athletics noticed the pitcher, who then moved on to Miami-Dade Community College. One year before baseball began its annual amateur draft, the skinny left-hander signed with St. Louis for a $5,000 bonus that seems meager by modern standards, but was big bucks for a college kid who seemed to have the wingspan of a condor.

Carlton catapulted through Rock Hill, Winnipeg, and Tulsa before reaching the major leagues in his second professional season. Used sparingly, he had no record for the 1965 Cardinals, but he did throw a gopher ball to Pittsburgh third baseman Bob Bailey on his first pitch as a major leaguer, on April 12, 1965. He also recorded the first of 4,136 strikeouts – fourth on the lifetime list behind Nolan Ryan, Randy Johnson, and Roger Clemens.

In 1966, Carlton started the year at Tulsa, struck out 10 Minnesota Twins during the Hall of Fame exhibition game in Cooperstown, then returned to the majors to stay. He won his first game on August 5, 1966, a 7-1 win over the Mets.

Carlton pitched for pennant-winning teams in 1967 and 1968, then won 20 for the first time in 1971. But he alienated Cardinals owner Gussie Busch with his salary demands, stating that he was at least half as good as St. Louis ace Bob Gibson and should therefore be entitled to at least half as much salary.

With the advent of free agency still five years away, and the reserve clause still ruling contract negotiations, Carlton and the Cardinals could not bridge a $5,000 gap. The pitcher wanted $60,000 while the club held firm at $55,000.

Busch, still bristling over a Carlton holdout that caused him to miss spring training and produce a 10-19 season in 1971, decided to put the pitcher on the market. Both he and Jerry Reuss, another Cardinal involved in a contract squabble, were dealt in separate trades after the 1971 season.

On his website, www.SteveCarlton32.com, the pitcher said the trade shocked him. "I was mentally committed to winning 25 games with the Cardinals and now I had to re-think my goals," he wrote. "I decided to stay with the 25-win goal and won 27. I consider that season my finest individual achievement."

The Cardinals thought they were punishing Carlton by dealing him to a last-place club, but the fans in Philadelphia were experiencing their own outrage. Informed that their team had traded Rick Wise, a veteran right-hander whose 17 wins in 1971 included a no-hitter, the fans bombarded the Phillies switchboard with angry messages. Some of them threatened to hang Phillies General Manager John Quinn in effigy. But Quinn's last deal turned out to be his best.

During a tenure that lasted more than 14 years with the Phillies, Carlton claimed 242 wins, all four of his Cy Young Awards, and virtually all of the club's lifetime and single-season pitching records. He threw 39 shutouts, fanned 3,031 hitters, and posted a 3.09 ERA. He also came within a whisker of a no-hitter on April 25, 1972. San Francisco leadoff man Chris Speier singled to open the game, but was the only Giant to hit safely as Carlton won, 3-0.

Robin Roberts, the team's star pitcher at the time of the 1950 World Series, saw most of his records erased. "I played with a lefty named Curt Simmons who had a big year in 1950," said Roberts, a 286-game winner himself. "They started calling him Lefty and he certainly deserved it. But so did Steve. I never saw a better delivery than Carlton had. He had some real years in Philadelphia."

Armed with the devastating slider that he had added to his repertoire after the 1969 season, Carlton became the second National League pitcher to strike out 300 men in a season and pitched the game that clinched the first world championship in Phillies history.

His workouts were as legendary as his record. Carlton created his own weight-training regimen before that technique proved popular in other clubhouses. An advocate of martial arts and Asian meditation techniques, he spent hours before and after games in the trainer's room, sometimes squeezing metal balls so hard that he left an imprint. McCarver once told reporters that Carlton was visualizing "fertile lanes" on the inside and outside of home plate.

"He stuck his arm into a barrel of rice," Green said. "That's where he built the strength of his forearms, wrists, and fingers. I think it helped his slider tremendously.

"When I was director of minor leagues and scouting in 1972, it seemed like he won every game by scores of 1-0 or 2-1. He had to pitch nine innings because we didn't have a guy who could close for us. It was an unbelievable performance that will probably never be duplicated by anyone."

The rice regimen helped his arm so much that Carlton tried it for his legs – often the first body part to fail an older pitcher. He'd walk back and forth in a box with his legs buried three feet deep in rice. According to Phillies historian and author Rich Westcott, he also did more than 1,000 sit-ups at a time with 15-pound weights strapped to his wrists and ankles. Stretching and flexibility exercises followed.

"Whoever put that man together genetically did one helluva job," Gus Hoefling told Westcott. "He's not only one of the greatest athletes I ever worked with but one of the best-conditioned."

That conditioning, plus strong defense on the left side of the infield, were the major factors in Carlton's best season, 1972. Helped immensely by the fine fielding of shortstop Larry Bowa and third baseman Don Money, Carlton could have won 30 games with better batting support. He somehow lost 10 times, though the Phillies seemed to find a sudden spark when he was on the mound. The only honor that eluded Carlton that summer was league leadership in winning percentage. Cincinnati's Gary Nolan went 15-5 for a .750 mark, 20 points ahead of Carlton's .730.

Carlton won 22 of his last 25 that year to finish in a tie with Sandy Koufax for the most wins in a season by a National League left-hander (27). The fifth pitcher to win 20 games for a last-place team, Carlton also topped 300 strikeouts for the only time in his career.

Make no mistake, though: Carlton was a strikeout pitcher even before coming to Philadelphia. On September 15, 1969, he fanned 19 men, then a one-game record, against the Mets, but lost, 4-3, when Ron Swoboda hit a pair of two-run homers. He finished that season with more wins, more strikeouts, and a lower ERA than he had in any previous season.

In addition to his pitching prowess, Carlton helped himself in other ways. He had 13 career homers, one of them a grand-slam against Fernando Valenzuela, and 346 hits for a respectable .201 batting average. He also helped himself with a pickoff move that bordered on a balk, but was rarely called one.

One of the most consistent pitchers in baseball history, Carlton reached double digits in wins for 18 consecutive seasons. During that timeframe, he also had more than 160 strikeouts and 190 innings pitched per season.

He was a 10-time All-Star, and a familiar figure on Opening Day, finishing second to Seaver with 14 first-game assignments.

Carlton completed 254 of his 709 starts, blanked opponents 55 times, and posted a 3.22 career earned run average. A no-brainer for the Hall of Fame, he rang up 95.82 percent of the vote in 1994, with 436 votes of 455 ballots cast.

Among left-handers, only Warren Spahn had more wins and only Randy Johnson had more strikeouts.

The only rap against Carlton, in addition to the silent treatment he gave the press, was his reluctance to leave the game. Unable to win more than he lost in his last years, the Phillies released him when he refused to retire. He then bounced to the Giants, White Sox, Indians, and Twins without much distinction, adding 11 wins to his career total. He even failed to make the Phillies staff after a spring training tryout. Those last few years just delayed the inevitable.

Hall of Fame rules require a five-year waiting period after retirement. During that time, even the best athletes have much to contemplate about their careers.

For Carlton, whose teams won four pennants and two world championships as well as three divisional titles after the leagues adopted divisional play in 1969, there was much to think about. His mind must have flashed back to his 300th win, his 4,000th strikeout, his partnership with McCarver, the three seasons he coped with a sore elbow, the 1985 rotator cuff strain that sent him to the disabled list for two months, and the night the Phillies retired his No. 32.

Writing on his website, Carlton described standing at the Cooperstown lectern as "every skinny kid's dream. My baseball life's memories came flooding back to me while standing at that podium. It was the pinnacle of my career."

Box Score of 300th Win

Carlton Baseball Almanac Box Score
Philadelphia Phillies 6, St. Louis Cardinals 2

Game played on Friday, September 23, 1983, at Busch Stadium II

Philadelphia Phillies	ab	r	h	rbi	St. Louis Cardinals	ab	r	h	rbi
Morgan 2b	4	1	1	0	Smith L. lf	4	0	0	0
Garcia 2b	1	0	1	0	Smith O. ss	3	0	1	0
Matuszek 1b	5	0	2	0	McGee cf	4	0	1	0
Schmidt 3b	5	2	3	1	Hendrick 1b	4	1	1	0
Lefebvre rf	5	1	2	0	Green rf	4	1	2	2
Matthews lf	5	2	3	1	Sexton 2b	4	0	0	0
Holland p	0	0	0	0	Lyons 3b	4	0	0	0
Gross cf,lf	3	0	2	1	Brummer c	4	0	3	0
Diaz c	4	0	1	2	Andujar p	1	0	0	0
DeJesus ss	4	0	1	0	Lahti p	0	0	0	0
Carlton p	4	0	1	1	Rayford ph	1	0	0	0
Dernier cf	0	0	0	0	Von Ohlen p	0	0	0	0
Totals	40	6	17	6	Oberkfell ph	1	0	0	0
					Totals	34	2	8	2

Philadelphia	0	1	1		0	3	1	0	0	0	–	6	17	0
St. Louis	0	0	0		2	0	0	0	0	0	–	2	8	0

Philadelphia Phillies	IP	H	R	ER	BB	SO
Carlton W (15-15)	8.0	7	2	2	1	12
Holland	1.0	1	0	0	0	2
Totals	9.0	8	2	2	1	14

St. Louis Cardinals	IP	H	R	ER	BB	SO
Andujar L (6-16)	4.1	11	5	5	1	3
Lahti	2.2	4	1	1	0	1
Von Ohlen	2.0	2	0	0	0	0
Totals	9.0	17	6	6	1	4

E–None. DP–St. Louis 4. PB–Brummer (3). 2B–Philadelphia Matthews (18,off Andujar); Morgan (19,off Lahti); Schmidt (15,off Lahti). 3B–St. Louis O Smith (6,off Carlton). HR–St. Louis Green (8,4th inning off Carlton 1 on, 0 out). SH–Andujar (5,off Carlton). SB–Schmidt (7,3rd base off Andujar/Brummer); Lefebvre (5,2nd base off Andujar/Brummer). U-HP–Jim Quick, 1B–Bob Engel, 2B–Dave Pallone, 3B–Paul Runge. T–2:31. A–27,266.

Career Statistics

CARLTON, Steve				Steven Norman "Lefty" Carlton; B: 12/22/1944, Miami, FL; BL/TL, 6'4"/(178-220); Debut: 4/12/1965; HOF 1994										

YEAR	TM-L	W	L	PCT	G	GS	CG-SHO	SV-BS	IP	H	R	HR	SO	ERA
1965	StL-N	0	0	...	15	2	0	0-0	25	27	7	3	21	2.52
1966	StL-N	3	3	0.500	9	9	2-1	0-0	52	56	22	2	25	3.12
1967	StL-N	14	9	0.609	30	28	11-2	1-0	193	173	71	10	168	2.98
1968	StL-N	13	11	0.542	34	33	10-5	0-0	232	214	87	11	162	2.99
1969	StL-N	17	11	0.607	31	31	12-2	0-0	236	185	66	15	210	2.17
1970	StL-N	10	19	0.345	34	33	13-2	0-0	253	239	123	25	193	3.73
1971	StL-N	20	9	0.690	37	36	18-4	0-0	273	275	120	23	172	3.56
1972	Phi-N	27	10	0.730	41	41	30-8	0-0	346	257	84	17	310	1.97
1973	Phi-N	13	20	0.394	40	40	18-3	0-0	293	293	146	29	223	3.90
1974	Phi-N	16	13	0.552	39	39	17-1	0-0	291	249	118	21	240	3.22
1975	Phi-N	15	14	0.517	37	37	14-3	0-0	255	217	116	24	192	3.56
1976	Phi-N	20	7	0.741	35	35	13-2	0-0	252	224	94	19	195	3.13
1977	Phi-N	23	10	0.697	36	36	17-2	0-0	283	229	99	25	198	2.64
1978	Phi-N	16	13	0.552	34	34	12-3	0-0	247	228	91	30	161	2.84
1979	Phi-N	18	11	0.621	35	35	13-4	0-0	251	202	112	25	213	3.62
1980	Phi-N	24	9	0.727	38	38	13-3	0-0	304	243	87	15	286	2.34
1981	Phi-N	13	4	0.765	24	24	10-1	0-0	190	152	59	9	179	2.42
1982	Phi-N	23	11	0.676	38	38	19-6	0-0	295	253	114	17	286	3.10
1983	Phi-N	15	16	0.484	37	37	8-3	0-0	283	277	117	20	275	3.11
1984	Phi-N	13	7	0.650	33	33	1	0-0	229	214	104	14	163	3.58
1985	Phi-N	1	8	0.111	16	16	0	0-0	92	84	43	6	48	3.33
1986	Phi-N	4	8	0.333	16	16	0	0-0	83	102	70	15	62	6.18
	SF-N	1	3	0.250	6	6	0	0-0	30	36	20	4	18	5.10
	Year	5	11	0.313	22	22	0	0-0	113	138	90	19	80	5.89
	Chi-A	4	3	0.571	10	10	0	0-0	63	58	30	6	40	3.69
1987	Cle-A	5	9	0.357	23	14	3	1-3	109	111	76	17	71	5.37
	Min-A	1	5	0.167	9	7	0	0-0	43	54	35	7	20	6.70
	Year	6	14	0.300	32	21	3	1-3	152	165	111	24	91	5.74
1988	Min-A	0	1	0.000	4	1	0	0-0	9	20	19	5	5	16.76
TOTAL	24	329	244	0.574	741	709	254-55	2-3	5217	4672	2130	414	4136	3.22

Courtesy of Ronnie Joyner

The Ryan Express

Nolan Ryan – 324 Wins

Nolan Ryan had such power behind his pitches that he was named after a speeding train.

In a career that stretched a record 27 seasons, "The Ryan Express" struck out more men and threw more no-hitters than any other pitcher. The thought of facing him terrorized virtually everyone who dared to approach the plate when he was pitching.

A native Texan who spent most of his career pitching for the two teams based in that state, the Texas Rangers and the Houston Astros, Ryan was just 19 when he broke into the major leagues with the New York Mets. Equipped with electric stuff he couldn't control, Ryan showed flashes of brilliance, pitching well out of the bullpen in the 1969 postseason and throwing a pair of shutouts in 1970, but losing more often than he won.

Worried that he might never find the strike zone consistently, the Mets packaged the pitcher with Frank Estrada, Don Rose, and Leroy Stanton and swapped him to the California Angels for infielder Jim Fregosi. To put it politely, the Mets were fleeced.

"Our club should never have let him go," future 300-game winner Tom Seaver said. "It was just a matter of time until he harnessed his potential. All the Angels did was give him the ball every fourth day."

Working with pitching coach Tom Morgan and catcher Jeff Torborg in Anaheim, Ryan quickly proved himself a heavenly find for the Angels. In his first year with the team, he threw a career-best nine

Nolan Ryan

shutouts while finishing 19-16 with a 2.28 earned run average. He also led the league with 329 strikeouts, a figure he would boost to a record 383 the following season.

By the time he retired, "The Ryan Express" had 5,714 strikeouts, 324 wins, 222 complete games, 61 shutouts, seven no-hitters, three saves, and a more-than-respectable 3.19 earned run average – especially since he spent all but one of his 13 American League seasons during the age of the designated hitter.

Had he not allowed 2,795 walks and thrown 277 wild pitches – both major-league records – his numbers would have been better. Playing for poor teams didn't help his win total, either.

Ryan started thinking about joining the 300-win club relatively early. "Once I got to 250," he said, "I felt that I could do it. Staying healthy was the whole key. An injury can always shorten a career. I think that is always in the back of a pitcher's mind. I knew I needed to stay healthy and pitch long enough."

Unlike most pitchers who reach a certain age, Ryan also fattened his win total by keeping his power at full throttle. "A lot of that is genetic," said the 12-time strikeout king. "The aging process affects each and every one of us differently. What it really came down to for me was staying away from any career-threatening injury that might have taken away from my ability to maintain my style of pitching."

Sportswriter Blackie Sherrod once suggested that Ryan go to Harvard medical school "not to study, but to be studied." Ryan reached the 300-win plateau on July 31, 1990, while pitching for the Texas Rangers. "I was very honored I was able to do that," said Ryan, who defeated the Milwaukee Brewers, then an American League club. "The 300 club is a very exclusive group."

Getting there was not easy for Ryan, whose lone 20-win seasons came consecutively, with the Angels of 1973 and 1974. "Looking back, I think 1973 was my best year," he said, "because of the two no-hitters, the fact that I won 20 games for the first time, and the 383 strikeouts. I grew up a Sandy Koufax fan, so when I passed Sandy with the strikeout record and later tied him by pitching my fourth no-hitter in 1975, those records meant a lot to me."

Luck played a part in Ryan's ability to erase the Koufax strikeout mark. His last start lasted 11 innings, allowing the right-hander to fan Minnesota's Rich Reese for his 16th strikeout of the game and 383rd of the season, one more than Koufax had in 1965.

"Pitching is the art of instilling fear," Koufax told *The Washington Post* in 1974. "If your control is suspect like Ryan's is, and the thought of being hit is in the batter's mind, you'll go a long way."

In three different seasons, Ryan reached double figures in hit batsmen but only led his league once, with eight in 1982. His inability to control his pitches was a factor, but so was his notion of keeping batters loose by pitching them inside and preventing them from digging in at the plate. No one dug in against Ryan.

"The type of hitter who gave me the most trouble was a left-handed contact hitter who hit the ball where it was thrown," he said recently. "I'm talking about Pete Rose, George Brett, Rod Carew, Don Mattingly, or Tony Gwynn. Those kinds of guys."

Although he split his career evenly between leagues, Ryan preferred the National League.

"I was a National Leaguer as a kid," he said, "and if you ask me which league I favored, I'd have to go with the National League, especially because I got the opportunity to live at home during my nine years in Houston. I am not a fan of the designated hitter, so I preferred National League baseball, which doesn't have it."

As a batter, Ryan rarely helped himself, smacking only two home runs. But he despised the idea of disenfranchising American League pitchers.

Ryan actually recorded a better career ERA (3.17) against American League opposition, with a higher mark (3.23) during his 14 National League campaigns.

Similar in style to Bob Feller, who blew hitters away but was wild enough to walk many others, Ryan pitched his first no-hitter by beating the Kansas City Royals, 3-0, on May 15, 1973, and his second by topping the Detroit Tigers, 6-0, on July 15 of the same season. He then came within a whisker of duplicating Johnny VanderMeer's feat of pitching consecutive no-hitters, but Baltimore's Mark Belanger ruined his bid in the eighth inning.

Instead, Ryan's third no-hitter was a 4-0 decision over the Minnesota Twins in his final appearance of the 1974 season, on September 28. The fourth – the one that tied Koufax – came on June 1, 1975, a 1-0 victory against the Baltimore Orioles.

Ryan's record fifth no-hitter came on national television, a 5-0 win for the Houston Astros over the Los Angeles Dodgers on September 26, 1981. He got his last two with Texas, beating the Oakland Athletics by a 5-0 score on June 11, 1990, and the Toronto Blue Jays, 3-0, on May 1, 1991.

"They all came as a surprise because it's not something you can anticipate or prepare for," Ryan recalled. "When it happened, I just called it a magical day when everything came together.

"I don't know which of my no-hitters stands out the most but it would probably have to be the second one, because I was so dominating in that game (17 strikeouts), or the last one, because it happened so late in my career. I had really thought that part of my career was behind me."

Had he not faced designated hitters instead of pitchers during 12 of his 13 seasons in the American League, Ryan might have had even more no-hitters. In 1989 alone, he took five no-hitters into the eighth inning, blowing two of them in the ninth. He wound up with two of his 12 one-hitters that season.

Ryan also lost a no-hitter to an official scorer's decision. On August 29, 1973, the only hit Ryan yielded to the Yankees was a pop-up that dropped safely between two infielders who called for it, then stopped to avoid a collision. Had the scorer not ruled it a hit, Ryan would have become the only man in baseball history to pitch three no-hitters in the same season.

By the time a bad elbow forced him out of the game for good late in 1993, Ryan's record for no-hit games was one of 53 he owned or shared. They included 27 years played, 19 low-hit games (one hit or no hits), six 300-strikeout seasons, and most strikeouts per nine innings in both a season (11.48) and career (9.55). A challenger to his strikeout mark would have to *average* 285.7 whiffs for 20 years just to forge a tie. That record seems as safe as Cy Young's 511 wins.

The oldest man to pitch a no-hitter (he was 44 when he got his last), Ryan led his league in shutouts three times, earned run average twice, and innings pitched and complete games once each. Add the dozen strikeout crowns and the 12 times he led the league in strikeouts per nine innings, and it seems that a Cy Young Award should also be on Ryan's resume. It never happened.

He finished second in the annual Cy Young voting once, third twice, and fourth once, but did much better when his name graced the

Hall of Fame ballot for the first time. He got into the Hall with 98.8 percent of the vote (491 of the 497 ballots cast).

The six writers who ignored him might have been dissuaded by Ryan's 292 losses, his meager .526 winning percentage, or his penchant for wildness – two seasons of 200+ walks, plus league leadership in bases on balls eight times.

"In close games, walks can be the difference in wins or losses," conceded Ryan, who held hitters to the league's lowest batting average a dozen times. "Hard throwers usually walk more people than others do, especially early in their careers. I know Bob Feller had a problem with that and I did, too."

When Ryan pitched for the Mets, the plate jumped around on him so much that he managed only a 29-37 record. His fortunes changed in California, largely because of pitching coach Tom Morgan.

"He made my delivery more compact and made it easier for me," Ryan said. "We were together about four or five years with the Angels."

Ryan also received wise counsel from Jeff Torborg, a catcher who later became a respected coach and manager. "There's no fatigue factor with him," said Torborg, who caught him with the 1973 Angels. "He is extremely well-conditioned and he has exceptionally strong legs that help him push off the rubber with extra velocity."

Torborg said the pitcher's release point, follow-through, and weight distribution accounted for the high velocity of his pitches. But he had no favorite catcher, pitching each of his no-hitters to a different one.

"The only time I had a catcher for any length of time on a regular basis was with the Astros, with Alan Ashby," Ryan remembered. "If somebody catches you on a regular basis, you don't shake them off a lot because they know how you like to pitch. But I didn't really have that. In fact, John Russell, who caught my sixth no-hitter, had never caught me before that game. He would just initiate pitches. But as the game went on, we fell into a pattern and I wasn't shaking him off very much at all."

Ryan spent eight years with the Angels before returning to the National League as a free agent signee with the Houston Astros, who gave him the first seven-figure salary on November 19, 1979. He lasted nine seasons in Houston before heading north to Dallas-Ft. Worth, also via free agency, to finish his career with the Rangers.

Picking a logo for his Hall of Fame cap wasn't hard for Ryan. "When I went to the Rangers, I planned to stay one year but lasted for five," he explained. "I enjoyed it because the Rangers gave me the chance to continue to play in Texas and so many neat things happened to me there: the sixth and seventh no-hitters, the 300th win, and the 5,000th strikeout. I just felt it was appropriate for me to go in as a Ranger."

Ryan was wearing a Texas uniform when he got his 300th win on July 31, 1990, at Milwaukee County Stadium. Although Milwaukee's lineup included future Hall of Famers Paul Molitor and Robin Yount, Ryan coasted to an 11-3 victory, yielding six hits, two walks, and one earned run in 7 $^2/_3$ innings.

"It was a relief to get it the second time I tried," said Ryan, who left tickets for friends and family hoping to witness history. "I didn't want my people to have to adjust their schedules while waiting for me to get it done."

He struck out eight Brewers in that game, but Ryan often fanned many more on a given night. He struck out 19 men in a game four times, three of them in extra innings. It was hardly surprising when he was timed at 100.8 miles an hour in 1974, at the peak of his career.

That was the year he won a career-best 22 games, more than a third of California's total of 65, and became the only man to fan at least 300 hitters three years in a row. Working in the four-man rotation that was then in vogue, the fireballer led the league with 332 $^2/_3$ innings pitched, the most of his career. Ryan had 26 complete games, tying his personal high of the previous year, but didn't always win them. He lost seven games by one run, including a 1-0 setback in a 19-strikeout game against Detroit.

For the most part, the league's best hitters couldn't handle him.

Reggie Jackson, who eventually joined Ryan in Cooperstown, admitted he was afraid to step into the box when the 6'2" right-hander was working. "He was the only guy who could put fear into me," said Jackson, known as "Mr. October" for his clutch postseason slugging. "It was not just because he could get me out but because he could kill me. There are no words to describe what it feels like to stand up there and see that ball come at you. I like fastballs, but that's like saying I like ice cream – just not a whole truckload of it."

Even Rod Carew, a confident contact hitter who won seven batting crowns, struggled against Ryan. "He can get you to chase a lot of bad pitches," said Carew after fanning 15 times in a stretch of 39 at-bats against Ryan. Carew fanned twice and walked twice when Ryan no-hit the Minnesota Twins.

Cecil Cooper, another talented hitter, whiffed 11 times in 16 trips and a record six times in a single game against Ryan in 1973. "You're really not sure where he'll throw the ball," Cooper complained. "When a guy is throwing that hard, you just can't get out of the way of it like you can with other guys. If he had Catfish Hunter's control, he'd be completely unhittable. I think he could win 35 games."

Larry Hisle griped about Ryan's curve, saying the extra weapon gave him an unfair advantage.

"I was a fastball hitter but I hated to face him," said Texas slugger Jeff Burroughs. "He was just so much faster than anyone else."

Norm Cash, who hit a league-best .361 in 1961, was so intimidated by Ryan that he once sawed off a table leg in the clubhouse and substituted it for his bat. Umpire Ron Luciano said, "You can't hit with that." Cash had a quick response: "What difference does it make? I can't hit him, anyway."

Cash finally popped out to short with a real bat, ending Ryan's no-hitter against Detroit.

A blazing fastball didn't always translate into wins. When he led the National League with 270 strikeouts and a 2.76 earned run average for the 1987 Astros, Ryan received such poor support from his teammates that he wound up with an 8-16 record – a mark that killed his candidacy for the Cy Young Award that season.

"That was very frustrating," said Ryan. He was 40 years old then and didn't know if or when he'd get another chance. Neither did the Astros, who wanted to reduce his salary. The Rangers, recognizing Ryan's value as a gate attraction and as a pitcher, decided to take a flyer on the flamethrower.

They were rewarded with 51 victories, two of them no-hitters, and a miraculous 301-strikeout season when Ryan was 42. It was during his Texas tenure that Ryan became the only man to throw no-hitters in three different decades. The eight-time All-Star also stood alone with 2000 strikeouts in both leagues.

Despite a well-publicized brawl with Robin Ventura, who charged the 46-year-old pitcher after a Ryan pitch grazed his arm, the Rangers eventually retired Ryan's number – an honor also accorded him by the Angels and Astros.

Named Lynn Nolan Ryan, Jr., when he was born in Refugio, Texas, on January 31, 1947, he showed an early ability to rocket the ball past rivals trying to hit it – or at least trying to see it. As a schoolboy at Alvin High, his fastball once fractured a hitter's arm. But he also fanned 19 men in a seven-inning game, convincing the New York Mets to take him in the 12th round of the June 1965 amateur draft. Players picked so late in the process rarely succeed, let alone succeed as brilliantly as Ryan.

He gave a hint of things to come by starring in the farm system, fanning 272 men in 183 innings at Greenville, South Carolina, and whiffing 21 Double-A batters in a stint that lasted $9 \, ^1/_3$ innings. Ryan was 19 when he made his debut on September 11, 1966, but he provided a better hint of things to come on May 18, 1968, when he fanned 14 Cincinnati Reds. He got the first of 61 career shutouts and the first of a dozen one-hitters by blanking Philadelphia on April 18, 1970. But the taciturn Texan, used as both a starter and reliever in New York, chafed from lack of work and lacked confidence in his control. He did contribute to the euphoria of the Mets' 1969 miracle, however.

Ryan worked seven stellar innings of relief, picking up the win in the decisive third playoff game against the Atlanta Braves and giving the Mets their first National League pennant. Then he relieved again in Game 3 of the World Series against Baltimore, working 2 $^1/_3$ scoreless frames behind Gary Gentry in a game made memorable by Tommie Agee's one-for-the-ages catch.

"Anytime you're on a World Championship team, it has to be a highlight of your career," said Ryan, who had lifetime 1-1 marks in both the Division Series and Championship Series. "If you look at the 1969 Mets team, very few of those players were ever in another World Series or on another World Series winner. So I think it shows how hard it is and how unique it is to be on a World Championship team."

Ryan came close to reaching the Fall Classic with the 1979 Angels and the Astros of 1980, 1981, and 1986, but never won a game in the World Series.

Ryan's career was curtailed several times by strikes and lockouts, most notably the 1981 work stoppage that cut seven weeks off the schedule. The pitcher later revealed that he had come close to quitting the game.

"If it had gone on for another week, I would have gone back to Alvin (Texas)," said Ryan, who later became a cattle rancher and minor-league team owner. "Once I had done that, I wouldn't have come back. That would have been it."

Ryan's career-best 1.69 ERA that season led the National League, but he made only 21 starts, far from his norm. Six years later, when he had the league's best ERA again, Ryan reverted to a more familiar form, winning the first of four straight strikeout titles. He was 43 and pitching for the Rangers when he won the last one.

The fifth man to throw two no-hitters in the same season, Ryan had many epic battles.

He cited a one-hitter he pitched against the Boston Red Sox at Anaheim Stadium on July 9, 1972. In the first inning, Tommy Harper walked, Doug Griffin fanned, and Carl Yastrzemski sneaked a roller through the shift on the right side of the infield. Then the pitcher retired 26 men in a row, fanning 16 of them and getting eight of those in succession.

"That was more overpowering than the no-hitters," said Ryan, who had at least 15 strikeouts in a game an amazing 26 times.

On May 2, 1979, in his last year with the Angels, Ryan outdueled defending Cy Young Award winner Ron Guidry of the Yankees, 1-0, in Anaheim.

"I was sitting in the dugout when Nolan got the last out," Guidry said. "I picked up my stuff and started to walk to the locker room. When I got to the end of the dugout, Nolan was in front of his dugout. He looked at me and took off his cap. I waved to him and gave him a thumbs up. That didn't happen often.

"I saw Nolan in the outfield the next day and went over to him, shook his hand, and said, 'I didn't want to lose but I didn't mind losing to you.' He said, 'It was a game neither of us should have lost. I was fortunate that I came out on top but I wouldn't have minded losing 1-0 to you.'"

Four years later, in 1983, Ryan broke Walter Johnson's career strikeout record, which had lasted 56 years, and never looked back. Rickey Henderson, also en route to the Hall of Fame, became his 5,000th strikeout victim on August 22, 1989.

Ryan whiffed 49 men who won Most Valuable Player awards, 21 who reached Cooperstown, and five father-and-son tandems.

He couldn't name his crowning achievement, with 5,000 strikeouts, 300 wins, 27 years played, and the seven no-hitters all vying for the honor.

"It's hard for me to classify one over the other because of the fact my career was so long," he explained. "To win 300 games, you have to have longevity. To throw seven no-hitters, maybe not so much. If somebody were to break that record, I don't think it would take longevity."

Since no one else has pitched more than four, Ryan was just being modest. His hitless prowess started in 1973, when he was 26, and extended to 1991, when he was 44.

Named to the All-Century team in a 1999 fan vote, Ryan retired with numbers that seem ridiculous: 215 games with double-digit strikeouts, 331 frames when he fanned three men in a row, 37 games yielding two or fewer hits, and a career ratio of 9.55 strikeouts per nine innings.

When the popular pitching legend became president of the Texas Rangers in 2008, he also became the first Hall of Famer to run a team since Christy Mathewson, a 300-game winner of earlier vintage, headed the Boston Braves in 1925.

Whether anyone else joins the 300 Club is problematic, according to Ryan.

"It's a bigger challenge today," said Ryan, who often topped 200 pitches per start and worked in a four-man rotation. "Because of the number of innings starters are pitching, the way they are used, and the number of bullpen pitchers who come in and get involved with the game, winning 300 is definitely a bigger challenge than it once was."

Box Score of 300th Win

Ryan Baseball Almanac Box Score
Texas Rangers 11, Milwaukee Brewers 3

Game played on Tuesday, July 31, 1990 at County Stadium

Texas Rangers	ab	r	h	rbi	Milwaukee Brewers	ab	r	h	rbi
Huson ss	4	0	1	2	Molitor 1b	5	2	3	0
Daugherty ph	1	1	1	1	Yount cf	5	1	1	1
Green ss	0	0	0	0	Sheffield 3b	4	0	0	0
Franco 2b	5	1	1	4	Parker dh	4	0	1	0
Palmeiro 1b	5	0	2	0	Vaughn lf	4	0	0	0
Sierra rf	5	2	3	0	Gantner 2b	3	0	2	1
Baines dh	5	1	1	0	Felder rf	3	0	0	0
Incaviglia lf	3	2	2	2	O'Brien c	3	0	0	0
Petralli c	2	1	0	1	Hamilton ph	1	0	0	0
Buechele 3b	4	2	2	1	Spiers ss	4	0	0	0
Pettis cf	3	1	0	0	Bosio p	0	0	0	0
Ryan p	0	0	0	0	Mirabella p	0	0	0	0
Arnsberg p	0	0	0	0	Knudson p	0	0	0	0
Totals	37	11	13	11	Fossas p	0	0	0	0
					Totals	36	3	7	2

Texas	0	0	0	0	4	1	0	0	6	–	11	13	3
Milwaukee	0	0	1	0	0	0	0	2	0	–	3	7	1

Texas Rangers	IP	H	R	ER	BB	SO
Ryan W (11-4)	7.2	6	3	1	2	8
Arnsberg SV (3)	1.1	1	0	0	0	0
Totals	9.0	7	3	1	2	8

Milwaukee Brewers	IP	H	R	ER	BB	SO
Bosio L (4-9)	5.1	6	5	5	1	1
Mirabella	2.2	4	2	2	1	1
Knudson	0.0	1	2	1	0	0
Fossas	1.0	2	2	2	0	1
Totals	9.0	13	11	10	2	3

E–Franco 2 (12), Buechele (5), Knudson (2). DP–Milwaukee 1. 2B–Texas Sierra (22,off Bosio). 3B–Texas Huson (2,off Bosio); Palmeiro (3,off Bosio), Milwaukee Yount (5,off Ryan). HR–Texas Incaviglia (17,9th inning off Mirabella 0 on, 0 out); Franco (7,9th inning off Fossas 3 on, 0 out). SH–Pettis (8,off Knudson). SF–Petralli (3,off Bosio). SB–Gantner (7,2nd base off Ryan/Petralli). WP–Ryan (5). U-HP–Al Clark, 1B–John Hirschbeck, 2B–Rocky Roe, 3B–Dave Phillips. T–3:05. A–51,533.

Career Statistics

RYAN, Nolan		Lynn Nolan Ryan; B: 1/31/1947, Refugio, TX; BR/TR, 6'2"/195 lbs.; Debut: 9/11/1966; HOF 1999												

YEAR	TM-L	W	L	PCT	G	GS	CG	SH	SV	IP	H	R	HR	SO	ERA
1966	NY-N	0	1	0.000	2	1	0	0	0	3	5	5	1	6	15.00
1968	NY-N	6	9	0.400	21	18	3	0	0	134	93	50	12	133	3.09
1969	NY-N	6	3	0.667	25	10	2	0	1	89	60	38	3	92	3.53
1970	NY-N	7	11	0.389	27	19	5	2	1	131	86	59	10	125	3.42
1971	NY-N	10	14	0.417	30	26	3	0	0	152	125	78	8	137	3.97
1972	Cal-A	19	16	0.543	39	39	20	9	0	284	166	80	14	329	2.28
1973	Cal-A	21	16	0.568	41	39	26	4	1	326	238	113	18	383	2.87
1974	Cal-A	22	16	0.579	42	41	26	3	0	332	221	127	18	367	2.89
1975	Cal-A	14	12	0.538	28	28	10	5	0	198	152	90	13	186	3.45
1976	Cal-A	17	18	0.486	39	39	21	7	0	284	193	117	13	327	3.36
1977	Cal-A	19	16	0.543	37	37	22	4	0	299	198	110	12	341	2.77
1978	Cal-A	10	13	0.435	31	31	14	3	0	234	183	106	12	260	3.72
1979	Cal-A	16	14	0.533	34	34	17	5	0	222	169	104	15	223	3.60
1980	Hou-N	11	10	0.524	35	35	4	2	0	233	205	100	10	200	3.35
1981	Hou-N	11	5	0.688	21	21	5	3	0	149	99	34	2	140	1.69
1982	Hou-N	16	12	0.571	35	35	10	3	0	250	196	100	20	245	3.16
1983	Hou-N	14	9	0.609	29	29	5	2	0	196	134	74	9	183	2.98
1984	Hou-N	12	11	0.522	30	30	5	2	0	183	143	78	12	197	3.04
1985	Hou-N	10	12	0.455	35	35	4	0	0	232	205	108	12	209	3.80
1986	Hou-N	12	8	0.600	30	30	1	0	0	178	119	72	14	194	3.34
1987	Hou-N	8	16	0.333	34	34	0	0	0	211	154	75	14	270	2.76
1988	Hou-N	12	11	0.522	33	33	4	1	0	220	186	98	18	228	3.52
1989	Tex-A	16	10	0.615	32	32	6	2	0	239	162	96	17	301	3.20
1990	Tex-A	13	9	0.591	30	30	5	2	0	204	137	86	18	232	3.44
1991	Tex-A	12	6	0.667	27	27	2	2	0	173	102	58	12	203	2.91
1992	Tex-A	5	9	0.357	27	27	2	0	0	157	138	75	9	157	3.72
1993	Tex-A	5	5	0.500	13	13	0	0	0	66	54	47	5	46	4.88
TOTAL	27	324	292	0.526	807	773	222	61	3	5386	3923	2178	321	5714	3.19

Sandy's Heir

Don Sutton – 324 Wins

Though it may be hard to believe, Don Sutton had something in common with Nolan Ryan.

Both were right-handers from the South who pitched more than 20 years while appearing in both major leagues. Both finished with 324 victories without collecting a Cy Young Award or collecting 20-win seasons. And both suffered such lack of run support that they logged more than 250 losses.

Unlike Ryan, a fireballer with whom he teamed briefly in Houston, Sutton sailed into the 300 club softly – by practicing techniques learned at an early age.

"I was always a goal setter," Sutton said. "When I was 15 years old, I knew I could pitch in the big leagues. When I heard there was a Hall of Fame, that was my goal. I wanted to win 300 and make the Hall of Fame. And that was before I got out of high school."

Henry Roper was one of the three men who molded Sutton into a major-leaguer.

"I played shortstop in Little League when I was 11 and wasn't a real good hitter or a real good fielder," Sutton said. "But I did have a good arm so if I caught the ball, I could throw you out. Between the fifth and sixth grade, somebody told me that my sixth-grade teacher, new to the country school I was going to, had played in the Giants organization as a pitcher.

Don Sutton

Photo courtesy of National
Baseball Hall of Fame Library
Cooperstown, N.Y.

"I hounded him from the day after Labor Day until Little League started. I said, 'Mr. Roper, I want to learn to pitch.' Every day at the break, he put on an old catcher's mitt and had me throw. He taught me the very same mechanics and the very same philosophy that I carried to my final day in the big leagues: put the fastball in the right spot and throw the curveball for strikes."

Sutton's dad also encouraged him. "The day I left to go to my first spring training in 1965, I had to take a bus from Pensacola, Florida, to Vero Beach. Dad took me to the bus station and said to me, 'There will always be people out there better than you, but don't let anyone ever outwork you.' And I didn't."

Sutton, who received a meager $7,500 to sign as an amateur free agent in 1964, was always ready when handed the ball. "My father was a farmer who became a construction worker," he said. "He went to work every day and stayed until the job was finished. I worked on a farm and did construction work, too, so the only thing I was doing was transferring what my dad had taught me about work – to do a good job. It didn't make any sense just being happy to be there. I was taught that if the job was worth doing, it should be done well and until it was finished. In baseball, the mindset I was taught dictated that we finish what we start. The game is nine innings, isn't it? You're the starting pitcher, right? Go nine innings."

Sutton twice topped 40 starts and reached double digits in complete games 10 times. Once, in 1972, he pitched nine shutouts in one season. He had an impressive 58 in his career.

A stickler for physical conditioning, Sutton never spent a day on the disabled list until an elbow injury ended his career at age 43 in 1988. He lasted 23 seasons, four of them ending in the World Series, and pitched in the playoffs five times.

That's not a bad resume for a guy who never won more games than he lost until his fifth season in the majors.

Sutton spent only five months in the minors before reaching the majors with the 1966 Dodgers, a team coming off a World Championship year spearheaded by future Hall of Fame pitchers Sandy Koufax and Don Drysdale. But Sutton's timing was perfect, as the two aces staged a double holdout that spring and yielded plenty of exhibition game innings to the rookie.

Walter Alston, the Dodgers' manager, gave Sutton 35 starts as the No. 4 starter behind Koufax, Drysdale, and Claude Osteen.

"I appreciated Walt giving such responsibility to a 21-year-old rookie in a pennant race," said Sutton, who split 24 decisions that season. "I appreciated the encouragement he gave me. I even appreciated the times he told me, 'You are so stubborn, you are going to kill yourself one day.' He also said, 'I know I can count on you.' That was the greatest compliment I received during my life as a pitcher. The day he retired, he brought me a copy of his book and wrote on the inside cover, 'To Don Sutton, when it is on the line, I want you to have the ball.'"

Alston, who managed the Dodgers for 24 years, reminded Sutton of his father.

"My dad believed in discipline, but you could talk to him," he said. "Walt was like that. He once told me I was the second most stubborn person he ever met. And I, in one of my belligerent moments, said, 'Oh yeah, who's first?' Alston said, 'I am, and you might want to remember that.'"

Dodgers pitching coach Red Adams also influenced the young Sutton.

"He was a guy who almost single-handedly put me into the Hall of Fame," said Sutton. "He had the ability to deal with 10 personalities in a unique way, remembering what we did best and helping us get better. He had a marvelous knowledge of pitching and mechanics and a great sense of humor. Red never let us take ourselves too seriously. His humor and bits of wisdom stuck with me for the rest of my life."

When he made his debut on April 14, 1966, Sutton departed with a 2-1 lead at Dodger Stadium, but left with two men on. Ron Perranoski, in a rare blown save, yielded a three-run homer to Rusty Staub and Sutton lost his first decision.

"When I first went out to the mound, I was wondering what took me so long," he told *Baseball Digest* editor John Kuenster. "I had been in the minors all of five months and remembered what my managers, Norm Sherry and Roy Hartsfield, told me: 'Throw strikes, change speeds, and back up third if you have to.' I figured pitching in the majors would be no different from what they told me. Actually, my greatest fear was failure."

Sutton's first major-league win came against future Hall of Famer Robin Roberts, then with Houston. "Roberts, Camilo Pascual, and Dick Donovan were the three right-handers who influenced what I was as a pitcher," Sutton said. "And I learned to pitch by listening to the radio. The broadcasters would say what those three guys were doing while they were pitching and I would go out and throw against the garage or chimney. Using what was natural for me, I would try to incorporate what the broadcaster had told me about those guys. He would say, 'Robin Roberts pitches up with a fastball. He's going to give up some home runs, but he'll come at you with strikes.' Or 'Pascual tips that front shoulder back. Here comes the curveball over the top, straight down.' And I remember hearing Donovan interviewed on Mutual's Game of the Day and saying, 'You gotta pitch inside. I'd knock my mom down if it would help me win.'"

Sutton spent his first 15 seasons in Los Angeles, winning a career-best 21 games in 1976. He led the National League in starts, shutouts, earned run average, and hits per nine innings once each. He also led the National League in ratio of strikeouts to walks three times.

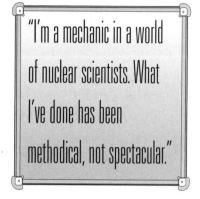

"I'm a mechanic in a world of nuclear scientists. What I've done has been methodical, not spectacular."

"I'm a mechanic in a world of nuclear scientists," he once said. "What I've done has been methodical, not spectacular."

The 6'1", 185-pound right-hander was merely being modest. He had plenty of big games, from the American League East title-clincher in 1982 to his 300th win, on June 18, 1986.

He wore three different uniforms in the World Series but always delivered as advertised. He wasn't Koufax or Drysdale, but neither was anyone else.

"The most important thing I learned from either of them," Sutton said, "was that I couldn't be them. Having grown up in Alabama and northwest Florida, there was a lot I didn't know about being a big-leaguer. I will always be grateful to Sandy, to Don, and to Claude Osteen, a country boy himself, for not letting me embarrass myself.

"I wasn't aware of the etiquette of being a major-leaguer – even little things like tipping the clubhouse guys or what clothes to wear when I wasn't playing. So many times I'd be eating alone somewhere and ask for the check but the server would say, 'The big gentleman over there has already picked it up for you.' They taught me how to think like a major-leaguer. But the most important thing they taught me was to keep on doing what got me there. Those 20 or 30 wins in the minors meant something. They told me to never change."

Sutton listened so well that his rookie year included more strike-outs than any National League rookie since Grover Cleveland Alexander in 1911. "Being compared to somebody else didn't enter my mind until I got deeper into my career," said Sutton. "But all of a sudden the names that were mentioned became more important to me than the numbers themselves."

En route to 3,574 career strikeouts, Sutton passed Koufax as the career Dodger leader. He also had many more victories, winning just 50 fewer games by himself than Koufax and Drysdale did together.

Sutton was with the California Angels when he joined the 300 club on June 18, 1986, with a three-hit, 5-1 victory over the Texas Rangers in Anaheim.

"I don't remember most of my games, but I do remember that one," said Sutton. "I was so comfortable with (catcher) Bob Boone that night. And I remember going nine – that was important to me.

"I pitched on Saturday against Kansas City the weekend before and got a no-decision. We were going to play Texas on Monday, Tuesday, and Wednesday in Anaheim before going on the road. After I came out of the Saturday game, Marcel Lachemann, the pitching coach, came over and said, 'Gene Mauch wants to see you.' I wondered what (the manager) wanted; I had pitched pretty well but just didn't win. I went into his office and sat down. He had a notepad with two or three columns of numbers on it. He said, 'The way I figure it, you start every fifth day and pitch every 116 hours. We just played a day game, but if you pitch on Wednesday night, that would be 96 hours. Are those eight or nine fewer hours going to make a difference in your preparation?' I said no, but wanted to know why.

"He said, 'I want you to win it in Anaheim. So I am going to bring you back a day early. I just had to satisfy my mind with how many hours it was going to be.' That's why I won my 300th game in California."

Because of that, supporters from Sutton's old Dodger days – including owner Peter O'Malley – were in attendance. O'Malley bought the top row behind the home dugout for an entourage of Sutton supporters.

He also remembered that Boone, the catcher, had a plan for the final out after the Rangers had two outs in the ninth and a 1-2 count on Gary Ward. "You kind of get into a rhythm with that kind of a game," Sutton said, "and I was rocking into my motion. But Bob Boone wouldn't flash a sign. He was staring straight at the ground. He told me later he was trying to think of a pitch that would fit there so that the batter would swing and miss, allowing him to hold the final out of my 300th win."

Although Pete Incaviglia ruined the shutout with a solo homer in the seventh, it was a gala night for the veteran pitcher.

Just 10 days later, Sutton marked another milestone when he and Phil Niekro became the first members of the 300 club to face each other since Tim Keefe and Pud Galvin in 1892.

"We laughed about it before and after the game," Sutton said. "I still have pictures that he and I took that weekend. We had some great match-ups over the years. It seemed every time I went to Atlanta, I had to face Niekro. We had tons of 2-1, 2-0, 3-1, and 3-2 ballgames. That's why you pitch; those are the games that are supposed to bring out the best in you."

Because he was always around the plate, Sutton surrendered 472 home runs. But he does not include Willie Mays, Mickey Mantle, or other immortals in his list of toughest opponents. "In the context of my pitching and my game," Sutton said, "Roberto Clemente was my toughest out. The next four were Bill Madlock, Bob Horner, Bill Buckner, and Rance Mulliniks."

Rance Mulliniks? "He wore my butt out," Sutton said of the utility infielder, who hit .272 with 73 home runs over 16 seasons. "He killed me. I swear he knew what was coming."

Sutton defeated every other team – a feat he ascribes to longevity. "If you play long enough and change teams often enough, you have a shot at doing it," he said. "That's a bi-product of being a free agent and being traded three times more than anything else."

No matter where he went, Sutton was consistent. He won at least 15 games a dozen times and reached double digits in victories and triple digits in strikeouts in 21 seasons. Sutton started and finished with the Dodgers, making intermediate stops in Houston, Milwaukee, Oakland, and California. He won 233 games for the Dodgers and 91 for everyone else, with 44 of those wins coming after age 40.

His Milwaukee stop was memorable because the Brewers, then in the American League, were locked in a fierce title fight with the Baltimore Orioles. The Brewers held a three-game lead with four to play, all in Baltimore. After dropping the first three games of the series, Milwaukee matched Sutton, a waiver wire pickup on August 31, against Orioles' ace Jim Palmer.

"They had traded for me just for an event like that," Sutton recalled. "I felt privileged to have that responsibility – and would have been disappointed not to have a shot at it. It turned out far better than I performed. They put a bunch of runs up early but Robin Yount, who never said anything, came up and jabbed me in the chest and said, 'We'll kick his butt.' Boom, he's got two home runs in the first few innings. I remember needling (manager) Harvey Kuenn when he came walking by. I said, 'Ain't you got anything for me?' He said, 'This is why we got you.'"

Sutton's title-clinching victory, his fourth in five Milwaukee decisions, pushed the Brewers into the playoffs. His defeat of the Angels in the American League Championship Series helped them win their only pennant.

Four years later, the 41-year-old pitcher made two starts for the Angels in a championship series they lost to Boston after taking three of the first four games.

In his career, Sutton was 3-1 in the National League Championship Series, 1-0 in the American League Championship Series, and 2-3 in the World Series. His cumulative postseason ERA was 3.68, considerably higher than his 3.26 regular-season mark.

Sutton did his best work in the 1974 postseason, posting a 2-0 record against Pittsburgh as the Dodgers lost only once in the best-of-five NLCS. Sutton's four-hit shutout in the opener marked the first postseason appearance by the Dodgers since divisional play began in 1969. When he followed by combining with Mike Marshall on a three-hitter in the decisive fourth game, Sutton's NLCS ERA stood at 0.53. He followed up by taking the lone Dodger win in a five-game World Series loss to the Oakland A's.

"The best game I ever pitched was the opening game of the playoffs against the Pirates in 1974," he said. "That was the one where I did more of what I wanted to do than in any other game. My second most memorable game came as a junior in high school. My little school in northwest Florida got to go to the state tournament for the first time and won because I pitched a 13-inning two-hitter and won, 3-1. There was no pitch count. And I was fine the next day."

In 1977, Sutton beat both the Philadelphia Phillies in the playoffs and the New York Yankees in the World Series without defeat. A year later, however, the pitcher's luck changed, leaving him with an 0-3 mark against the same two opponents. Sutton returned to the postseason winner's circle in 1982, when he beat the Angels in the third game of Milwaukee's five-game triumph.

"I went to the World Series in 1966, but didn't get to pitch," said Sutton. "So the 1974 World Series stands out for me because that was my first one. When I think of the World Series, I am pleased that I got to play in four of them. That's all I used to (dream about) when I threw the ball against the wall as a kid. I was always pitching in a World Series game. Growing up, I was pitching for the Yankees, not against them. I had two goals growing up in the Baptist Bible Belt: To pitch for the Yankees and punt for Notre Dame. But I couldn't talk about it at family reunions."

Nor could Sutton ever talk about winning a World Series. His teams went 0-4, creating the lone void in a career that was otherwise highly fulfilling.

He won the last three games of his career for the Dodgers in 1988, but retired before they won the Fall Classic – costing him his last chance at a ring.

The only 300-game winner who had only a single 20-win season, Sutton stood for consistent excellence. Proficient but not flashy, he threw five one-hitters, nine two-hitters, and eight scoreless innings in his four All-Star appearances. He started seven season openers and belonged to seven pitching staffs that led the National League in earned run average. He also belonged to the only starting quartet in which each member eventually would pitch at least 40 shutouts (1966 Dodgers).

"When I pitch during the regular season, it's work," he once said, "like going to an office or walking into a factory. You have a job to do and you try to do it. But the All-Star Game, playoffs, and World Series are just plain fun."

Sutton's resume suggests he had a lot of fun.

Years after both retired, Nolan Ryan was asked about Sutton. His answer was definitive: "He may have been the best finesse pitcher I ever saw."

But was it finesse or chicanery?

Finesse pitchers don't usually strike out 200 men per season – a level Sutton reached five times, with a personal high of 217. He ended his career with 3,574, seventh on the lifetime list.

Surprisingly, Sutton had to wait five years for the gates of the Hall of Fame to swing open. His entry might have been delayed by accusations that he doctored the baseball. In fact, he was ejected from a 1978 contest for that very violation.

Only when the outspoken pitcher threatened to sue the National League did the pitcher escape a probable fine and suspension. Sutton got off with a warning.

He and Gaylord Perry, also accused of ball-tampering, just smiled. "When I met Gaylord," Sutton said, "he gave me a jar of Vaseline. I thanked him and gave him a piece of sandpaper."

Both pitchers played the psychological angle to the hilt, hoping that batters would think a ball that dropped as it crossed the plate was illegally scuffed or "wet." Long-time Pittsburgh pitching coach Ray Miller even called Sutton "a fine example of defiance."

All Sutton would say is: "I got everything I could out of what I was given. I was taught to exhaust every effort and leave it all out there. When you look at the list of recent 300-game winners, Phil Niekro and I sit on the same ledge. He was a freak with the knuckleball, a battler. Neither of us threw that hard, had the Carlton slider, the Seaver fastball, the Gaylord Perry guile, the Nolan Ryan heater, or whatever Roger Clemens had. Nor could we throw 100 miles an hour like Randy Johnson.

"Carlton was one of the first, I think, to use creative conditioning to make himself stronger and better. Seaver was a classic pitcher. I don't mean to slight anybody but if I had one game to win, I would give the ball to him. Ryan was one of the most dominating, fear-invoking pitchers I was ever around and Clemens was very talented. Randy Johnson was just a different style of Steve Carlton, an over-powering left-hander.

"Greg Maddux was the greatest artist I ever saw pitch and Tom Glavine was the consummate professional, a guy who watched, observed, and had a plan for everything."

They could be the last of a breed, according to Sutton.

Asked whether the 300 club will have any new members, Sutton said, "I doubt it. Pitchers don't go nine innings now because the environment does not encourage it. It almost does not allow it. We glorify 200 innings pitched and a 4.50 earned run average. In the past, that would've gotten you a ticket back to Triple-A. We are conditioning pitchers to go six innings – two-thirds of their job – and glorifying a level of performance that is not conducive to winning 300 games."

Box Score of 300th Win

Sutton Baseball Almanac Box Score
Chicago Cubs 1, Milwaukee Braves 2

Game played on Friday, August 11, 1961, at County Stadium

Chicago Cubs	ab	r	h	rbi	Milwaukee Braves	ab	r	h	rbi
Heist cf	4	0	0	0	Cimoli cf	4	1	2	1
Zimmer 2b	4	0	2	0	Bolling 2b	4	0	0	0
Santo 3b	3	1	0	0	Mathews 3b	4	0	1	0
Altman rf	4	0	1	0	Aaron rf	2	0	1	0
Williams lf	4	0	1	0	Adcock 1b	2	0	0	0
Rodgers 1b	4	0	1	1	Thomas lf	3	0	1	0
Kindall ss	4	0	1	0	Torre c	3	1	0	0
Bertell c	3	0	0	0	McMillan ss	3	0	1	0
Banks ph	1	0	0	0	Spahn p	2	0	0	1
Curtis p	2	0	0	0	Totals	27	2	6	2
McAnany ph	1	0	0	0					
Totals	34	1	6	1					

Chicago	0	0	0	0	0	1	0	0	0	–	1	6	1
Milwaukee	0	0	0	0	1	0	0	1	x	–	2	6	2

Chicago Cubs	IP	H	R	ER	BB	SO
Curtis L (7-7)	8.0	6	2	1	2	6
Totals	8.0	6	2	1	2	6

Milwaukee Braves	IP	H	R	ER	BB	SO
Spahn W (12-12)	9.0	6	1	1	1	5
Totals	9.0	6	1	1	1	5

E–Williams (9), Bolling (8), Mathews (10). **DP**–Chicago 2. **HR**–Milwaukee Cimoli (3,8th inning off Curtis 0 on, 1 out). **SH**–Santo (1,off Spahn). **Team LOB**–8. **SF**–Spahn (2,off Curtis). **Team**–4. **CS**–Heist (2,2nd base by Spahn/Torre). **SB**–Aaron (17,2nd base off Curtis/Bertell). **U-HP**–Shag Crawford, **1B**–Al Barlick, **2B**–Bill Jackowski, **3B**–Ed Vargo. **T**–2:25. **A**–40,775.

Career Statistics

SUTTON, Don	Donald Howard Sutton; B: 4/2/1945, Clio AL; BR/TR, 6'1"/185 lbs.; Debut: 4/14/1966; HOF 1998

YEAR	TM-L	W	L	PCT	G	GS	CG	SH	SV	IP	H	R	HR	SO	ERA
1966	LA-N	12	12	0.500	37	35	6	2	0	225	192	82	19	209	2.99
1967	LA-N	11	15	0.423	37	34	11	3	1	232	223	106	18	169	3.95
1968	LA-N	11	15	0.423	35	27	7	2	1	207	179	64	6	162	2.60
1969	LA-N	17	18	0.486	41	41	11	1	0	293	269	123	25	217	3.47
1970	LA-N	15	13	0.536	38	38	10	1	0	260	251	127	38	201	4.08
1971	LA-N	17	12	0.586	38	37	12	1	1	265	231	85	10	194	2.54
1972	LA-N	19	9	0.679	33	33	18	9	0	272	186	78	13	207	2.08
1973	LA-N	18	10	0.643	33	33	14	3	0	256	196	78	18	200	2.42
1974	LA-N	19	9	0.679	40	40	10	5	0	276	241	111	23	179	3.23
1975	LA-N	16	13	0.552	35	35	11	4	0	254	202	87	17	175	2.87
1976	LA-N	21	10	0.677	35	34	15	4	0	267	231	98	22	161	3.06
1977	LA-N	14	8	0.636	33	33	9	3	0	240	207	93	23	150	3.18
1978	LA-N	15	11	0.577	34	34	12	2	0	238	228	109	29	154	3.55
1979	LA-N	12	15	0.444	33	32	6	1	1	226	201	109	21	146	3.82
1980	LA-N	13	5	0.722	32	31	4	2	1	212	163	56	20	128	2.20
1981	Hou-N	11	9	0.550	23	23	6	3	0	158	132	51	6	104	2.61
1982	Hou-N	13	8	0.619	27	27	4	0	0	195	169	75	10	139	3.00
	Mil-A	4	1	0.800	7	7	2	1	0	54	55	21	8	36	3.29
1983	Mil-A	8	13	0.381	31	31	4	0	0	220	209	109	21	134	4.08
1984	Mil-A	14	12	0.538	33	33	1	0	0	212	224	103	24	143	3.77
1985	Oak-A	13	8	0.619	29	29	1	1	0	194	194	88	19	91	3.89
	Cal-A	2	2	0.500	5	5	0	0	0	31	27	13	6	16	3.69
	Year	15	10	0.600	34	34	1	1	0	226	221	101	25	107	3.86
1986	Cal-A	15	11	0.577	34	34	3	1	0	207	192	93	31	116	3.74
1987	Cal-A	11	11	0.500	35	34	1	0	0	191	199	101	38	99	4.70
1988	LA-N	3	6	0.333	16	16	0	0	0	87	91	44	7	44	3.92
TOTAL	23	324	256	0.559	774	756	178	58	5	5282	4692	2104	472	3574	3.26

The Knuckleballer

Phil Niekro – 318 Wins

Phil Niekro played 24 years in the major leagues without ever reaching the World Series – a drought unmatched in baseball history. But that was hardly his fault.

Pitching primarily for the Braves, first in Milwaukee and then in Atlanta, he bamboozled batters with a knuckleball so effective that he was able to pile up 318 career victories – a record 121 of them after age 40.

The only knuckleballer in the 300 Club, he was also the only man to gain admittance with a shutout, beating the Toronto Blue Jays, 8-0, on the last day of the 1986 season. That win made him the oldest man ever to pitch a shutout, and the first man to win No. 300 while playing for the New York Yankees.

Although he pitched two seasons for New York, Niekro looked strange in pinstripes. He had won his first 284 games for the Braves, and even bridged the gap between two other 300-game winners, Warren Spahn and Tom Glavine. Niekro was his teammate in Spahn's last year with the Braves, in 1964, and Glavine's first, in 1987. He admitted disappointment that he didn't win his own 300th for the franchise.

"I was born a Brave and wanted to walk off the field with a Braves hat on," he said long after his retirement. "I walked in wearing a Milwaukee hat with that raised logo. But after 1983, they released me and the Yankees picked me up. I stayed there two years, then went to

Photo courtesy of National
Baseball Hall of Fame Library
Cooperstown, N.Y.

Phil Niekro

Cleveland for a couple of years. I pitched a few games for Toronto, then went back to Atlanta for a farewell game. I wanted to retire with a Braves hat on."

After winning a $500 contract at a tryout camp, Niekro found the inspiration he needed in the minor leagues. Pitching for Jacksonville in 1960, manager Red Murff – the same man who signed Nolan Ryan – told Niekro he could win in the majors if he learned to control the knuckler. "That was my motivation," Niekro recalled. "He was around a long time and I figured he must know something. I was hoping that what he told me would get me to the big leagues, and eventually it did."

Niekro reached the Milwaukee Braves as a reliever in 1964, but found the team had no catcher capable of handling his pet pitch. "Catchers wouldn't call for the knuckleball in the late innings with a runner on third because it might get away and cost us a ballgame," he said. "Things didn't change until they traded Gene Oliver to the Phillies for Bob Uecker.

"Uke told me, 'They don't care if I hit .150 as long as I call for the knuckleball. I don't care what the count is or what the situation is. I'm going to call for it and I know you can win with it.'"

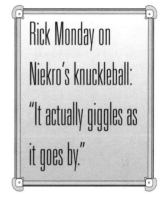

Rick Monday on Niekro's knuckleball: "It actually giggles as it goes by."

In 1967, Niekro had a new catcher in Uecker, and a new responsibility. When veteran starter Ken Johnson was scratched by illness in Philadelphia, manager Billy Hitchcock named Niekro the emergency starter. In the first of 20 starts he made that season, the 6'1" right-hander blanked the Phillies on two hits and proceeded to record the best earned run average of his career, a 1.87 mark that was also the best in the National League that season.

Two years later, when the Braves won the National League West title in the first year of divisional play, Niekro won a career-best 23 games, lost two other leads to rainouts, and finished second to 25-game winner Tom Seaver of the "Miracle Mets" in the voting for the Cy Young Award.

Niekro had two other 20-win seasons, one of them in a year when he led the league in both wins and losses (21-20 when the team was truly the "Bad News" Braves in 1979). The league's first 20-20 pitcher in 73 years, he joined Steve Carlton as the only National Leaguers since 1901 to have 20-win campaigns with last-place teams.

Except for surprise title seasons in 1969 and 1982, the Braves were so bad during most of Niekro's tenure that they tried to squeeze every ounce out of his right arm. Eight times after his transfer into the starting rotation, Niekro made at least 40 appearances, often working on short rest because the knuckler put so little strain on his arm. In 1977, one of two years when he *lost* 20 games, he struck out a career-best 262 – a Braves franchise record never challenged by Glavine or Greg Maddux, the future 300-game winners who followed him, or Warren Spahn, the 300-game winner who preceded him.

Neither Glavine nor Maddux ever pitched a no-hit game, but Niekro did, against San Diego in 1973. It was hardly his best game. "I don't know how I got it or why I got it," he said. "I didn't pitch real well and a couple of balls that were hit real hard were caught. Everything I threw that day just happened to be hit right at someone. I never had a lot of strikeouts. I think I struck out 10 or 11 guys in a game twice in my career."

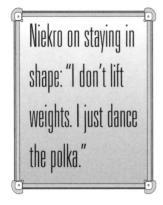

Niekro on staying in shape: "I don't lift weights. I just dance the polka."

His best work came during the Braves' division title years. He was the winning pitcher in the 1969 division clincher, with relief help from fellow knuckleballer Hoyt Wilhelm, and pitched consecutive shutouts in San Francisco and San Diego to finish his 1982 season with a flourish. He even hit a key home run against the Padres as the Braves went 5-2 on their season-ending West Coast road trip.

Though disabled earlier that year when a line drive bruised his ribs during batting practice, Niekro managed to win 17 of 21 decisions in 1982.

His good fortune would not last in October. Niekro nursed a 1-0 lead into the fifth inning of the playoff opener in St. Louis, but the umpires halted play with two outs, presumably because they didn't want the weather to influence the best-of-five series. Not nearly as effective when he returned with only one day of rest, Niekro had a 4-3 lead when he left his second start, eventually lost by the Atlanta bullpen.

Swept by both the 1969 Mets and the 1982 Cardinals, the Braves never won a playoff game during Niekro's tenure. Officially, the records show he never won a postseason game, going 0-1 with a 3.86 ERA in two official starts. The first was a 5-4 loss to Seaver in Game 1 of the 1969 National League Championship Series, when Niekro could not count on the ineligible Wilhelm, acquired on waivers after August 31, to close out the game.

"I learned a lot from Hoyt," said Niekro of Wilhelm, the first knuckleballer to reach the Hall of Fame. "Any knuckleball pitcher can learn some things from another knuckleball pitcher, things like how to throw it or how not to throw it. Another guy who helped me was Bobby Tiefenauer. We were roommates up in Milwaukee for a little bit. I couldn't ask a John Smoltz or Tom Seaver about pitching because I was not going to get the batters out the same way. But knuckleball pitchers can talk about what hitters look for in counts, in speed, and things like that."

When Niekro's brother, Joe, joined the knuckleball fraternity in mid-career, he participated in some of those conversations. Teammates briefly with the Braves and Yankees, the Niekros combined for 538 victories, a record for brothers. Joe won five of their nine matchups, thanks to a home run against Phil that was the only one of his career.

Phil Niekro's plaque hangs in the National Baseball Hall of Fame.
Photo courtesy of National Baseball Hall of Fame Library, Cooperstown, N.Y.

"It was the only hit he ever got against me," Phil said. "It was the seventh inning with two men out and a man on second. I threw him a knuckleball and he just took it. I yelled at him, saying, 'You can't hit the darn thing if you don't swing at it.' Then I threw him my best one – it would have hit his left toe if he didn't swing. He hit it like he was using a 9-iron golf club. I saw Ralph Garr backing up in left field and going to the track. I said, 'No way. There's no darn way.' It went out of the ballpark and I looked at Joe. He rounded first base and came back – he had missed first base. Then he circled the bases with the hit that beat me, 4-3."

Normally, the toughest hitter for Phil was Bill Buckner. "His objective was to get to first base," Niekro said. "He wasn't worried about doubles, triples, home runs, or stolen bases. The guy who comes up and will do anything to get to first base is the toughest guy to get out. I don't know if I ever struck him out."

Niekro never looked ahead. "I never looked at rivals, I looked at teams," he said. "I had to face Joe Morgan, Johnny Bench, Tony Perez, and Mike Schmidt one at a time. I never looked at the next inning. The only thing I looked at was what inning we were in, what the score was, and what the count was."

Able to avoid serious injury, Niekro topped 300 innings pitched four times, completed 245 of 716 starts, led his league in complete games four times, and tied Cy Young's record of working at least 200 innings in 19 different seasons. He pitched 45 shutouts, but was on the wrong end of shutouts 49 times, trailing only fellow 300-game winners Walter Johnson and Nolan Ryan in that dubious department.

"Knucksie" – the name his teammates gave him for obvious reasons – did his best work late in his career. The oldest man ever to play regularly in the majors, he was 48 when he got his last win, as a member of the Cleveland Indians, and a no-decision in a specially-arranged Atlanta farewell game, both in 1987. Always a slow starter, he went 0-7 in Opening Day assignments.

"The two things I remember most are winning 121 games after the age of 40 and teaming with Joe to win the most games by brothers," he said. "I never believed in any age limit. I was still playing at 46, 47, and 48. I always believed in hiring the best man available, regardless of age. If a 50-year-old guy is better than anybody else, he should get the job."

"I aimed for the plate and hoped for the best," said the pitcher, who seemed so relaxed on the mound that teammates thought he might doze off. "I didn't know whether the ball would jump up or down or go sideways. The best part is that the batter didn't know, either."

Neither did the catcher: in 1977, Niekro became the ninth National Leaguer to strike out four men in one inning. He also threw more wild pitches in his career (200) than anyone else.

Well-liked by both teammates and opponents, Niekro never had a problem with a manager, pitching coach, or player. "I got along with each and every one of them," said the pitcher, who survived Ted Turner's tempestuous tenure as owner of the Braves and his one-night stand as manager. "I knew managers had jobs to do and didn't always like coming out of games. I respected everybody for the way they played the game, but I also knew that if they kicked the (crap) out of me I just picked up my head and knew I was going to come back at them again.

"I always looked at pitching pitch-by-pitch. I couldn't throw the second pitch before I threw the first one, I couldn't pitch the second inning before I pitched the first one, and I couldn't pitch the second game before I pitched the first game. I learned from my mistakes and I made a lot of them: I lost 274 games in the big leagues. Fortunately, I won a few more than I lost."

Pitching primarily for one-year contracts provided incentive to succeed.

"One year I started 44 games and got 41 decisions," he said. "I pitched 340 innings. Other pitchers were doing that, too. Guys didn't have arm problems in those days. Maybe our arms were stronger because we pitched more often. When I look at the Carltons, the Seavers, and the Spahns, I just don't remember those guys missing many games because they had sore arms, upset stomachs, or pimples on their (butt). Nobody said he was tired.

"You might know you were tired. Your manager might know you were tired. But the other team didn't know you were tired when you were sticking it up their you-know-what. All they wanted to know is how to get that guy out of there."

A great fielder who helped his own cause with five Gold Gloves, Niekro once held two dozen Atlanta pitching records. One of them, most wins in a season, fell when John Smoltz won 24 games in 1996, 30 years after the Braves moved from Milwaukee to Atlanta. Niekro's career records for games, innings, and wins, on the other hand, seem secure. Including two wins recorded in Milwaukee, Niekro gave the Braves 268 wins, 43 of them shutouts, and a 2.30 ERA.

"I really enjoyed Milwaukee," said the pitcher. "There were a lot of Polish people there and a lot of Polish food, from kielbasa to pierogies. I was in heaven up there. But I roomed with a guy named Cecil Butler who was from Atlanta and told me what a great town that was. I always liked to hunt and fish so when they moved down there, it was a good move for me."

The cozy dimensions of Atlanta Fulton County Stadium, plus the habitual bad play of the Braves, made winning more difficult for Niekro, but he found a way. It wasn't long before the poetry-writing pitcher, born on April Fool's Day in 1939, was the ace of the staff – a position he kept for more than 15 seasons.

"One year I started 0-7 and got a letter from a lady in Chicago who watched our games on WTBS," Niekro said. "She wrote, 'I want you to think of two things: You can't always control what happens to you but you can control how you react to what happens to you. And you're going to have to accept your losses without being defeated.'

"The more I thought about it, the more it made sense. Even if I lost, I still had the bat, glove, and ball. And I'll keep coming at you. You can knock me down, but I'm getting back up. And eventually, no matter how long it takes, I'm going to beat you. That was my thinking the rest of my career."

Still, Niekro admitted, the long years of losing were tough. He countered by trying to transform himself into a complete pitcher, capable of helping himself at bat or in the field. "I took pride in my hitting, fielding, bunting, and base-running," he said. "I also worked on my pick-off move. And I knew that if I got on base, someone from the top of the order might knock me in and win a ballgame."

Niekro almost got his second no-hitter in 1979. But Cincinnati centerfielder Cesar Geronimo ruined it with a one-out double down the left-field line in the ninth inning. Niekro's reaction? "The first thing that came to my mind after the hit was how great it would have been for Dale Murphy to catch a no-hitter his first month in the 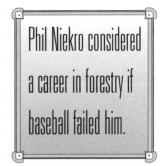 big leagues. He told me afterward that when Geronimo got the hit, he felt like we had just lost the ballgame."

Murphy, who later won consecutive MVP awards as an outfielder, provided most of Niekro's offense through the 1983 season, the pitcher's last as an Atlanta mainstay. The team's decision to release the pitcher plunged him into a depression. "It was my darkest day in baseball," he said later. "I didn't want to leave."

But the Braves thought Niekro, coming off an 11-10 season with a 3.97 ERA, would only decline further. Needing 32 wins to reach 300, he got the chance with the Yankees, who gave him a two-year contract. Unfamiliar with his assortment of slow, slower, and slowest pitches, American League hitters proved easy prey for the crafty veteran. In 1984, he won 16 games to reduce by half the number needed to reach 300. But he wondered whether he could do it again.

Approaching 300 as the 1985 season wound down, the veteran started to fall prey to the vagaries of time. Saddled with more losses and a higher earned run average in 1985, he needed five tries to reach 300. Constantly flying back to Ohio with brother Joe to visit their hospitalized father, Niekro saw his quest come down to October 6, 1985, the last day of the season. The Toronto Blue Jays had beaten the Yankees the day before to clinch the American League East crown and had been celebrating into the wee hours. That helped, since Niekro put his famous knuckleball on hold to make the match more even.

"I knew that might be my last game in the big leagues since I was 46 and I didn't know if the Yankees were going to re-sign me," he remembered. "If I didn't get it that day, I'd have to go to spring training, make a ballclub, and maybe not get a chance to win it until April. I didn't think my dad was going to hang on that long."

The Yankees made Niekro's job easy, piling up an early lead. It was 8-0 entering the ninth, but Tony Fernandez kept the Blue Jays alive with a two-out double. Yankee manager Billy Martin sent Joe Niekro to the mound with a message. "I just found out that if you pitch a shutout, you'll be the oldest guy in the history of baseball to throw one," Joe said.

With two strikes on Jeff Burroughs, a one-time American League MVP who already had one of four Toronto hits in that game, catcher Butch Wynegar wanted Niekro to finish with a flourish. He did, throwing the only knuckleball of the game for strike three.

Thanks to a special telephone line arranged by the Yankees, Niekro's gem was pumped into his father's hospital room. His mom, listening to the play-by-play on the phone, relayed the information to his comatose dad, who hadn't spoken in four weeks. In the seventh inning, he suddenly opened his eyes and said, "Sonny's pitching a helluva game, isn't he?"

By the time Phil and Joe flew back to Ohio, the elder Niekro was sitting up and talking. "My dad saw everything he was waiting to see," said Phil, whose dad lived two more years. "He saw one of his boys win 300, one pitch in a World Series, and both get the record for wins by brothers. After that, we lost him."

It was Niekro's dad who taught him the rudiments of the knuckler. An amateur pitcher for a coal-mining team, he learned the pitch from a fellow miner and showed it to his 11-year-old son. Phil was fascinated, but never could have dreamed that the unusual pitch would make him famous.

Blessed with both baseball ability and a huge helping of humility, Niekro credited his close family ties for his success. "Looking back on my career," he said, "I did it not so much for myself, but for the whole town of Lansing, Ohio. I did it for my mom, my dad, my sister, and my brother, plus my high school coach and my uncle Ed, who had a butcher shop across the street from the school.

"Every time I won a game, I figured, 'Boy, everything's going to be all right back in Lansing.' My mother always told me how my father reacted when Joe or I won a game. 'When your dad gets up in the morning and has a cup of coffee and a donut, the coffee really tastes good if he knows you won the night before.' When I won a game, I'd say to myself, 'Dad's going to have a good cup of coffee in the morning.'

"I was very fortunate and very blessed that I was able to sign a contract with the Milwaukee Braves when I was young, to get that opportunity, that break. There are so many young boys playing Little League, American Legion, high school ball, and college ball who want to get there. But only a few of them will.

"How many of them will sign a professional contract? How many will stay X amount of years in the major leagues? And how many will become Hall of Fame players?

"I was always very thankful that I had that opportunity. It was an honor to play the game that long. I spent five years in the minors and wanted to get to the big leagues and get my picture taken in a Braves uniform for my hometown paper. I wanted everybody to see that I played in the big leagues. Once I got there, I just hoped I was good enough to be there another day, another week, another month, or another year. I didn't even look at the long-range end of it."

When he looks long-range now, Niekro thinks the era of the 300-game winner is over. "Our job was pitching nine innings," said the 1997 Hall of Famer, who spent most of his career in a four-man rotation. "When we got the ball, we had the pride not to give it back to the manager before the game was over. Now that doesn't happen anymore. There's a long man, a middle man, a set-up guy, and a closer. With a pitch count, guys don't get to pitch as much, which means they aren't going to have as many chances to win."

Phil Niekro got all the chances he needed.

Box Score of 300th Win

Niekro Baseball Almanac Box Score
New York Yankees 8, Toronto Blue Jays 0

Game played on Sunday, October 6, 1985, at Exhibition Stadium

New York Yankees	ab	r	h	rbi	Toronto Blue Jays	ab	r	h	rbi
Henderson cf	3	0	0	0	Garcia 2b	3	0	0	0
Pasqua lf	2	0	0	0	Iorg 2b	1	0	0	0
Mattingly 1b	5	3	4	1	Leach lf	3	0	0	0
Winfield rf	5	0	0	0	Thornton rf	4	0	0	0
Baylor dh	4	1	0	0	Fielder 1b	2	0	1	0
Robertson 3b	2	1	0	0	Fernandez ph	1	0	1	0
Pagliarulo ph,3b	3	1	1	2	Burroughs dh	4	0	1	0
Randolph 2b	0	1	0	1	Gruber 3b	3	0	0	0
Cotto lf,cf	4	1	2	4	Shepherd cf	3	0	0	0
Wynegar c	3	0	0	0	Hearron c	3	0	0	0
Meacham ss	4	0	0	0	Lee ss	2	0	1	0
Niekro p	0	0	0	0	Cerutti p	0	0	0	0
Totals	35	8	7	8	Acker p	0	0	0	0
					Caudill p	0	0	0	0
					Davis p	0	0	0	0
					Totals	29	0	4	0

New York	3	0	0		0	2	0		0	2	1	–	8	7	0
Toronto	0	0	0		0	0	0		0	0	0	–	0	4	1

New York Yankees	IP	H	R	ER	BB	SO
Niekro W (16-12)	9.0	4	0	0	3	5
Totals	9.0	4	0	0	3	5

Toronto Blue Jays	IP	H	R	ER	BB	SO
Cerutti L (0-2)	4.0	2	3	0	3	3
Acker	2.0	2	2	2	1	2
Caudill	2.0	2	2	2	1	0
Davis	1.0	1	1	1	0	1
Totals	9.0	7	8	5	5	6

E–Garcia (12). **DP**–New York 2. **2B**–Toronto Burroughs (9,off P Niekro); Fernandez (31,off P Niekro). **HR**–New York Pagliarulo (19,5th inning off Acker 1 on, 2 out); Cotto (1,8th inning off Caudill 1 on, 0 out); Mattingly (35,9th inning off Davis 0 on, 0 out). **HBP**–Randolph (4,by Cerutti). **SB**–Randolph (16,2nd base off Acker/Hearron). **WP**–Cerutti 2 (2). **HBP**–Cerutti (1,Randolph). **T**–2:25. **A**–44,422.

Career Statistics

NIEKRO, Phil										Philip Henry Niekro; B: 4/1/1939, Blaine, OH; BR/TR, 6'1"/180 lbs.; Debut: 4/15/1964; HOF 1997					
YEAR	TM-L	W	L	PCT	G	GS	CG	SH	SV	IP	H	R	HR	SO	ERA
1964	Mil-N	0	0	...	10	0	0	0	0	15	15	10	1	8	4.80
1965	Mil-N	2	3	0.400	41	1	0	0	6	74	73	32	5	49	2.89
1966	Atl-N	4	3	0.571	28	0	0	0	2	50	48	32	4	17	4.11
1967	Atl-N	11	9	0.550	46	20	10	1	9	207	164	64	9	129	1.87
1968	Atl-N	14	12	0.538	37	34	15	5	2	257	228	83	16	140	2.59
1969	Atl-N	23	13	0.639	40	35	21	4	1	284	235	93	21	193	2.56
1970	Atl-N	12	18	0.400	34	32	10	3	0	229	222	124	40	168	4.27
1971	Atl-N	15	14	0.517	42	36	18	4	2	268	248	112	27	173	2.98
1972	Atl-N	16	12	0.571	38	36	17	1	0	282	254	112	22	164	3.06
1973	Atl-N	13	10	0.565	42	30	9	1	4	245	214	103	21	131	3.31
1974	Atl-N	20	13	0.606	41	39	18	6	1	302	249	91	19	195	2.38
1975	Atl-N	15	15	0.500	39	37	13	1	0	275	285	115	29	144	3.20
1976	Atl-N	17	11	0.607	38	37	10	2	0	270	249	116	18	173	3.29
1977	Atl-N	16	20	0.444	44	43	20	2	0	330	315	166	26	262	4.03
1978	Atl-N	19	18	0.514	44	42	22	4	1	334	295	129	16	248	2.88
1979	Atl-N	21	20	0.512	44	44	23	1	0	342	311	160	41	208	3.39
1980	Atl-N	15	18	0.455	40	38	11	3	1	275	256	119	30	176	3.63
1981	Atl-N	7	7	0.500	22	22	3	3	0	139	120	56	6	62	3.10
1982	Atl-N	17	4	0.810	35	35	4	2	0	234	225	106	23	144	3.61
1983	Atl-N	11	10	0.524	34	33	2	0	0	201	212	94	18	128	3.97
1984	NY-A	16	8	0.667	32	31	5	1	0	215	219	85	15	136	3.09
1985	NY-A	16	12	0.571	33	33	7	1	0	220	203	110	29	149	4.09
1986	Cle-A	11	11	0.500	34	32	5	0	0	210	241	126	24	81	4.32
1987	Cle-A	7	11	0.389	22	22	2	0	0	123	142	83	18	57	5.89
	Tor-A	0	2	0.000	3	3	0	0	0	12	15	11	4	7	8.25
	Year	7	13	0.350	25	25	2	0	0	135	157	94	22	64	6.10
	Atl-N	0	0	...	1	1	0	0	0	3	6	5	0	0	15.00
TOTAL		24	318	274	0.537	864	716	245	45	29	5404	5044	2337	482	3342	3.35

Have Arm, Will Travel

Gaylord Perry – 314 Wins

Did he or didn't he?

For virtually his entire 22-year career in the major leagues, Gaylord Perry perplexed opposing hitters by making them think he was applying an artificial substance to his pitches. He even wrote a book about it: *Me and the Spitter*.

Frequently accused, but rarely caught, Perry outfoxed the opposition so effectively that he won 314 games – an amazing total for a pitcher often saddled with less-than-stellar offensive support.

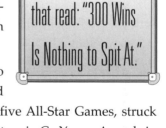

Perry once had a shirt that read: "300 Wins Is Nothing to Spit At."

Like Phil Niekro, a contemporary who also won 300 games, Perry never pitched in the World Series. But he appeared in five All-Star Games, struck out 3,534 hitters, and was the first pitcher to win Cy Young Awards in both leagues. Fellow 300-game winners Roger Clemens and Randy Johnson did it years later, along with Pedro Martinez.

Influenced by teammate Juan Marichal, with whom he formed a devastating 1-2 punch in San Francisco, Perry spent his best years

Gaylord Perry

Photo courtesy of National
Baseball Hall of Fame Library
Cooperstown, N.Y.

with the Giants. But he also pitched for seven other clubs, winning Cy
Youngs in Cleveland and San Diego and earning No. 300 for Seattle.

The son of a North Carolina sharecropper who pitched semipro
ball when he wasn't harvesting tobacco, corn, or peanuts, Perry was
a three-sport high school star whose first position was third base.
After switching to pitching, Perry got a $73,500 bonus from the Giants
in 1958 and reached the major leagues four years later. But he failed
to make the San Francisco pitching staff that lost a seven-game World
Series to the New York Yankees.

Perry's early career path resembled a roller coaster, riding up and
down the West Coast between the Bay Area and Pacific Northwest,
where Tacoma was the top Giants farm team.

Only in 1964 did Perry stick – thanks to an unexpected 10-inning
relief job against the New York Mets at the new Shea Stadium. In the
second game of an April 23 doubleheader, Perry was the last man

standing when manager Alvin Dark needed bullpen help in the 14th inning. The young right-hander had worked two innings the previous day, but thought he could throw a couple more. Ten innings later, the Giants had a win and Perry had a new job.

"That was my breakthrough game," the pitcher said years later. "I had just gotten called back from the minor leagues a couple of weeks before that. There was nobody else in the bullpen, so they had to let me pitch. I thought I would pitch one inning and win the game because we had men on first and second with nobody out and Orlando Cepeda hitting. We tried a hit-and-run and he hit into a triple play. So I had to keep pitching. But it all worked out."

Marichal, then in his fourth full season with the team, proved a good man to emulate.

"I learned so much from watching him," Perry said. "He was a great gentleman and a great friend. I never picked my leg up high until I saw him pitch. A friend of mine from another team said he didn't see anything but arms and legs when Marichal pitched. The next day, I started practicing arms and legs, too."

During their 10 years as teammates, the Marichal-Perry tandem won 336 games, placing them in the Top 10 duos of baseball history. While still with the Giants, Perry led the National League in wins once and innings pitched twice, usually finishing games he started.

"That's how we were trained," he said. "It's not the same anymore. Even in the minor leagues, pitchers are trained to go six innings. We were trained to go nine. We were expected to do it. If you didn't go nine at least 50 percent of the time, you got demoted to the bullpen, traded, or released."

Perry posted his first win on April 25, 1962, beating Pittsburgh, and pitched the first of his 53 career shutouts two years later against the Mets, winning 5-0 on a three-hitter. He had 134 victories for San Francisco when they decided he was too old at age 33.

The Giants conveniently forgot that Perry had pitched four straight shutouts, and 39 consecutive scoreless innings, in the last month of the 1970 season, when Marichal was idled by illness.

Shortly after Perry posted a 1-1 record against Pittsburgh in the 1971 National League Championship Series, the Giants traded him – much to the pitcher's regret.

"I cried," said Perry. "I had a home in California, my kids were in school, and the kids had their horses and animals. We were having a great time, doing well, and I had a two-year contract for 1970-71 and had won 40 games. I thought I was safe."

Instead, Perry and shortstop Frank Duffy were packaged to Cleveland for "Sudden Sam" McDowell, a left-handed flamethrower with a drinking problem. Though McDowell was four years younger than the 32-year-old Perry, his flame flickered so quickly that the deal soon became known as one of the worst in baseball history – at least from the Giants' perspective. Perry won 180 games after the trade, while McDowell won just 24.

Perry prospered in his new environment. In 1972, his first year with Cleveland, the 6'4" right-hander won the American League's Cy Young Award with career bests in victories and earned run average. In 41 outings, he went 24-16 in 342 innings, one off his personal high; recorded the only save of his long career; and had one-third of the wins posted by the fifth-place Indians.

Also that year, Perry joined Cy Young and Jack Chesbro as the only men to have led both leagues in victories. He led in complete games, too, with 29, but finished second to knuckleballer Wilbur Wood in innings pitched, 377-343, and to Luis Tiant in ERA, 1.92 to 1.91. Perry's best effort was a 14-inning, 2-0 shutout over the Texas Rangers on July 14.

After giving the Indians another 20-win season two years later, Perry was sent packing in a move spurred by worry over his age and salary. Traded to the Texas Rangers for three pitchers and $100,000 on June 13, 1975, Perry moved on to the San Diego Padres for Dave Tomlin and $100,000 less than three years later.

The return to the National League suited Perry perfectly; he went 21-6 with a 2.73 ERA, which earned him a second Cy Young Award and made him the first man to win the trophy in both leagues. He also joined Grover Cleveland Alexander and Carl Mays as the only men to post 20-win seasons for three different teams.

"I always had great respect for the National League," Perry said during his post-career tenure as coach of the baseball team at Limestone College in Gaffney, South Carolina. "They played more aggressive ball. The American League became tougher after it got the designated hitter in 1973. That meant pitchers had to get an extra out. The National League had a lot of hit-and-run plays and guys stealing bases."

Those sentiments are not surprising for a player whose hat in the Hall of Fame gallery bears the logo of the San Francisco Giants.

"That's how I think of myself," said Perry, who also played for the Atlanta Braves, Kansas City Royals, New York Yankees, and Seattle Mariners. "I enjoyed all the places I went to. I found new friends. It was a great job, but a job in which I knew I had to travel from time to time. I did a lot of traveling."

Along the way, Perry pitched a no-hitter, riding a rare Ron Hunt homer to a 1-0 win over Bob Gibson and the St. Louis Cardinals at San Francisco's Candlestick Park on September 17, 1968. That game was followed by another pitching gem the next night. When the Cardinals' Ray Washburn returned the favor, he and Perry became the first men to exchange no-hitters on consecutive nights of the same series. Excluding Marichal's 1963 no-hit game, Perry was the first Giant to author a no-hitter since Carl Hubbell in 1929.

Gaylord also teamed with his brother, Jim, three years his senior, to win 529 games, a major-league record for brothers before Phil and Joe Niekro teamed for 10 more.

The Perrys, who had more strikeouts and shutouts than any fraternal tandem, were Cleveland teammates in 1974, when Gaylord won 21 games with the help of a 15-game winning streak (one short of the American League record). After losing his first outing, Gaylord pitched 15 straight complete games – on a taped ankle that was badly sprained in his first start – to boost his record to 15-1. He then went all the way in a 10-inning game but lost, 4-3, dashing his hopes of tying the American League mark for consecutive wins.

At the same time, Jim won 17, giving the Perrys nearly half the club's wins.

Before they turned pro, the Perry brothers had been offered college basketball scholarships. They starred in both baseball and basketball for Williamston High School before leaving North Carolina.

Early in their careers, while pitching for different teams, the Perrys won three games (two by Jim) in one day. The date was July 20, 1969, the same day astronaut Neil Armstrong set foot on the moon. Gaylord punctuated the occasion by hitting the first home run of his career – six years after Alvin Park had facetiously predicted that the day the weak-hitting Perry homered would be the day man walked on the moon.

Gaylord's pitching was so sensational that his hitting hardly mattered. Working in a four-man rotation, he collected innings like a kid collecting shells on the beach, topping 300 six times. Perry made five All-Star appearances, winning the 1966 game in relief, and had eight seasons with at least 200 strikeouts – a level never reached by fellow 300-game winner Warren Spahn, his teammate late in the 1965 season.

"Gaylord is a great pitcher," said Ken Aspromonte, his manager with the 1974 Indians, "but he also is a great competitor. Nobody wants to win more than Gaylord."

Aspromonte's departure from Cleveland foreshadowed Perry's. When the Indians landed Frank Robinson on September 12, 1974, Perry immediately angered Robinson by saying his next contract should be "a dollar more than Robinson's." Things got worse the next spring, when Perry objected to rules imposed by Robinson, by then a player-manager.

"I'm not about to let some superstar who never pitched a game in his life tell me how to get ready to pitch," said Perry, still miffed that Robinson was earning $100,000 more than the pitcher's $85,000 deal.

Saddled with poor offensive support in Cleveland, Perry turned the lemons he was given into lemonade. He completed 86 of his 118 starts – 73 percent – and won a whopping 39 percent of all Cleveland victories while he was there. After running afoul of Robinson, Perry moved on. He continued to pitch well for the Rangers and Padres, two more teams accustomed to losing more often than they won. In fact, San Diego never had a winning record until Perry arrived in 1978.

Although the pitcher turned 40 before that season ended, he was so encouraged by his 21-6 record and league-best .778 winning percentage that he started to think about getting 300 wins.

But he had to keep his suitcase packed.

Perry was traded twice in 1980, first to Texas during spring training and then to the Yankees in midseason. In 1981, he moved to Atlanta via free agency and pitched in the same rotation as Phil Niekro, who was also grasping at 300 wins. He missed his shot at winning 300 for the Braves because a player strike cut seven weeks off the schedule, leaving Perry three victories short.

Anxious to rework its aging rotation, Atlanta released Perry, apparently ending his career. But the cagey right-hander, who still had his health, also had more determination than ever. After a winter of phone calls, he finally persuaded his old Texas general manager, then with Seattle, to bring him west as a gate attraction.

Dan O'Brien didn't regret the move. Even though Perry missed most of spring training and lost his first two starts for the Seattle Mariners, he followed with a pair of complete-game wins, moving him to 299. Finally, on May 6, 1982, Gaylord Perry became the oldest of the 15 men who then had membership in the 300 Club. At the age of 43 years and 8 months, he pitched a complete game to beat the New York Yankees, 7-3, yielding nine hits and six walks while becoming the first pitcher to win 300 since Early Wynn in 1963. The game attracted only 27,369 – less than half the Kingdome's capacity – but it did attract a telegram from former teammate Fergie Jenkins that read CONGRATULATIONS YOU OLD GOAT.

Always thinking ahead, Perry changed jerseys every inning in an effort to create more memorabilia from the historic contest. He got future major-league manager Willie Randolph for the last out.

The man of many motions won 14 more times, wearing the uniforms of both the Mariners and Kansas City Royals, before calling it a career. In 1983, his last year, Perry reached another milestone, passing Walter Johnson on the career strikeout list.

His climb to 300 wins was slowed by making 79 relief outings during his first four seasons, but he eventually became the first man to win at least 15 games for 13 consecutive seasons (1966-78) in the modern era. Greg Maddux, also en route to 300 wins, later topped that mark by doing it 17 years in a row (1988-2004).

The spitball, allegedly taught to him by Giants teammate Bob Shaw in 1964, might have helped Perry prolong his career after his fastball faded. Or maybe the *thought* of the spitball gave him enough ammunition against enemy batters.

Because the spitball had been banned since 1920, Perry answered all questions about the illegal delivery with a wink and a smile. He referred to his darting pitch as a "super slider" and used it to complement a standard repertoire of fastball, curveball, and changeup. But he also hinted that he should have been doing commercials for Vaseline and K-Y Jelly, intimating that he kept at least one of the slick substances in two separate places – in case the umpires uncovered one of them. Perry might not have been kidding when he said he applied everything to the ball but chocolate sauce.

> After a tube of Vaseline was found in his clubhouse cubicle, Perry said:
>
> "Leave it alone — that's a two-hit shutout."

Although Billy Williams bashed more home runs against Perry than any other player, the pitcher said singles hitter Rod Carew gave him more grief. "He's the only player in baseball who consistently hits my grease," Perry said of Carew, who, ironically, was in the same Hall of

Fame class as the pitcher. "He sees the ball so well, I guess he can pick out the dry side."

Official baseball was so convinced Perry was cheating that it passed two rules pertaining to a pitcher's behavior on the mound. It didn't stop him from doing whatever he was doing, prompting rival manager Gene Mauch to say Perry's Hall of Fame plaque should have a tube of K-Y attached to it. His only suspension, 10 days for doctoring a ball, came in 1982, his 21st season.

Like Lew Burdette, the 1957 World Series star also accused of spitball chicanery, Perry fidgeted so frequently on the mound that neither hitter, catcher, nor umpire could keep track of what parts of his uniform he was touching before delivering the ball.

"The hitter is up there looking for one thing and I throw him something else," Perry said. "That's why I go through all those motions, touching my belt, cap, and neck. I picked up the habit from Don Drysdale, who used to make a big thing tugging away at his cap and belt."

Ralph Houk, Billy Martin, and Dick Williams were among the managers who suspected Perry and protested loudly enough to prod the umpires into action. Martin even earned a three-day suspension of his own for criticizing the American League's failure to discipline Perry.

"I watched Gaylord like a hawk," said umpire Bill Haller. "He never goes to his mouth. I never see him get any foreign substance. When we umpire, we check balls as well as the catcher's glove. I never found anything. He's got a good curve, a fine fastball, a good change, and a fine sinker. But the sinker is no better than Mel Stottlemyre's and nobody complains about his. I'll tell you what Gaylord Perry is: one helluva pitcher."

When Perry retired in 1983, he left the game with this parting shot: "The league will be a little drier now, folks." Whether he had his tongue in his cheek, or his hand under the bill of his cap, remains a mystery to this day.

Box Score of 300th Win

Perry Baseball Almanac Box Score
New York Yankees 3, Seattle Mariners 7

Game played on Thursday, May 6, 1982 at Kingdome

New York Yankees	ab	r	h	rbi	Seattle Mariners	ab	r	h	rbi
Randolph 2b	5	1	1	0	Cruz J. 2b	3	1	0	0
Griffey rf	4	2	3	1	Castillo 3b	4	2	2	2
Mumphrey cf	4	0	2	0	Bochte lf	4	0	2	1
Mayberry 1b	4	0	0	0	Zisk dh	4	0	1	0
Winfield lf	4	0	1	1	Cruz T. ss	4	1	2	2
Gamble dh	4	0	1	1	Cowens rf	4	0	1	1
Smalley 3b	3	0	1	0	Simpson cf	4	0	0	0
Cerone c	4	0	0	0	Maler 1b	3	1	1	0
Dent ss	2	0	0	0	Bulling c	3	2	2	1
Murcer ph	1	0	0	0	Perry p	0	0	0	0
Milbourne ss	1	0	0	0	Totals	33	7	11	7
Alexander p	0	0	0	0					
May p	0	0	0	0					
Totals	36	3	9	3					

New York	0	0	0		0	0	1		0	2	0	–	3	9	1
Seattle	0	0	5		0	0	0		2	0	x	–	7	11	1

New York Yankees	IP	H	R	ER	BB	SO
Alexander L (0-2)	3.0	6	5	1	0	2
May	5.0	5	2	2	0	2
Totals	8.0	11	7	3	0	4

Seattle Mariners	IP	H	R	ER	BB	SO
Perry W (3-2)	9.0	9	3	3	1	4
Totals	9.0	9	3	3	1	4

E–Cerone (2), Castillo (5). **DP**–New York 1, Seattle 1. **2B**–Seattle Bochte (4,off Alexander); Zisk (4,off May); Bulling (2,off May); Castillo (7,off May). **3B**–New York Mumphrey (1,off Perry), Seattle Maler (2,off Alexander); Cowens (2,off Alexander). **HR**–New York Griffey (1,6th inning off Perry 0 on, 1 out). **SH**–J Cruz (1,off Alexander). **WP**–May (2). **U-HP**–Ken Kaiser, **1B**–Bill Haller, **2B**–Jerry Neudecker, **3B**–George Maloney. **T**–2:29. **A**–27,369.

Career Statistics

PERRY, Gaylord			Gaylord Jackson Perry; B: 9/15/1938, Wilmington, NC; BR/TR, 6'4"/215 lbs.; Debut: 4/14/1962; HOF 1991												
YEAR	TM-L	W	L	PCT	G	GS	CG	SH	SV	IP	H	R	HR	SO	ERA
1962	SF-N	3	1	0.750	13	7	1	0	0	43	54	29	3	20	5.23
1963	SF-N	1	6	0.143	31	4	0	0	2	76	84	41	10	52	4.03
1964	SF-N	12	11	0.522	44	19	5	2	5	206	179	65	16	155	2.75
1965	SF-N	8	12	0.400	47	26	6	0	1	195	194	105	21	170	4.19
1966	SF-N	21	8	0.724	36	35	13	3	0	255	242	92	15	201	2.99
1967	SF-N	15	17	0.469	39	37	18	3	1	293	231	98	20	230	2.61
1968	SF-N	16	15	0.516	39	38	19	3	1	291	240	93	10	173	2.44
1969	SF-N	19	14	0.576	40	39	26	3	0	325	290	115	23	233	2.49
1970	SF-N	23	13	0.639	41	41	23	5	0	328	292	138	27	214	3.20
1971	SF-N	16	12	0.571	37	37	14	2	0	280	255	116	20	158	2.76
1972	Cle-A	24	16	0.600	41	40	29	5	1	342	253	79	17	234	1.92
1973	Cle-A	19	19	0.500	41	41	29	7	0	344	315	143	34	238	3.38
1974	Cle-A	21	13	0.618	37	37	28	4	0	322	230	98	25	216	2.51
1975	Cle-A	6	9	0.400	15	15	10	1	0	121	120	57	16	85	3.55
	Tex-A	12	8	0.600	22	22	15	4	0	184	157	70	12	148	3.03
	Year	18	17	0.514	37	37	25	5	0	305	277	127	28	233	3.24
1976	Tex-A	15	14	0.517	32	32	21	2	0	250	232	93	14	143	3.24
1977	Tex-A	15	12	0.556	34	34	13	4	0	238	239	108	21	177	3.37
1978	SD-N	21	6	0.778	37	37	5	2	0	260	241	96	9	154	2.73
1979	SD-N	12	11	0.522	32	32	10	0	0	232	225	90	12	140	3.06
1980	Tex-A	6	9	0.400	24	24	6	2	0	155	159	74	12	107	3.43
	NY-A	4	4	0.500	10	8	0	0	0	50	65	33	2	28	4.44
	Year	10	13	0.435	34	32	6	2	0	205	224	107	14	135	3.68
1981	Atl-N	8	9	0.471	23	23	3	0	0	150	182	70	9	60	3.94
1982	Sea-A	10	12	0.455	32	32	6	0	0	216	245	117	27	116	4.40
1983	Sea-A	3	10	0.231	16	16	2	0	0	102	116	60	18	42	4.94
	KC-A	4	4	0.500	14	14	1	1	0	84	98	48	6	40	4.27
	Year	7	14	0.333	30	30	3	1	0	186	214	108	24	82	4.64
TOTAL	22	314	265	0.542	777	690	303	53	11	5350	4938	2128	399	3534	3.11

The Franchise

Although no one has ever won admission to the Baseball Hall of Fame with a unanimous vote, Tom Seaver came close. In 1992, the same year the New York Mets retired his No. 41 jersey, Seaver received a record 98.84 percent of the vote. He was named on all but two of the 427 completed ballots, and also left off three blank ballots that were submitted as a protest against Major League Baseball's exclusion of Pete Rose, the suspended-for-life leader in career hits.

Seaver was the anti-Rose, a paragon of pitching perfection and personal purity that prompted Mets fans to dub him "The Franchise."

The Fresno, California, native registered 198 of his 311 career wins with the Mets, for whom he pitched a dozen years in separate stints, and also earned three Cy Young Awards and his lone World Series ring while wearing a Mets uniform.

He was "Tom Terrific" almost from Day One, arriving at age 22 in 1967 to a clubhouse conditioned to losing. But Seaver, hardened by a stint in the Marines, shunned all association with the team's image as "lovable losers." He hated the ingrained defeatist attitude and said so. Then he proved he could pitch like a winner, even when the rest of the staff couldn't.

Five years after the Mets went 40-120 under the grandfatherly Casey Stengel, Seaver brought youth, vitality, and ability into the ranks. The team finished last, with 61 wins in a 10-team league, but he

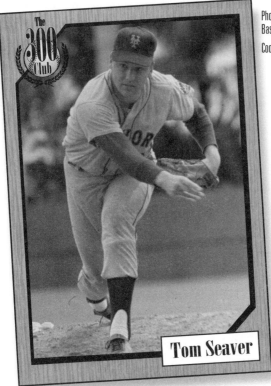

Tom Seaver

finished first in the 1967 Rookie of the Year voting, thanks to a 16-13 record and 2.76 earned run average. For George Thomas Seaver, that was just the tip of the iceberg.

With a year of experience under his belt, the 6'1", 206-pound pitcher shrunk his ERA to 2.20, won 16 again, and posted the first of nine straight seasons with 200 strikeouts.

By the spring of 1969, veteran catcher Jerry Grote already was sensing a trip to the World Series. "In spring training, he knew," Seaver recalled. "He said we were going to win it. We all thought he was nuts. But it made sense. He was the one who had caught us all the year before and he was catching us now in spring training. He just knew."

Grote was right. Under the guiding hand of Gil Hodges, the Mets parlayed young pitching (Seaver, Jerry Koosman, Gary Gentry, and

Nolan Ryan) into the least-likely championship season in the history of baseball.

Seaver was nothing short of sensational, leading the league with 25 wins and a hits-per-game ratio of 6.7. His 25-7 mark, 2.21 ERA, and 208 strikeouts enabled the Mets to win 100 games, rising from ninth in the former 10-team league to first in their new six-team division. They took the first National League East title by eight games, swept the favored Atlanta Braves in the best-of-five National League Championship Series, and bested the Baltimore Orioles in a five-game World Series. Seaver was the winning pitcher in the NLCS opener and in the fourth game of the Series.

After the cheering drifted into a memorable winter echo, the right-hander was rewarded with the first of three Cy Young Awards (he also won in 1973, when the Mets reached the World Series but lost to Oakland, and again in 1975). He finished second in two other seasons and third once.

Seaver always seemed to be in contention for something – even when his team wasn't. He made the All-Star team 12 times, won five strikeout crowns, led the league in wins three times, and twice posted the best winning percentage. The five-time 20-game winner allowed  the fewest hits per nine innings three times, and threw the most shutouts in a season twice.

An expert on pitching mechanics, Seaver's *modus operandi* was simple: "Out of a sound delivery comes a sound arm." He made maximum mileage from his motion. He worked out of a compact windup, generating velocity by driving off his powerful legs and often scraping the ground with his knee. Early in his 20-year tenure, he varied the speeds on his fastball, which he threw at three different speeds, before developing a changeup grip that he discovered while playing catch in the outfield with Jon Matlack.

"As a pitcher, I feel I'm creating something," said Seaver. "I don't enjoy it until I can stand back and look at what I've created. Pitching is work – it's not enjoyable while you're doing it."

His Mets records are almost too numerous to mention; he had more wins (105) and more strikeouts (1,370) at Shea Stadium than any other pitcher and placed second to Matlack with a 2.50 career ERA at Shea, where the Mets played from 1964-2008. Seaver holds single-season club records for wins (25 in 1969), complete games (21 in 1971), innings (290 2/3 in 1970), and strikeouts (289 in 1971). His 1.76 ERA in 1971 was bettered only by Doc Gooden's 1.53 in 1985.

So consistent that he pitched five shutouts five times, with a career high of seven, Seaver topped 200 strikeouts a record nine years in a row. He also made 36 starts, tied with Jack Fisher for the club record, three times. He hurled shutouts in successive starts four times and pitched five one-hitters – one of them during the pressure-packed National League East title chase of 1969.

On the night of July 9, 1969, when the Mets were trying to reduce the four-game margin that separated them from the first-place Chicago Cubs, Seaver pitched a game that was most likely the best of his career. Overcoming a stiff shoulder that bothered him early in the evening, he found his rhythm and retired 25 men in succession.

"I knew what was going on," Seaver said later. "How could I not know? You try to isolate yourself from the crowd noise, to retain your concentration, but as that game continued, it got harder and harder. By the seventh inning, the crowd was cheering every pitch. I could feel the tension, the excitement, and the expectation of the crowd more than I had ever sensed it before. It was stimulating, but it also put pressure on me."

Seaver, a capable hitter who knocked in a second-inning run with a double, carried a 4-0 lead into the ninth. Randy Hundley, a catcher not known for his speed, tried to bunt for a surprise base-hit but hit the ball directly to the pitcher. That brought up Jimmy Qualls, who had hit Seaver hard twice, lining out to deep right and smacking a sharp grounder to first.

Qualls, playing center only because regular Don Young made two misplays the previous night, slapped a sharp single to left-center on the first pitch he saw.

If not for that quirk of fate, Qualls would have disappeared into the dustbin of history. He played only three seasons, batting .233 with 31 hits – including that ninth-inning single against Seaver.

"I wanted to keep the fastball away but the ball didn't sink," said the pitcher, whose father and wife were among 59,083 frenzied spectators who packed Shea Stadium beyond capacity. "Qualls got the bat on it and it fell for a single. I would have liked the perfect game – anybody would – but I don't have any regrets about pitching a one-hitter in the middle of a pennant race."

Five years earlier, in Shea's first season, Philadelphia right-hander Jim Bunning had pitched a perfect game in the ballpark. But Seaver's bid failed, keeping alive the prevailing jinx that said no pitcher could throw a no-hitter in a Mets uniform.

He suddenly understood the comment of Bob Feller, who pitched a dozen of them, that throwing a one-hitter is like being the second man on the moon. Or, as teammate Ron Swoboda said, the difference between a no-hitter and a one-hitter is like the difference between virginity or lack of it. It's not much, but it's *something*.

"At 25, I was too old to cry," Seaver said, "but inside I still hurt. Never in any aspect of my life, in baseball or otherwise, had I experienced such a disappointment. I thought I would have another chance. In fact, I couldn't have kept playing without that goal."

Seaver one-hit the Cubs twice more in his career, but perfection would elude him.

Like Ryan, Gooden, Mike Scott, and other talented pitchers who started with the Mets, Seaver did pitch a no-hitter – but only after he left New York. It came on June 16, 1978, a year and a day after New York sent him to Cincinnati for four fringe players in a move dictated by a salary dispute. M. Donald Grant, who engineered that trade, proved as popular in New York as Robert Moses, whose refusal to build a new stadium for the Brooklyn Dodgers forced the team to move to Los Angeles after the 1957 season.

Although the Qualls game cemented Seaver's reputation as a star capable of success in any situation, he was even more impressive a year later, on the afternoon of April 22, 1970. Pitching before a sparse early-season crowd of 14,197 at Shea, the pitcher was protecting a 2-1 lead against the San Diego Padres with two outs in the sixth inning. He finished the frame by fanning Al Ferrara for his 10th strikeout of the game.

Then the fun began: Seaver whiffed Nate Colbert, Dave Campbell, and Jerry Morales in the seventh; Bob Barton, Ramon Webster, and Ivan Murrell in the eighth; and Van Kelly, Cito Gaston, and Ferrara in the ninth. That gave him a record 10 strikeouts in a row, erasing a record that stood for 86 seasons, and a total of 19, tying a one-game mark since broken. "He kept building as the game went on," Grote said of Seaver, who threw 136 pitches. "The cool weather helped and by the end of the game, he was stronger than ever."

The pitcher won the first of his three ERA crowns that season, finishing at 2.82, and retained the title a year later with a career-best 1.76 mark. He also won his first two strikeout crowns in those same seasons, 1970 and 1971.

With Seaver anchoring the young pitching staff, the Mets were expected to contend. They won a wild five-team title chase in 1973, barely finishing over .500 but saving enough energy to surge past Cincinnati in a National League Championship Series marred by a fight between Pete Rose and Bud Harrelson. Coming off a 19-win season that included a 2.08 ERA, Seaver split two decisions while posting a 1.62 ERA in the NLCS. But he lost his only decision in the World Series against the Oakland A's.

One of Seaver's best-pitched games was a no-decision in Los Angeles on May 1, 1974. "I made one bad pitch the entire game," said Seaver, who had held the Dodgers hitless until Steve Garvey hit a leadoff homer in the fifth inning. "I threw a hanging slider to Garvey and he hit it out. Every other pitch I threw exactly where I wanted it." Yielding just two other hits (both singles), Seaver fanned 16 Dodgers while working 12 innings of a 1-1 tie against Andy Messersmith. Los Angeles won, 2-1, in 14 innings. Slowed by a sore hip later that season, he bounced back nicely in 1975, when he went 22-9. It was the second time he led the National League in wins.

Although Seaver was such a Mets icon that he seemed destined to spend his entire career with the club, the advent of free agency in 1976 created new perceptions for both players and management. Seeking to renegotiate his contract, Seaver was skewered by New York columnist Dick Young, a friend of M. Donald Grant, and the team unloaded him at the June 15 trading deadline of 1977 to the Cincinnati Reds. Going the other way were Pat Zachry, a former Rookie of the Year, plus Steve Henderson, Doug Flynn, and Dan Norman. Yes, that's all the Mets got for the future Hall of Famer.

"He didn't like me and I didn't like him," Seaver said of Grant. "He had a real plantation mentality. He even called me a Communist. I stuck up for the players and stuck up for myself and he didn't like it. So he traded me. But I hated to leave."

After bringing a 7-3 record to the Reds, Seaver went 14-3 with his new club to finish the 1977 season with a sparkling 21-6 mark – the fifth and final time he would win 20 in a season.

Sparky Anderson, his first manager in Cincinnati, said of him, "My idea of managing is giving the ball to Tom Seaver and then sitting down and watching him work."

He followed his 20-win summer with a pair of 16-win seasons, dropped to 10 when his shoulder was hurt in 1980, then posted his best winning percentage (a league-leading .875) by going 14-2 with a 2.54 ERA during the strike-shortened 1981 season. Media darling Fernando Valenzuela of the Dodgers won "The Cy Young That Got Away" – at least in the eyes of Seaver supporters.

Well past the days of domination by The Big Red Machine, Cincinnati did not sample the vintage Seaver. Proving the baseball adage that what counts most is not what a player has done, but what he has done lately, Cincy swapped Seaver back to New York after his

5-13 season, also marked by injury, in 1982. The Mets sent only Charlie Puleo, Lloyd McClendon, and Jason Felice to the Reds.

Even though he had a losing record for a bad team, Seaver immediately rekindled his romance with Mets fans thrilled to have "The Franchise" back. But their euphoria turned to shock when the Chicago White Sox claimed the 39-year-old pitcher as compensation for losing Dennis Lamp in the free agent re-entry draft (a system since abandoned). The Mets, figuring no one would take an aging pitcher with a big salary, had left Seaver off their list of protected personnel, preferring to guard against the selection of a younger player.

Both Seaver and his enormous New York fan base were incensed, with the pitcher even threatening retirement in the heat of the moment. Given time to contemplate, he relented, especially with 300 wins on the horizon.

Seaver needed a dozen victories to hit the magic number, but was coming off consecutive seasons without double-digit victory totals. Though suddenly forced to face nine batters instead of eight – designated hitters batted for American League pitchers – Seaver found his unfamiliarity to the league worked in his favor. In his first two seasons with the White Sox, he won 31 games, including the historic 300th.

It was a strange game – perhaps the only one in which fans in Yankee Stadium rooted for the opposing team.

"I wasn't totally surprised about that," Seaver said. "Mets fans could buy tickets, too. Some people are Mets fans, some people are Yankees fans, and some people are baseball fans. I had made my name in New York, so people came out to see me pitch there."

Seaver's bid for history on August 4, 1985, coincided with Phil Rizzuto Day, an event that guaranteed a huge crowd, anyway. Rizzuto, the diminutive announcer famous for his "Holy Cow" catchphrase, was knocked over by a real-life cow before the game, then watched a pitcher named Joe Cowley face the determined Seaver.

"It meant more to me than I was willing to admit," Seaver said after stopping the Yankees, 4-1, with a complete-game, six-hit effort.

"It was a constant emotional drain. The last time I'd felt like that was when I had that perfect game going against the Cubs in 1969. It was nice to win (my 300th game) in New York, in front of some fairly sophisticated fans."

Winning his 12th game in 20 decisions, Seaver silenced leadoff man Rickey Henderson and cleanup hitter Dave Winfield, holding them hitless in eight at-bats, while walking one and fanning seven. It hardly mattered that Tony LaRussa, then managing the White Sox, got thrown out of the game for arguing an umpire's call.

"I really enjoyed my time in Chicago," said Seaver. "You develop relationships with all the people you play with and that White Sox team had Pudge (Carlton Fisk), Harold Baines, Greg Walker, and Ozzie Guillen at short.

"I also appreciated the opportunity to play in Comiskey Park and Fenway Park, being able to participate in the history of the game. The first time I went to Yankee Stadium, I didn't go to the clubhouse. I went right to the monuments. I really have a love of the history of the game."

As a youth in California, Seaver idolized Sandy Koufax. "I knew about Christy Mathewson, Cy Young, and Rube Waddell," he said. "Baseball history was part of my life. Hank Aaron was one of my heroes, too, but that idolatry ended after the first home run. One line drive brings you back to reality. (Hank) hit me pretty well, but Willie McCovey was my toughest out. He was a very aggressive hitter who looked for my best pitch – the low fastball. Since he was basically a low-ball hitter, he had a high number of pitches in his wheelhouse each time we faced each other."

The first man since Don Newcombe to win both a Rookie of the Year award and Cy Young Award, Seaver never won an MVP trophy. Nor did Seaver ever win the Triple Crown of pitching, though he did lead his league in all three components (wins, strikeouts, and ERA) in separate seasons.

He was 41 and fading when traded for the final time on June 29, 1986. He changed his socks, from white to red, when Chicago sent him to Boston for Steve (Psycho) Lyons. Devoid of his fearsome fast-ball, he won five more games, hurt his knee, and never pitched again – chafing on the unfamiliar visitor's bench at Shea Stadium when the Red Sox faced the Mets in the World Series that fall.

Called back to Shea in 1987, when his old team needed pitching help, the 42-year-old pitcher knew his skills were gone. His last win, the 311th of his career, had come against the Minnesota Twins on the previous August 17.

At the time he retired, Seaver's winning percentage was the best of any 300-game winner since Lefty Grove – a stretch that spanned nearly 50 years. He also stood third on the career strikeout list.

Seaver said he succeeded not only because of natural ability, but also because of lessons he learned as a Marine. "I hated boot camp," he said, "but I learned in the first couple of days the importance of discipline and focus. I took the traits the Marine Corps gave me right into the game I love. I learned that it didn't make any difference (to me as a pitcher) whether we were one game out or 40 games out. It didn't make any difference if it was April or September."

One of the most articulate athletes of any generation, Seaver kept his mind sharp by working crossword puzzles in the locker room – often while being interviewed. He was friendly to fans, popular with the press, and cordial in the clubhouse. He even exchanged auto-graphs, getting one from home run king Hank Aaron while giving one to stolen base king Rickey Henderson.

In retrospect, it's hard to believe that Seaver once earned $2.05 an hour lifting heavy boxes packed with raisins. His father Charles, a former Walker Cup golfer, was an executive with the Bonner Packing Company, one of many Fresno, California, firms processing local farm produce for sale. Although the physical routine helped build his stamina, Seaver was anything but a big-league pitching prospect.

His 6-5 record as a senior at Fresno High earned him a back-up spot on the all-city team and failed to attract the attention of major league scouts. That changed after Seaver served a six-month stint in the Marine Reserve that toughened him up, physically and emotionally. He was 6'1" and 195 pounds when he finished that tour at Twenty-Nine Palms, near Palm Springs.

After attending Fresno State, where his eight-game winning streak left him with an 11-2 record, Seaver switched to the University of Southern California, where the baseball program was run by legendary coach Rod Dedeaux. Earning a USC scholarship by starring for the Alaska Goldpanners, an advanced semipro club that sent many players into the professional ranks, Seaver went 10-2 as a sophomore. He supplemented his skills by studying big-league pitchers at Dodger Stadium, practicing various grips, and lifting weights. The scouts, attracted by his rare combination of brains and brawn, paid attention.

Drafted by the Los Angeles Dodgers in the first amateur free agent draft, in June of 1965, Seaver declined a bonus he deemed insufficient. The following February, however, the Atlanta Braves signed him to a contract worth more than $50,000. Before the pitcher could report to Triple-A Richmond, Commissioner William D. (Spike) Eckert nullified the deal.

According to NCAA rules, no team could sign a college player once his season had started. Although he hadn't pitched in either game, USC had already played two exhibitions. So Eckert conducted a lottery, allowing any team to match Atlanta's offer. The Cleveland Indians, Philadelphia Phillies, and New York Mets agreed, throwing their names into a hat. On April 3, 1966, the Mets won the drawing.

Temporarily shelving his plans to pursue dentistry, Seaver bought a new car, invested the rest of his signing money, and headed for Jacksonville to start his pro career. He spent only one year in the minors, making a major impression on the managers who witnessed his debut on April 25.

"We heard a college pitcher was going to pitch against us and I thought we'd have an easy night," said Rochester manager Earl Weaver, later enshrined in Cooperstown for his success in Baltimore. "He beat us, 4-2. His slider was low outside, his fastball was up and in. He never missed a corner all night, never threw the ball down the middle. I got on the phone to the Orioles farm director and said, 'I've just seen a guy who's going to the Hall of Fame pitch one ball game. Nobody can be this good. If you ever get a chance to get him, do it.'"

Seaver's poise also impressed Jacksonville manager Solly Hemus, a former big-league player: "He reminds me of Bob Gibson – in command all the time. Tom Seaver has a 35-year-old head on top of a 21-year-old body. Usually we get a 35-year-old arm attached to a 21-year-old head."

During their time together, Hemus helped Seaver establish the work habits that gave him a leg up on the opposition. "I told him to keep a record of everything he did – how many wind sprints he ran, how much sleep he got, what he ate – and see how they affected his pitching," Hemus said. Seaver did, adding notes on every pitch he threw and how each hitter handled it. Among pitchers who followed, only Greg Maddux, another 300-game winner, proved such a student of the game.

According to Bing Devine, then general manager of the Mets, "We were lucky to get him. Seaver impressed me. I thought we could take advantage of (the situation) and it paid off very quickly and to an extreme. Seaver was a very smart guy who could have done anything. He was a student of the game and a student of pitching. He had a lot of things going for him that a lot of young ballplayers didn't and probably never would – aside from his ability to pitch and the stuff he had on the ball."

The only rookie to make the roster of the 1967 Mets, Seaver won his first game in his first start, which came in the second game of the season. He beat Pittsburgh, 3-2, for the first of his 311 career victories.

Seaver was so good so fast that he made the National League All-Star team, saving a 2-1 victory for the Nationals in the 15th inning by getting three men out without yielding a hit.

"He was a finished product when he came here," said Ron Swoboda, remembered for his ninth-inning catch that saved Seaver's World Series win in 1969. "I don't ever recall the sense of him being a rookie. He came out of the box a big-league pitcher and there was this golden glow about him. This was clearly a big talent, intelligent, capable, and controlled."

When the Mets retired his No. 41 jersey on July 24, 1988, they recounted his litany of achievements: more wins (198), complete games (171), innings (3,045), strikeouts (2,541), and shutouts (44) than anyone in club history, plus a better earned run average (2.57).

Seaver later spent six seasons in the team's broadcast booth, never encountering anyone who could challenge his reputation as "the Franchise."

Career Statistics

SEAVER, Tom	George Thomas "Tom Terrific" Seaver; B: 11/17/1944, Fresno, CA; BR/TR, 6'1"/206 lbs.; Debut: 4/13/1967; HOF 1992

YEAR	TM-L	W	L	PCT	G	GS	CG	SH	SV	IP	H	R	HR	SO	ERA
1967	NY-N	16	13	0.552	35	34	18	2	0	251	224	85	19	170	2.76
1968	NY-N	16	12	0.571	36	35	14	5	1	277	224	73	15	205	2.20
1969	NY-N	25	7	0.781	36	35	18	5	0	273	202	75	24	208	2.21
1970	NY-N	18	12	0.600	37	36	19	2	0	290	230	103	21	283	2.82
1971	NY-N	20	10	0.667	36	35	21	4	0	286	210	61	18	289	1.76
1972	NY-N	21	12	0.636	35	35	13	3	0	262	215	92	23	249	2.92
1973	NY-N	19	10	0.655	36	36	18	3	0	290	219	74	23	251	2.08
1974	NY-N	11	11	0.500	32	32	12	5	0	236	199	89	19	201	3.20
1975	NY-N	22	9	0.710	36	36	15	5	0	280	217	81	11	243	2.38
1976	NY-N	14	11	0.560	35	34	13	5	0	271	211	83	14	235	2.59
1977	NY-N	7	3	0.700	13	13	5	3	0	96	79	33	7	72	3.00
	Cin-N	14	3	0.824	20	20	14	4	0	165	120	45	12	124	2.34
	Year	21	6	0.778	33	33	19	7	0	261	199	78	19	196	2.58
1978	Cin-N	16	14	0.533	36	35	8	1	0	259	218	97	26	226	2.88
1979	Cin-N	16	6	0.727	32	32	9	5	0	215	187	85	16	131	3.14
1980	Cin-N	10	8	0.556	26	26	5	1	0	168	140	74	24	101	3.64
1981	Cin-N	14	2	0.875	23	23	6	1	0	166	120	51	10	87	2.54
1982	Cin-N	5	13	0.278	21	21	0	0	0	111	136	75	14	62	5.50
1983	NY-N	9	14	0.391	34	34	5	2	0	231	201	104	18	135	3.55
1984	Chi-A	15	11	0.577	34	33	10	4	0	236	216	108	27	131	3.95
1985	Chi-A	16	11	0.593	35	33	6	1	0	238	223	103	22	134	3.17
1986	Chi-A	2	6	0.250	12	12	1	0	0	72	66	37	9	31	4.38
	Bos-A	5	7	0.417	16	16	1	0	0	104	114	46	8	72	3.80
	Year	7	13	0.350	28	28	2	0	0	176	180	83	17	103	4.03
TOTAL	20	311	205	0.603	656	647	231	61	1	4782	3971	1674	380	3640	2.86

Box Score of 300th Win

Seaver Baseball Almanac Box Score
Chicago White Sox 4, New York Yankees 1

Game played on Sunday, August 4, 1985, at Yankee Stadium

Chicago White Sox	ab	r	h	rbi	New York Yankees	ab	r	h	rbi
Law lf	3	0	2	0	Henderson cf	4	0	0	0
Nichols ph,lf	1	0	1	0	Griffey dh	4	0	1	1
Little 2b	2	0	1	2	Mattingly 1b	4	0	2	0
Fletcher ph,2b	1	0	0	0	Winfield rf	4	0	0	0
Baines rf	5	0	2	0	Pasqua lf	4	0	1	0
Walker 1b	3	0	1	0	Hassey c	4	0	0	0
Fisk c	5	1	1	0	Randolph 2b	3	0	0	0
Gamble dh	2	1	1	0	Pagliarulo 3b	3	1	1	0
Kittle ph,dh	1	0	0	0	Meacham ss	3	0	1	0
Hulett 3b	4	1	2	1	Baylor ph	1	0	0	0
Guillen ss	4	0	1	1	Cowley p	0	0	0	0
Salazar cf	4	1	1	0	Fisher p	0	0	0	0
Seaver p	0	0	0	0	Shirley p	0	0	0	0
Totals	35	4	13	4	Allen p	0	0	0	0
					Totals	34	1	6	1

Chicago	0	0	0		0	0	4		0	0	0	–	4	13	1
New York	0	0	1		0	0	0		0	0	0	–	1	6	0

Chicago White Sox	IP	H	R	ER	BB	SO
Seaver W (12-8)	9.0	6	1	1	1	7
Totals	9.0	6	1	1	1	7

New York Yankees	IP	H	R	ER	BB	SO
Cowley L (9-5)	5.1	7	2	2	5	2
Fisher	0.2	4	2	2	1	0
Shirley	2.0	2	0	0	0	2
Allen	1.0	0	0	0	0	1
Totals	9.0	13	4	4	6	5

E–Hulett (14). **DP**–New York 1. **2B**–Chicago Salazar (7,off Cowley); Hulett (13,off Fisher); Fisk (14,off Shirley). **HBP**–Randolph (2,by Seaver). **CS**–Law (5,2nd base by Cowley/Hassey). **HBP**–Seaver (6,Randolph). **T**–3:20. **A**–54,032.

Precision on the Hill

Tom Glavine – 305 Wins

Hockey's loss was baseball's gain. The only 300-game winner once drafted by a professional hockey franchise, Tom Glavine guessed correctly that he would go further with baseball.

The biggest name ever to step out of Billerica, Massachusetts, and into the celebrity spotlight, Glavine spent all but five of his 22 major-league seasons letting his live left arm carve out a career path certain to end in the Baseball Hall of Fame.

He started in June 1984, when the Atlanta Braves picked Glavine in the second round of the amateur free agent draft and then outbid the Los Angeles Kings, the National Hockey League team that selected Tom in the fourth round of that sport's draft. Three years later, the 6', 205-pound left-handed pitcher was summoned to the major leagues, where the Atlanta franchise was barely hanging on. In his second start, Glavine earned his first win, a 10-3 decision over the Pittsburgh Pirates on August 22, 1987, at Atlanta Fulton County Stadium.

Glavine got a taste of the majors that fall, going 2-4, but became a full-time starter a year later. He went 7-17, the team lost 106 games, and bookmakers weren't besieged with bettors willing to bank on the soft-throwing Glavine eventually winning 300 games.

With some experience under his belt, however, he improved to 14-8 in 1989, then reverted to his losing ways with the defensively

Photo courtesy of National Baseball Hall of Fame Library Cooperstown, N.Y.

Tom Glavine

challenged Braves of 1990. As a rule, young lefties with 33-41 records don't turn into superstars. But Glavine was determined to prove himself an exception.

After Braves general manager John Schuerholz bolstered the defense through a series of savvy deals and shrewd free-agent acquisitions before the 1991 season, the Braves stopped giving away games for a young pitching corps that included Glavine, John Smoltz, and Steve Avery. Thanks mainly to those arms, Atlanta was rising from the ashes for the second time in its history.

By season's end, Glavine had won 20 games and the Braves had completed the first worst-to-first climb in National League history. Then in the National League West Division, Atlanta beat the Pittsburgh Pirates in the league championship series and took a full seven games before losing to the Minnesota Twins in the World Series. The last game, a 1-0 decision, took 10 innings.

The 1991 season was the first of 14 consecutive division crowns – an unprecedented achievement in any professional sport – for the Braves. Glavine was a major figure in 11 of them.

He won two Cy Young Awards, twice was runner-up for the pitching trophy, and twice placed third. He led the league in wins five times – in each of his 20-win seasons – and finished first in starts six times.

In 1991, he was the National League Pitcher of the Month after a 6-0 May, the starting pitcher in the All-Star Game in July, and the second man in franchise history (after Warren Spahn) to win a Cy Young.

A year later, he won 13 games in a row, tying a franchise record; pitched a league-high five shutouts; yielded only six home runs; and became the first lefty to pitch two complete games in the World Series since Mickey Lolich in 1968. He lost his bid for a second straight Cy Young to Greg Maddux, who would go on to win four straight.

In 1993, the Braves outlasted the Giants, winning 104 games to San Francisco's 103, in a grueling National League West race that went down to the last day. Glavine's 5-3 win over Colorado gave the Braves a sweep of their 13-game season series and allowed Atlanta to win the division by one game when the Dodgers beat the Giants.

In a career filled with good fortune, Glavine's shining moment came in 1995, when he came within a whisker of duplicating Don Larsen's World Series no-hitter. Facing the powerful Cleveland Indians in the sixth game, he yielded only a bloop single to Tony Pena before exiting after eight innings with a 1-0 lead. Relief pitcher Mark Wohlers worked a 1-2-3 ninth inning to clinch the only world championship in Atlanta Braves history. Glavine, also the winning pitcher in Game 2, was named World Series MVP for his 2-0 record, 1.29 earned run average, and 11 strikeouts in 14 innings.

"We'd had so many disappointments," he said. "We had this group of guys who'd played together and been around each other in the (minor league) system and then the majors. We finally tasted success. That's what made it so special to win the World Series and run out on the field (celebrating) with my buddies."

Glavine said that he felt strong warming up before the deciding game. "I knew I had good stuff," he said. "But with me, you never knew. The first inning was always my Achilles heel. When I got through the first that night, I thought, 'Okay, the stuff's the same I had in the bullpen. Here we go.' As each inning went on, I got more and more confident. I was in the zone. Then David Justice gave us the big hit (a solo home run).

"There might have been one or two other games where I pitched nearly as well but to think that I did it, in that situation, with the pressure we were under, and what it meant to our team, to our city, and to me personally, made it the best game I ever pitched."

There were other contenders, including the clinching games of both the National League Division Series and the National League Championship Series in 1996. The latter capped a comeback for the Braves, who won three elimination games from the St. Louis Cardinals.

Glavine never pitched a no-hitter, but he came close.

"When I was with the (New York) Mets, I gave up my first hit with two outs in the eighth," he said, "but that was on a Sunday afternoon in August, not Game 6 of the World Series."

Glavine jumped to the Mets as a free agent after the 2002 season when the Braves seemed reluctant to match the money and years in New York's offer. As the National League's player union representative and a player who raised the ire of fans with his visibility during the 1994-95 player strike, the pitcher had to set an example by accepting the highest offer.

Glavine was such an Atlanta icon that he was asked to carry home plate from Atlanta Fulton County Stadium to Turner Field when the Braves opened their new stadium in 1997. For Atlanta fans, losing him was unthinkable – especially to the rival Mets.

For the pitcher, leaving his long-time home in suburban Atlanta wasn't easy, either. Nor was it easy to leave Bobby Cox, who managed the Braves through most of Glavine's tenure, or pitching coach Leo Mazzone.

"Bobby gave me every opportunity to go out there and be successful," Glavine said. "He was a positive guy who never said anything negative about anybody in the newspaper or on the radio. I lost 200 games in my career and a lot of them were under Bobby. There were some days when I got up and read the paper and thought, 'Oh my God, Bobby, were you watching the same game that I was pitching?'"

Mazzone's methods, considered unorthodox by many, also helped. "He was very instrumental in helping me understand my mechanics," Glavine said. "He was a proponent of the Johnny Sain theory about throwing twice between starts, throwing a lot, and playing catch. Just getting my feet on the mound that one extra time between starts and working on things got me to the point where I could make adjustments pitch-to-pitch or inning-to-inning.

"I never had to wait for Leo to come out in the middle of an inning to tell me what I was doing wrong. I had a pretty good sense of that. What really turned me into a good pitcher was the ability to understand the adjustments I needed to make during the course of the game – plus the ability to make those adjustments."

The first National League pitcher to start consecutive All-Star Games (1991-92) since Robin Roberts (1954-55), Glavine made the National League squad eight times with Atlanta and twice with the Mets. He pitched in five World Series, all with the Braves, while taking home Cy Young Awards in 1991 and 1998.

Glavine grabbed his first award – the first by an Atlanta pitcher – by winning more games than any Braves left-hander since Spahn went 23-7 in 1963. He placed second in innings pitched and third in strikeouts, earned run average, and batting average by opponents. He also won Game 5 of the World Series against Minnesota. But it wasn't the best of his two Cy Young seasons, according to Glavine.

"That 1998 season was a more consistent year for me," he said. "I would call 1991 a coming-out year, a season in which both the Braves and I put ourselves on the map. That might have been a more fun year, but in terms of consistency, time in and time out, 1998 was better. From start to finish in 1998, I was able to go out there and do what I wanted to do every time. That was the one year when I never felt like I got into any kind of a funk. I was comfortable every time out. That wasn't the case most years. I usually went through a stretch where I was just fighting myself or where something didn't feel quite right. It might have been my tempo, my leg kick, or something else. I never felt like I had any of that in 1998."

Glavine earned his second Cy Young Award with a 20-6 record and career-best 2.47 ERA, numbers that helped pitch the Braves into the playoffs.

Mazzone was especially proud of that team's pitching staff. "We won 106 games that year, leading the major leagues in ERA, shutouts, and strikeouts," he said. "We had five starters who won at least 16 games – something that happened only once before (the 1902 Pittsburgh Pirates). Glavine won the Cy Young for the second time and Mad Dog (Greg Maddux) won the ERA title.

"The reason we won so many games is we had a huge advantage once you got past the No. 3 starter. Our four and five holes were as good as the one and two holes on a lot of teams. You don't get into losing streaks when you're running five guys like that out there. You come to the ballpark feeling pretty confident and pretty good."

The five starters that season were Maddux, Glavine, John Smoltz, Denny Neagle, and Kevin Millwood. In his book, *Leo Mazzone's Tales from the Mound*, the former pitching coach called them "the greatest starting five since 1902."

Smoltz, acquired from the Detroit farm system, broke into the majors with the Braves in 1988, Glavine's first full season, while Maddux signed as a free agent after the 1992 season. During the decade of the 1990s, they gave the Braves six Cy Young Awards, five pennant wins, three division title wins, and a world championship. Glavine had been the ace of the staff when Maddux arrived as a free agent after winning his first Cy Young while pitching for the Chicago Cubs.

"I remember being excited about it," said Glavine of the Maddux signing. "We were already in a situation in Atlanta with Smoltzy, Steve Avery, and me where a lot of us could have been No. 1 pitchers anywhere. It just happened we were all on the same team. We were all the No. 1 guy when it became our turn to pitch. During the course of the year, there would always be a time where one of us was on our game and maybe the other guys were not quite on theirs. I remember hearing we got Greg and thinking, 'Man, we already have a good pitching staff, but now it's going to be really good.' None of us could have imagined how great Greg was going to be."

Although Maddux and Glavine rank among the top five pitching tandems of all time with 438 wins during their 10 years as teammates, Smoltz might have similar numbers if he hadn't spent four seasons as a closer. During their heyday, the talented threesome proved to be one of the most formidable pitching trios of all time.

"That's pretty flattering," Glavine said when asked about its historic significance. "There were some nice threesomes over the years: Feller, Lemon, and Wynn in Cleveland; Drysdale, Koufax, and Sutton in Los Angeles; and Palmer, Cuellar, and McNally in Baltimore. Not many other trios who pitched together as long as we did had three guys get into the Hall of Fame."

None of the Atlanta trio is enshrined yet, but it's only a matter of time. Winning 300 games is a virtual lock for election to the Hall, and Smoltz had the rare distinction of 200 wins and 150 saves.

Glavine, who won 244 games for the Braves, notched his 300th win while pitching for the Mets in front of an overflow crowd at Wrigley Field on August 5, 2007. He beat the Cubs, 8-3, yielding two runs in 6 $1/3$ innings and knocked in a run with a single. The fifth left-hander to win 300, but the first since Steve Carlton in 1983, Glavine won by hitting his spots and changing speeds – characteristics of a career-long style that accented control rather than velocity.

"I let the guys behind me do the work," he said. "It wasn't a dazzling performance in terms of striking people out. My feeling right now is (one of) relief. At some point in time, the historic side will sink in. I know the company I'm in and I'm proud to be in that company."

Glavine, who finished his career with 305 victories, realized that reaching 300 wins in an era of five-man rotations, interleague play, and frequent pitching changes was not easy. He also realized his five 20-win seasons helped.

"With five 20-win seasons, you're one-third of the way there," he said. "When you start to break it down into how many years it really takes, it is a hard thing to get your mind around. You have to talk about guys averaging 15 wins a year for 20 years. That puts into perspective how difficult a task it really is."

A fine fielder who was an annual contender for the Gold Glove, Glavine also helped himself as a batter, winning four Silver Slugger awards. (This award is given annually to the top offensive player at each position.)

Glavine could always hit. His triple with the bases loaded in the first inning of the final National League Championship Series game in 1996 set the tone for a 15-0 thumping of the St. Louis Cardinals. A year earlier, he had beaten John Smiley, 2-1, with the lone home run of his career.

"I was pitching against Cincinnati in late August and hit a home run to break a 1-1 tie in the seventh," Glavine remembered. "I got a curtain call and thought, 'Okay, this is the end of it for me.' The Atlanta fans had been booing me. I was involved in negotiations with the owners and was a spokesman for the Players Association. So I took a lot of heat. The first game back, people were throwing money at me in the bullpen. It lasted into the summer."

A finesse pitcher who threw to the outside part of the plate, Glavine struggled when baseball introduced the QuesTec machine as a means of checking umpire performance. Although he retained his repertoire of sinker, slider, and circle-change, plus a cut fastball taught by Maddux, he started pitching inside at the suggestion of Rick Peterson, pitching coach of the Mets.

The recommendation helped Glavine, who went 28-15 in his last two Mets seasons. Despite problems with his left ring finger and pitching shoulder, he won nine straight games in 2006, finished with a 15-7 record, and blanked St. Louis, 2-0, in the opener of the National League Championship Series. That game, Glavine's 14th postseason win, tied him with Andy Pettitte for second in postseason history, one behind Smoltz.

He took a huge pay cut to rejoin the Braves as a free agent in 2008, but wanted to be closer to his growing family. The Braves thought the return of the sentimental favorite would bring more fans to Turner Field. But the pitcher won only two games before a myriad of physical problems, including elbow trouble and a severe hamstring pull, forced him onto the disabled list for the first time in his 21-year career. He never returned, though he did complete a 2009 minor-league rehab assignment before the Braves released him.

Glavine said he started to think about winning 300 games many years before it happened. "Once I got to the 240 mark," he said, "I started doing the math, figuring out where I was in my career, my age, what it would take to get to 300, and what are the average amount of wins I would need in a given year. I really didn't think about it a whole lot until I got to 290. Once I needed just 10 wins, I felt it was more of an achievable thing. Of course, you're always one injury away from not having that opportunity."

To Glavine, where he won his 300th was less important than the fact that he was able to do it. "I was thankful to do it anywhere and not really concerned whether or not it should have been in a Braves uniform," he said. "I think things happen for a reason. I know people will always view me as a Brave, remember me as a Brave, and realize that most of my accomplishments came as a Brave. I loved playing in Atlanta, but I also loved playing in New York.

"For me, it was the best of both worlds. I was able to spend a great length of time in one place that I thoroughly enjoyed and had a lot of great games and teammates in a town that ended up becoming my home. At the same time, I got to play in one of the best cities in America and one of the best baseball towns."

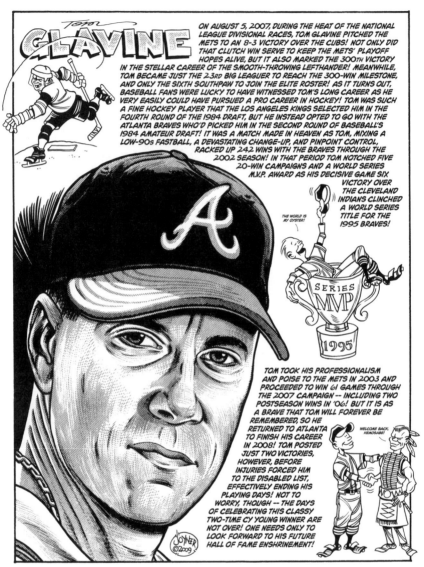

ON AUGUST 5, 2007, DURING THE HEAT OF THE NATIONAL LEAGUE DIVISIONAL RACES, TOM GLAVINE PITCHED THE METS TO AN 8-3 VICTORY OVER THE CUBS! NOT ONLY DID THAT CLUTCH WIN SERVE TO KEEP THE METS' PLAYOFF HOPES ALIVE, BUT IT ALSO MARKED THE 300TH VICTORY IN THE STELLAR CAREER OF THE SMOOTH-THROWING LEFTHANDER! MEANWHILE, TOM BECAME JUST THE 23RD BIG LEAGUER TO REACH THE 300-WIN MILESTONE, AND ONLY THE SIXTH SOUTHPAW TO JOIN THE ELITE ROSTER! AS IT TURNS OUT, BASEBALL FANS WERE LUCKY TO HAVE WITNESSED TOM'S LONG CAREER AS HE VERY EASILY COULD HAVE PURSUED A PRO CAREER IN HOCKEY! TOM WAS SUCH A FINE HOCKEY PLAYER THAT THE LOS ANGELES KINGS SELECTED HIM IN THE FOURTH ROUND OF THE 1984 DRAFT, BUT HE INSTEAD OPTED TO GO WITH THE ATLANTA BRAVES WHO'D PICKED HIM IN THE SECOND ROUND OF BASEBALL'S 1984 AMATEUR DRAFT! IT WAS A MATCH MADE IN HEAVEN AS TOM, MIXING A LOW-90s FASTBALL, A DEVASTATING CHANGE-UP, AND PINPOINT CONTROL, RACKED UP 242 WINS WITH THE BRAVES THROUGH THE 2002 SEASON! IN THAT PERIOD TOM NOTCHED FIVE 20-WIN CAMPAIGNS AND A WORLD SERIES M.V.P. AWARD AS HIS DECISIVE GAME SIX VICTORY OVER THE CLEVELAND INDIANS CLINCHED A WORLD SERIES TITLE FOR THE 1995 BRAVES!

THE WORLD IS MY OYSTER!

SERIES MVP
1995

TOM TOOK HIS PROFESSIONALISM AND POISE TO THE METS IN 2003 AND PROCEEDED TO WIN 61 GAMES THROUGH THE 2007 CAMPAIGN -- INCLUDING TWO POSTSEASON WINS IN '06! BUT IT IS AS A BRAVE THAT TOM WILL FOREVER BE REMEMBERED, SO HE RETURNED TO ATLANTA TO FINISH HIS CAREER IN 2008! TOM POSTED JUST TWO VICTORIES, HOWEVER, BEFORE INJURIES FORCED HIM TO THE DISABLED LIST, EFFECTIVELY ENDING HIS PLAYING DAYS! NOT TO WORRY, THOUGH -- THE DAYS OF CELEBRATING THIS CLASSY TWO-TIME CY YOUNG WINNER ARE NOT OVER! ONE NEEDS ONLY TO LOOK FORWARD TO HIS FUTURE HALL OF FAME ENSHRINEMENT!

WELCOME BACK, KEMOSABE!

Courtesy of Ronnie Joyner

Box Score of 300th Win

Glavine Baseball Almanac Box Score
New York Mets 8, Chicago Cubs 3

Game played on Sunday, August 5, 2007, at Wrigley Field

New York Mets	ab	r	h	rbi	Chicago Cubs	ab	r	h	rbi
Reyes ss	6	2	3	1	Soriano lf	2	0	1	0
Castillo 2b	5	2	4	0	Fontenot 2b	3	0	1	1
Gotay 2b	1	0	0	0	Theriot ss	4	0	1	0
Wright 3b	4	1	1	0	Lee 1b	4	1	1	0
Delgado 1b	4	1	2	4	Ramirez 3b	4	0	1	1
Alou lf	4	0	0	0	Floyd rf,lf	2	0	1	0
Green rf	5	0	1	1	DeRosa 2b,rf	4	0	0	0
Lo Duca c	5	0	1	1	Dempster p	0	0	0	0
Milledge cf	4	2	3	0	Pagan cf	4	1	1	0
Glavine p	2	0	1	1	Kendall c	4	1	2	0
Mota p	0	0	0	0	Marquis p	2	0	0	0
Feliciano p	0	0	0	0	Eyre p	0	0	0	0
Heilman p	0	0	0	0	Wood p	0	0	0	0
Anderson ph	1	0	0	0	Jones ph	1	0	0	1
Sosa p	0	0	0	0	Ohman p	0	0	0	0
Wagner p	0	0	0	0	Wuertz p	0	0	0	0
Totals	41	8	16	8	Murton rf	1	0	0	0
					Totals	35	3	9	3

New York	0	1	0	0	2	2	0	2	1	–	8	16	0
Chicago	0	0	0	0	0	1	2	0	0	–	3	9	0

New York Mets	IP	H	R	ER	BB	SO
Glavine W (10-6)	6.1	6	2	2	1	1
Mota	0.0	1	1	1	0	0
Feliciano	0.1	1	0	0	0	0
Heilman	0.1	0	0	0	0	0
Sosa	1.0	0	0	0	1	0
Wagner	1.0	1	0	0	0	1
Totals	9.0	9	3	3	2	2
Chicago Cubs	IP	H	R	ER	BB	SO
Marquis L (8-7)	5.1	9	5	5	3	1
Eyre	0.2	1	0	0	2	0
Wood	1.0	1	0	0	0	1
Ohman	0.1	3	2	2	1	1
Wuertz	0.2	1	0	0	0	0
Dempster	1.0	1	1	1	1	1
Totals	9.0	16	8	8	7	4

E–None. **2B**–New York Castillo (2,off Marquis); Delgado 2 (27,off Marquis,off Ohman); Green (25,off Marquis); Milledge (6,off Marquis)., Chicago Lee (33,off Glavine); Ramirez (26,off Glavine); Pagan (10,off Glavine); Fontenot (10,off Feliciano); Kendall (4,off Wagner).. **3B**–New York Reyes (11,off Dempster). **SH**–Glavine (9,off Wood). **SF**–Delgado (5,off Dempster). **IBB**–Wright (6,by Eyre); Alou 2 (3,by Eyre,by Ohman).. **Team LOB**–15. **Team**–7. **U-HP**–Marty Foster, **1B**–Fieldin Culbreth, **2B**–Paul Schreiber, **3B**–Tim McClelland. **T**–3:20. **A**–41,599.

Career Statistics

GLAVINE, Tom				Thomas Michael Galvine; B: 3/25/1966, Concord MA; BL/TL, 6'1"/190; Debut: 8/17/1987; ALL STAR											
YEAR	TM-L	W	L	PCT	G	GS	CG	SHO	SV	IP	H	R	HR	SO	ERA
1987	Atl-N	2	4	0.333	9	9	0	0	0	50	55	34	5	20	5.54
1988	Atl-N	7	17	0.292	34	34	1	0	0	195	201	111	12	84	4.56
1989	Atl-N	14	8	0.636	29	29	4	0	0	186	172	88	20	90	3.68
1990	Atl-N	10	12	0.455	33	33	1	0	0	214	232	111	18	129	4.28
1991	Atl-N	20	11	0.645	34	34	9	1	0	246	201	83	17	192	2.55
1992	Atl-N	20	8	0.714	33	33	7	5	0	225	197	81	6	129	2.76
1993	Atl-N	22	6	0.786	36	36	4	2	0	239	236	91	16	120	3.20
1994	Atl-N	13	9	0.591	25	25	2	0	0	165	173	76	10	140	3.97
1995	Atl-N	16	7	0.696	29	29	3	1	0	198	182	76	9	127	3.08
1996	Atl-N	15	10	0.600	36	36	1	0	0	235	222	91	14	181	2.98
1997	Atl-N	14	7	0.667	33	33	5	2	0	240	197	86	20	152	2.96
1998	Atl-N	20	6	0.769	33	33	4	3	0	229	202	67	13	157	2.47
1999	Atl-N	14	11	0.560	35	35	2	0	0	234	259	115	18	138	4.12
2000	Atl-N	21	9	0.700	35	35	4	2	0	241	222	101	24	152	3.40
2001	Atl-N	16	7	0.696	35	35	1	1	0	219	213	92	24	116	3.57
2002	Atl-N	18	11	0.621	36	36	2	1	0	224	210	85	21	127	2.96
2003	NYM-N	9	14	0.391	32	32	0	0	0	183	205	94	21	82	4.52
2004	NYM-N	11	14	0.440	33	33	1	1	0	212	204	94	20	109	3.60
2005	NYM-N	13	13	0.500	33	33	2	1	0	211	227	88	12	105	3.53
2006	NYM-N	15	7	0.682	32	32	0	0	0	198	202	94	22	131	3.82
2007	NYM-N	13	8	0.619	34	34	1	1	0	200	219	102	23	89	4.45
2008	Atl-N	2	4	0.333	13	13	0	0	0	63	67	40	11	37	5.54
TOTAL	22	305	203	0.600	682	682	56	25	0	4413	4298	1900	363	2607	3.54

Flamethrower

Randy Johnson – 303 Wins

Randy Johnson was so overpowering that even the best left-handed batters quivered in their spikes when he took the mound.

Even before he unleashed his fearsome fastball, he looked like a formidable foe, standing 6'10" and glowering at opposing batters.

Tony Gwynn, the eight-time National League batting champion, took himself out of the lineup when Johnson was pitching. Wade Boggs, another perennial batting king, faced Johnson and struck out three times in a game for the first time in his career. John Kruk backed out of the batter's box at the 1993 All-Star Game with an "I give up" look on his face. Larry Walker, another batting champion, did the same thing four years later, twisting his batting helmet around and jumping to the right-handed hitter's box.

"There was nothing fun about facing him," said Washington slugger Adam Dunn, who had one hit and eight strikeouts against Johnson in his first 15 at-bats against him. "He's eight feet tall and when he comes from the side, it looks like the ball's coming from first. Not first base – the first row."

Even after he conquered the control problems that plagued his early years, Johnson struck fear into the hearts of experienced hitters. And he struck out thousands along the way – more than any pitcher not named Nolan Ryan.

Photo courtesy of National
Baseball Hall of Fame Library
Cooperstown, N.Y.

The only man to top 300 strikeouts five years in a row, the lethal left-hander from California tied Ryan with six 300-strikeout seasons, contributing to a career total of 4,875. He won nine strikeout crowns, led his league in winning percentage four times, and finished first in earned run average four times. He also won the Triple Crown of pitching, leading the National League in wins, earned run average, and strikeouts in 2002, seven years after nearly becoming the first American League Triple Crown winner since Hal Newhouser in 1945.

No pitcher ever won the rare triple in both leagues, but Randy Johnson was different. He gave his fans a roller-coaster ride, making the All-Star team 10 times, but also going on the disabled list just as often. The Big Unit, as he was known in big-league dugouts, wasn't always well-oiled. He had four knee operations, three back surgeries, and a lingering shoulder problem that cost him two months of the 2009 season.

When he was good, he was very, very, good. He pitched no-hitters in both leagues and won Cy Young Awards in both, even emulating the Greg Maddux feat of winning the National League trophy four times in a row (1999-2002).

A Cy Young Award runner-up three other times, Johnson also duplicated the Grover Cleveland Alexander feat of winning the second and sixth games of the World Series as a starter, then saving the seventh with an unexpected relief appearance.

Even as a schoolboy star, Randall David Johnson gave hints of things to come. He threw a perfect game in his final start for Livermore (California) High School, then turned down a chance to go pro when the Atlanta Braves picked him in the third round of the June 1982 amateur draft. Accepting a joint baseball/basketball scholarship to USC, Johnson played on the same college team as future home run king Mark McGwire.

His pro career began when the Montreal Expos, now the Washington Nationals, made him their second choice in the amateur draft of June 1985. Three years later, with a minor-league strikeout title under his belt, he won his big-league debut, beating the Pittsburgh Pirates on September 15, 1988. In his second start, five days later, he struck out 11 while pitching a complete game against the Chicago Cubs.

Like fellow 300-game winners Warren Spahn and Lefty Grove, Johnson was already 25 years old when he won his first game, so it seemed unlikely that we would attain 300 wins.

In parts of two seasons with the Expos, Johnson posted a 3-4 record. But he showed enough sizzle to solicit interest from the Seattle Mariners. On July 31, 1988, the Mariners sent veteran starter Mark Langston and minor-leaguer Mike Campbell to Montreal for Johnson, Gene Harris, and Brian Holman.

Johnson teamed with Alex Rodriguez and Ken Griffey, Jr., to give Seattle a trio of talented superstars, all of whom would make the Mariners a potent force in the American League West – even winning a league record 116 games in 2001 – but would eventually become too expensive to keep.

With free agency looming, Seattle fielded several offers for Johnson before dealing him to the Houston Astros at the trade deadline on July 31, 1998.

His return to the National League worked wonders for The Unit, who went 10-1 with Houston, but he went into free agency when the Astros couldn't meet his contract demands. Johnson signed a four-year, $53 million deal with the Arizona Diamondbacks, an expansion team coming off a debut season marred by 97 losses, and instantly created a rags-to-riches tale in the desert.

In his first year with Arizona, Johnson joined Gaylord Perry and Pedro Martinez as the only men to win Cy Young Awards in both leagues (Roger Clemens did it later). The award was well-earned: Johnson led the majors with 364 strikeouts and a dozen complete games while pitching to a National League-leading 2.48 earned run average. Often the victim of weak run support, Johnson won only 17 times in 26 decisions. But he pitched well enough for his team to win more.

Johnson was the losing pitcher in four straight shutouts, tying a record, from June 25 to July 10. Making the situation even more remarkable was the sequence of support Johnson received: no hits in the first game, then one hit, two hits, and three hits in order. It was the 10th time in major-league history, and the first time since 1980, that a starter was the loser in four consecutive shutouts.

Observers wondered how such a weak-hitting team could win 100 games. But adding Johnson added credibility, allowing the Diamondbacks to rise from worst to first in the National League West. Although Arizona failed to survive a postseason series with the New York Mets, it would be back with a vengeance two years later.

In 2001, Johnson and fellow pitcher Curt Schilling shared World Series MVP honors after going 4-0 against the Yankees in a seven-game set. Johnson won the last two, including Game 7 in relief, while

Schilling started twice on three days' rest. The left/right tandem had 43 wins and a record 665 strikeouts during the season, with Johnson averaging 13.4 strikeouts per nine innings, also a record.

Schilling, acquired by Arizona from Philadelphia during the 2000 season, was a perfect partner for Johnson. "I had already won the Cy Young in 1999 and was on my way to winning three more," said Johnson, "but his arrival created a lot of stability in the pitching rotation. That's one reason we went on to win the World Series."

It was the only time in Johnson's career he was part of a world championship team.

Schilling won the opener, 9-1, and Johnson followed with a 4-0 shutout. The Yankees then won all three games at Yankee Stadium. With their backs to the wall, the Diamondbacks walloped the over-confident Yankees, 15-2, as Johnson worked the first seven innings of the sixth game. The following night, New York was up by a 2-1 score in the eighth when Johnson came out of the bullpen. He got the final out of the eighth and worked a scoreless ninth inning, hoping Arizona could pull off the same last-inning rally that Seattle had for Johnson six years earlier.

Thanks in part to a throwing error by Yankees closer Mariano Rivera, the Diamondbacks scored twice to win, 3-2. As a result, Johnson became the first man to win three World Series games in the same year since Mickey Lolich in 1968.

Arizona reached the playoffs again in 2002, but failed to survive. In fact, such almost-but-not-quite performances became a pattern on Johnson's resume. Although he reached postseason play eight times, he advanced to the championship series only once in each league and to the World Series only in 2001.

An eight-time All-Star, Johnson started the mid-summer game twice for each league, never getting a decision but getting lots of unhappy looks from left-handed hitters.

Johnson's game peaked in 2001 en route to his only world championship.

On May 8, he fanned 20 men in nine innings, matching a major-league record shared by Roger Clemens and Kerry Wood, but received no credit for the performance because it was not a complete game. He left the game after nine innings with the score tied; the game went 11 innings before Arizona won. Baseball's commissioner later reversed the original ruling, giving The Big Unit the big credit he deserved.

Johnson's penchant for striking out hitters was proven again on July 19, when he smashed an 88-year-old record by fanning 16 San Diego Padres during a seven-inning relief stint. The game had actually started the previous night, with Schilling on the mound, when an explosion knocked out two light towers, forcing a suspension of play. When the game resumed, Johnson was on the mound.

At the end of the 2001 regular season, Johnson won his 200th game. But 300 still seemed out of reach for a 41-year-old power pitcher besieged by a bad back and the march of time.

Johnson finished 2001 with 372 strikeouts, 11 shy of Nolan Ryan's record for a single season. A year later, he would top 300 for the fifth straight year, a record.

For Johnson, those were the good old days, when Jerry Colangelo headed the group that owned the Diamondbacks. Like all good things, they didn't last forever.

When new ownership arrived in Arizona, Johnson's days were numbered. His age, his salary, and his history of injuries convinced the new owners to take a new direction. On January 11, 2005, he was traded to the New York Yankees for three players and cash. The Yankees were one of the few teams who could afford Johnson, who was then earning a career-best $16 million.

Johnson produced a pair of 17-win seasons in Yankee pinstripes, but felt suffocated by the New York media. Almost two years to the day after his arrival, Johnson retraced his steps. He went back to Arizona. He stayed only two seasons before free agency beckoned again.

Johnson, a Bay Area native who once rooted for Vida Blue and the Oakland A's, signed with the San Francisco Giants. He knew he'd be relatively close to his home in Paradise Valley, Arizona, and also knew the Giants were a contending team that could help him win the five games needed for membership in the 300 club.

June 3, 2009, was the appointed day. But the weather in Washington didn't cooperate. After waiting for three hours, the umpires consulted with Johnson. He decided the hour was too late and the forecast too uncertain to try, preferring to wait until the front end of a doubleheader the following day.

Again, Johnson felt raindrops falling on his head. But the weather delay was only 36 minutes long.

Pitching against a Washington Nationals team that was on its way to finishing last in its division, Johnson worked six innings, leaving with a 2-1 lead after suffering a minor injury. He barehanded a ball and threw while falling forward and landing on his pitching shoulder.

The bullpen kept the lead, giving the Giants a 5-1 victory, and allowing Johnson to become the first pitcher since Tom Seaver in 1985 to win his 299th and 300th games in consecutive starts. Johnson also joined Steve Carlton as the only 300-game winners to notch the milestone against the franchise with whom they started their careers.

"We watched history today," said Washington manager Manny Acta after the game. "He's probably going to be the last guy ever to do this. It was impressive to see. His longevity and everything he'd done for the game paid off today."

At age 45, Johnson was a year younger than Phil Niekro, the oldest man to win his 300th.

To his manager, Bruce Bochy, he was living proof that persever-ance pays off.

"I'm sure he had his eye on 300 for awhile," he said of Johnson, whose son, Tanner, served as batboy that day while his wife and three daughters watched. "He does an incredible job with keeping himself in shape. Pitching at 45 and still throwing the ball the way he's throw-ing is quite an accomplishment."

Johnson went into the season focused on the goal. "I came into the season with 295 and felt very competitive after winning 11 games while having two back surgeries in 2008," he said. "I threw 180 innings and made 30 starts. So I knew I only had to win five games. I thought if I stayed healthy, that would be very achievable."

Although he won three more games after the history-making game, Johnson went down in July with a partial tear of his rotator cuff. "After being out two months, I found my role had changed," said Johnson. "I was no longer a starting pitcher. It was a bit disap-pointing after being on such a high earlier in the year and the achieve-ment that I had accomplished."

A bigger disappointment for the pitcher was not winning his 300th for Arizona.

"My regrets really started in 2004," he said. "We lost 100 games that year, but I finished second in the Cy Young Award voting and had one more year on my contract. I was wondering what direction the team was going in and wanted to stay there, to get an extension that would take me to the end of my career – maybe two years beyond 2005. But the new ownership told me I would have to give back half of my salary and I didn't think that was right, considering everything I did for that franchise."

He spent two years with the Yankees, then came back to the Diamondbacks in another deal. When his contract expired, Arizona ownership could have had him back at a hometown discount, but they weren't interested.

"I was willing to come back and take a 50 percent pay cut," Johnson said. "I thought that would be a no-brainer for ownership to have me come back and win my 300th game in a Diamondbacks uniform. But they wouldn't do it. It was the second time I had to go through contract-type stuff with ownership, but now I know how they felt about me. It was unfortunate."

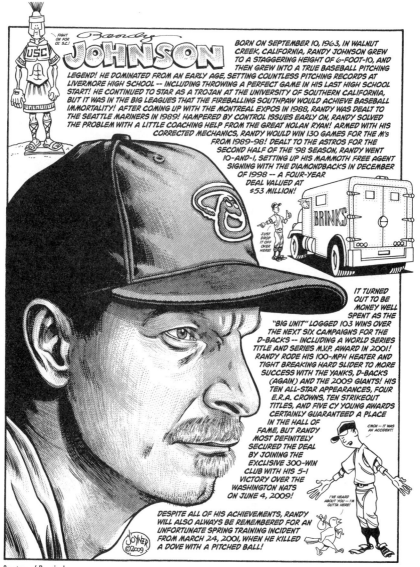

Courtesy of Ronnie Joyner

Signing with the Giants was hardly a tough call, he said.

"They pursued me from the get-go. And I thought it was a good fit. They were looking for a pitcher with experience to lend some credibility to their rotation and help some of the younger guys. I was able to help Matt Cain and I tutored Jonathan Sanchez from spring training until the last day of the season. The Giants trained in Scottsdale, which was close to my home in Arizona, and I had lot of family and friends in California who were able to come to games on a more regular basis."

Johnson's milestones are a mile long.

"Winning the World Series was a team accomplishment – being a part of it and being instrumental in winning is a very proud team moment," he said. "And there are several individual accomplishments that I am proud of because they reflect my durability and stamina and my ability to overcome adversity with the injuries I had.

"I am very proud of the perfect game because I was the oldest pitcher (40) ever to throw one. I would also have to include the 20-strikeout game and being able to strike out 300 batters six times to tie Nolan Ryan. These things reflect my ability to be able to go out there and be consistent every fifth day."

It was Ryan who set Johnson's career on the proper path.

"When I was with Seattle, I had a nice conversation with Ryan and (Texas pitching coach) Tom House about proper mechanics," Johnson said. "Later that year, 1992, I pitched against Ryan in a day game in Texas and struck out 18 in eight innings. That was the first big strikeout game of my career. We both got no-decisions but it was an honor to pitch against him. Later on, he hurt his arm in Seattle. That was the last game he would pitch, so I was there to see that as well."

Johnson also pitched against other 300-game winners, including Roger Clemens, Tom Glavine, and Greg Maddux.

"The most memorable games I had against Maddux and Glavine were both in the same year. It was in the 2001 National League

Championship Series. I faced Maddux in Arizona and shut the Braves out. Then I pitched against Glavine and won the clincher that put us into the World Series. I knew I was going to have to be on top of my game because of the respect that I had for both those pitchers. Being able to do it within five days was pretty special."

Johnson said he became more aware of the game's past as he approached 300 wins.

"Over time, when I heard myself compared to other people, I started opening books, reading a little bit more, and talked to people who knew the history of the game," he said. "I know mostly the players of the modern era, but I am a collector of memorabilia, too. I have autographs of Cy Young, Christy Mathewson, Babe Ruth, and Lou Gehrig. I know what their accomplishments were and what significance they had in the game."

Johnson was not considered an elite performer early in his career. In fact, his first days with Seattle were trying for the pitcher, whose frequent walks bloated his ERA and hurt his winning percentage.

"During my first four or five years in Seattle, I had growing pains," Johnson said. "The team hadn't finished over .500 and didn't even get over .500 until we went to the playoffs in 1995. My first breakout year was 1993 and from that point on, the next five years in Seattle I took some big steps in my career and was able to start showing my ability on a consistent basis. I was really becoming the pitcher that I ended up being."

Johnson first flashed his future form on June 2, 1990, when he threw a no-hitter against Detroit. He won his first four strikeout crowns from 1992-95, but walked well over 100 batters in each of his first three Seattle seasons. Then, in 1993, he reduced his walk total below triple digits, struck out 300 for the first time, and won 19 games. Johnson was on his way.

Over a span of 81 starts that stretched from May 1994 through the 1997 season, he went 53-9. The guy almost never lost, which thrilled manager Lou Piniella.

"I really enjoyed pitching for Lou," said Johnson of the man who managed the Mariners from 1993-2002. "Since he was a former player, I could see how much he wanted to win as a manager. That just said a lot about him as a person. I really enjoyed my time with him."

Johnson also lauded Mark Connor, Piniella's pitching coach in 1999 and 2000, and Dan Wilson, Seattle's catcher at the time. "We really worked well together," he said of Wilson. "Early in my career, when Scott Bradley caught me, I was still rough around the edges. But Dan was the catcher when I was coming into my own."

Like other pitchers who reached 300 wins by working in relief between starts, Johnson would make headlines with other relief roles later, most prominently in the 2001 World Series.

He also found other ways to top the baseball news cycle. For example:

☞ He once won 16 games in a row, one short of the American League record.

☞ Twice in 1997, he struck out 19 men in a game.

☞ He went 10-1 with a 1.28 ERA for the 1998 Astros after arriving in a trade.

☞ In 1999, he reached double digits in strikeouts 23 times, tying a record.

☞ In his career, he fanned at least 15 in a game a record 29 times and he won at least one game in a record 41 different ballparks.

Johnson would have reached 300 wins sooner had he avoided injuries that kept him sidelined for most of four different seasons, 1996, 2003, 2007, and 2009.

But he managed to make a series of amazing comebacks.

He retired before the start of the 2010 season with the fifth-best winning percentage among the 24 members of the 300 Club, trailing only Lefty Grove, Christy Mathewson, Roger Clemens, and John Clarkson.

"There's not a lot more for me to do," said Johnson, who just missed joining Nolan Ryan as the only men with 5,000 strikeouts.

The sixth left-hander to win 300, Johnson was also the fourth Giant, joining Mathewson and 19th century teammates Mickey Welch and Tim Keefe. Even if he had never pitched for San Francisco, Johnson will always be remembered as a giant, both in stature and accomplishment.

Career Statistics

JOHNSON, Randy	Randall David "Big Unit"Johnson ; B: 19/10/1963, Walnut Creek CA; BR/TL, 6'10"/225; Debut: 9/15/1988; ALL STAR

YEAR	TM-L	W	L	PCT	G	GS	CG	SHO	SV	IP	H	R	HR	SO	ERA
1988	Mon-N	3	0	1.000	4	4	1	0	0	26	23	8	3	25	2.42
1989	Tot-MLB	7	13	0.350	29	28	2	0	0	160	147	100	13	130	4.82
	Mon-N	0	4	0.000	7	6	0	0	0	29	29	25	2	26	6.67
	Sea-A	7	9	0.438	22	22	2	0	0	131	118	75	11	104	4.40
1990	Sea-A	14	11	0.560	33	33	5	2	0	219	174	103	26	194	3.65
1991	Sea-A	13	10	0.565	33	33	2	1	0	201	151	96	15	228	3.98
1992	Sea-A	12	14	0.462	31	31	6	2	0	210	154	104	13	241	3.77
1993	Sea-A	19	8	0.704	35	34	10	3	1	255	185	97	22	308	3.24
1994	Sea-A	13	6	0.684	23	23	9	4	0	172	132	65	14	204	3.19
1995	Sea-A	18	2	0.900	30	30	6	3	0	214	159	65	12	294	2.48
1996	Sea-A	5	0	1.000	14	8	0	0	1	61	48	27	8	85	3.67
1997	Sea-A	20	4	0.833	30	29	5	2	0	213	147	60	20	291	2.28
1998	Tot-MLB	19	11	0.633	34	34	10	6	0	244	203	102	23	329	3.28
	Sea-A	9	10	0.474	23	23	6	2	0	160	146	90	19	213	4.33
	Hou-N	10	1	0.909	11	11	4	4	0	84	57	12	4	116	1.28
1999	Ari-N	17	9	0.654	35	35	12	2	0	271	207	86	30	364	2.48
2000	Ari-N	19	7	0.731	35	35	8	3	0	248	202	89	23	347	2.64
2001	Ari-N	21	6	0.778	35	34	3	2	0	249	181	74	19	372	2.49
2002	Ari-N	24	5	0.828	35	35	8	4	0	260	197	78	26	334	2.32
2003	Ari-N	6	8	0.429	18	18	1	1	0	114	125	61	16	125	4.26
2004	Ari-N	16	14	0.533	35	35	4	2	0	245	177	88	18	290	2.60
2005	NYY-A	17	8	0.680	34	34	4	0	0	225	207	102	32	211	3.79
2006	NYY-A	17	11	0.607	33	33	2	0	0	205	194	125	28	172	5.00
2007	ARI-N	4	3	0.571	10	10	0	0	0	56	52	26	7	72	3.81
2008	Ari-N	11	10	0.524	30	30	2	0	0	184	184	92	24	173	3.91
2009	SFG-N	8	6	0.571	22	17	0	0	0	96	97	55	19	86	4.88
TOTAL	22	303	166	0.646	618	603	100	37	2	4135	3346	1703	411	4875	3.29

Box Score of 300th Win

R. Johnson Baseball Almanac Box Score									
San Francisco Giants 5, Washington Nationals 1									
Game played on Thursday, June 4, 2009									
San Francisco	**ab**	**r**	**h**	**rbi**	**Washington**	**ab**	**r**	**h**	**rbi**
Rowand cf	4	1	1	0	Gonzales ss	4	1	0	0
Renteria ss	4	1	1	0	Johnson 1b	2	0	1	1
Winn rf	4	1	1	2	R Zimmerman 3b	3	0	0	0
Molina c	4	0	1	0	Dunn lf	4	0	0	0
Lewis lf	3	1	1	0	Dukes cf	4	0	1	0
a-Sandoval ph 1b	0	0	0	1	Kearns rf	3	0	0	0
Ishikawa	3	1	1	0	Belliard 2b	4	0	1	0
b-Torres ph lf	1	0	0	0	Nieves c	4	0	1	0
Uribe 3b	4	0	0	1	J Zimmermann p	1	0	0	0
Burriss 2b	3	0	1	1	a-Hernandez ph	1	0	0	0
R Johnson p	2	0	0	0	Villone p	0	0	0	0
Medders p	1	0	0	0	MacDougal p	0	0	0	0
Affeldt p	0	0	0	0	b-Guzman ph	1	0	0	0
Wilson p	0	0	0	0	Hanrahan p	0	0	0	0
Totals	33	5	7	5	Beimel p	0	0	0	0
					Totals	31	1	4	1

San Francisco	0	2	0		0	0	0		0	0	3	–	5
Washington	0	0	0		0	0	1		0	0	0	–	1

San Francisco Giants	IP	H	R	ER	BB	SO	HR
Ra Johnson (W, 5-4)	6.0	2	1	0	2	2	0
Medders (H, 3)	1.0	1	0	0	0	2	0
Affeldt (H, 13)	0.2	0	0	0	1	0	0
Wilson (S, 13)	1.1	1	0	0	1	4	0
Totals	9.0	4	1	0	4	8	0
Washington Nationals	**IP**	**H**	**R**	**ER**	**BB**	**SO**	**HR**
J Zimmermann (L, 2-3)	6.0	3	2	2	0	7	0
Villone	1.0	0	0	0	0	1	0
MacDougal	1.0	0	0	0	0	1	0
Hanrahan	0.0	4	3	3	0	0	0
Beimel	1.0	0	0	0	0	0	0
Totals	9.0	7	5	5	0	9	0

San Francisco:
a-hit sacrifice fly to center for Lewis in the 9th.
b-flied out to center for Ishikawa in the 9th.
Washington:
a-grounded to pitcher for J Zimmermann in the 6th.
b-flied out to center for MacDougal in the 8th.
2B–San Francisco Ishikawa (4, J Zimmermann); Renteria (8,Hanrahan); Winn (Hanrahan), Washington N. Johnson (8 R Johnson). **SF**-Sandoval. **RBI**–San Francisco Uribe (10), Burriss (12), Winn 2 (23), Sandoval (21) Washington Johnson (27). **GIDP**-Washington Belliard. RISP-Washington 0-5 (Belliard 0-1, Nieves 0-1, R Zimmerman 0-1, Dunn 0-2). LOB- San Francisco 2; Washington 7.
T-2:30

By a Nose

Early Wynn – 300 Wins

Early Wynn pitched more innings and struck out more hitters than any pitcher who worked during the decade of the 1950s. But he still needed eight tries to push his way into the 300 Club.

Two things hurt him: wearing a Washington Senators' uniform for the first eight years of his major-league career, and periodic attacks of gout, a painful disease that plagued him from 1951 through the end of his career in 1963.

One of the few men to play in four decades, Wynn was 16 when he signed his first professional contract after walking into a Senators' tryout camp in Florida. Since Washington always seemed to be searching for pitching, scout Clyde Milan offered Wynn a contract. He spent five years in the minor leagues, pitching to American League hitters only for a three-game trial at age 19 in 1939. He did not win his first American League game until 1941.

Armed with only a one-pitch arsenal, Wynn found that even a flaming fastball could not compensate for a weak supporting cast. He went 77-87 for the Senators over six full seasons, with a year-and-a-half interruption caused by World War II. He also suffered his most severe setback when his wife, Mabel, died in an auto accident, leaving the 21-year-old pitcher with an infant son. Wynn, who later re-married, somehow managed to focus on baseball.

Early Wynn

Photo courtesy of National
Baseball Hall of Fame Library
Cooperstown, N.Y.

In 1948, Wynn did anything but personify his last name. He posted the most losses and worst earned run average of his career, finishing 8-19 with a 5.82 ERA.

Meanwhile, the Cleveland Indians were enjoying a championship season.

Bill Veeck, the eccentric Indians owner, wanted to keep his club ahead of the Yankees and Red Sox and thought Wynn would benefit from the better support he'd receive in Cleveland. But he also knew that conservative Washington Senators owner Clark Griffith disdained Veeck's penchant for publicity stunts, gimmicks, and outspoken comments about baseball.

Veeck knew he could acquire Joe Haynes, a sore-armed White Sox pitcher who also happened to be Griffith's son-in-law. Knowing Griffith wouldn't want his son-in-law playing for his team, Veeck obtained Haynes for catcher Joe Tipton. Griffith immediately dispatched his adopted nephew, Calvin, to negotiate a trade that would bring Haynes home to Washington.

The eventual deal sent Haynes, Eddie Robinson, and Ed Kleiman from the Indians to the Senators for Wynn and Mickey Vernon, a first baseman whom Veeck also coveted. As part of the agreement, Veeck said he'd pay for the surgery that Haynes required.

Veeck said he announced the trade at 4:45 a.m. because he didn't want to give Griffith time to change his mind.

While Haynes won 10 games in four years for Washington, Wynn won 163 for Cleveland and 59 more for Chicago, where his arrival helped the 1959 White Sox win their first pennant in 40 years. By that time, Veeck was the owner there, having left Cleveland for the St. Louis Browns before buying the White Sox.

The route Wynn took from walk-in at a Washington tryout camp to king of the hill was circuitous at best.

The son of an auto mechanic who dreamed of reaching the major leagues, Wynn picked cotton and worked various odd jobs, from peanut farmer to truck driver, while growing up in Hartford, Alabama. His hopes of playing professional football vanished when he broke his leg in high school. But baseball was another story. While visiting his aunt in Sanford, Florida, in 1937, Wynn went to the Senators' tryout camp and threw hard enough to win a contract that paid $100 a month and meal money of a dollar a day. That was big bucks for a farm boy who never finished high school.

Except for a 20-inning tryout with the 1939 Senators at age 19, Wynn wallowed in the minors for five years before reaching the majors to stay in 1941. He won three of four September decisions and crafted a 1.58 earned run average, persuading the Senators to make him a regular starter in the season that followed.

In 1942, he had more walks than strikeouts and, predictably, a losing record. A year later, he was 18-12 with a 2.91 earned run mark. In 1944, he kept the ERA respectable (3.38), but poor run support saddled him with an 8-17 record.

Ironically, he was in the military when Washington went to the final weekend of the season with a chance to win the 1945 American League pennant. He had winning records in both 1946, when he returned in the second half, and 1947 – even though he again had more walks than strikeouts. (Poor pitching control – wildness – plagued him throughout his career.) When the walks-to-strikeouts ratio grew to 2:1 in 1948, however, the won-lost record went with it (8-19), as did the patience of the Senators.

On December 14, they shipped Wynn westward, opening the door to immortality for the veteran right-hander.

Cleveland pitching coach Mel Harder, once a starter himself, convinced Wynn he could win by changing speeds and keeping batters off-balance. In addition to the changeup, Harder taught Wynn how to throw a slider, curveball, and even a knuckleball.

"He showed me how to improve my grip on the delivery of the curveball, and also encouraged me to throw the knuckleball," Wynn said years later.

Harder's advice took root, as Wynn blossomed into a consistent 20-game winner within two years. From 1950-56, Wynn won at least 20 games four times, 18 once, and 17 twice. He also teamed with Bob Lemon, Bob Feller, and Mike Garcia to give the Indians one of the most formidable foursomes in baseball history. During their seven seasons together, Lemon won 20 five times, Wynn three times, Garcia twice, and Feller once.

During his Cleveland tenure, Wynn led the American League in ERA (1950) and strikeouts (1957) and made the All-Star team three years in a row (1955-57). He won another strikeout crown with the White Sox (1958) and had the most wins a year later, when his 22-win season for a championship club earned the only Cy Young Award of his career. Wynn also made the All-Star team in his first three Chicago summers (1958-60).

A tough guy who intimidated hitters with a scowling countenance and a feared brushback pitch, Wynn blamed poor run support for his failure to win 300 much sooner. He might have been right: he finished on the wrong end of shutouts 45 times, mostly during his time with the Senators.

He had only 83 wins (and 94 losses) at age 30, but managed to win 217 more. He had 188 wins in the 1950s and more strikeouts (1,544) than any other pitcher of that decade. Wynn's bat helped him win: The switch-hitting pitcher pounded 17 home runs, collected 173 runs batted in, and made 90 appearances as a pinch-hitter during a career that lasted 23 seasons, longer than any other pitcher who worked exclusively in the American League. He was the only pitcher to both hit and give up a pinch-hit grand slam. Wynn connected against Detroit's Johnny Corsica in 1946 – a rare highlight of his nondescript tenure in the nation's capital – but returned the favor when Bob Cerv of the Yankees tagged him in 1961.

Known for his glowering demeanor on the mound, Wynn was one-quarter Cherokee, and always seemed to be on the proverbial warpath. He made no bones about his love for pitching inside, using the knockdown as a means of intimidation.

"You weren't about to scare the great ones, like (Ted) Williams or (Joe) DiMaggio," he once said, "but some of the others looked for your message and didn't like the ball high and tight any more than I did those shots through the (pitcher's) box."

Nicknamed Gus after a scowling cartoon character called Gloomy Gus, Wynn called the mound his "office" and came up with the preposterous concept of knocking down his grandmother if she dug in at the plate while batting against him.

"Wynn was a pretty tough pitcher," Casey Stengel once said. "He's got everybody in the league scared. He knows just about all there is to know about pitching."

Joe DiMaggio, a lifelong Yankee who completed his career under Stengel, said Wynn was the man who forced him to end his 13-year career after the 1951 campaign. "He found out I was no longer able to hit the high inside fastball," DiMaggio revealed after his retirement. "When I broke my left collarbone, I wasn't able to bring my arm around high enough to be ready for the tight pitch. In my younger days, I could murder the high inside hummer. I'd drive it to deep center or maybe right-center. A pitcher wouldn't dare throw it there because he knew there was a good chance I'd pickle it.

"I didn't tell anybody, not even our trainer, that I couldn't come all the way around. Pitchers wouldn't throw high and inside to me on purpose, but Wynn threw one and then another. I couldn't just stand there and he saw my grinding swing. It didn't take more than a week for the word to get around the American League. They all had me pegged and I was dead."

Wynn won 20 for the first time in 1951, helping the Indians finish second to the Yankees, and won a career-high 23 a year later, when the runner-up Indians narrowed the gap to two games. The Indians were second again in 1953 before their pitching prowess reached full flower in 1954. With a league-leading 23 wins from both Wynn and Lemon, Cleveland won 111 of its 154 games, good for an eight-game bulge over New York.

Though the Indians were heavily favored, Wynn didn't win a game in the 1954 World Series. Neither did Lemon or Garcia. The three pitchers, who had shared Cleveland's Man of the Year when all three were 20-game winners in 1951, came up empty against Leo Durocher's Giants. Lemon lost the first and last games.

"We won the pennant a couple of weeks before the season ended," Wynn said after suffering a 3-1 defeat in Game 2 of the World Series against the New York Giants. "I think we had a big letdown."

Wynn pitched well while Cleveland spent the next two seasons in its traditional runner-up spot, but both pitcher and team slipped under .500 in 1957, prompting the club to contemplate changes.

On December 4, 1957, Wynn was traded to the White Sox, along with Al Smith, for Minnie Minoso and Fred Hatfield. Al Lopez, who had managed Wynn in Cleveland, moved to the White Sox dugout earlier that season and wanted the burly right-hander on his pitching staff.

Although he won 14 games for the second straight season, Wynn still lost more often than he won. But he led the league in strikeouts, becoming the first pitcher to win consecutive strikeout crowns while working for different teams.

The White Sox finished second in 1958, then won their first pennant in 40 years when Wynn, at 39, surprised the world with one of his best seasons. Including a 1-0 one-hitter over the Red Sox that he won with a home run, Wynn led the American League in wins and innings pitched. He finished at 22-10 with a 3.17 ERA – good enough to win his only Cy Young Award – and blanked the Los Angeles Dodgers, 11-0, in the World Series opener. With a Series victory under his ever-expanding belt, Wynn had only one milestone in his sights: 300 wins.

Routed in the sixth and deciding game of the 1959 Series, the pitcher dropped to 13 wins in 1960, then eight in an injury-riddled 1961 season, before bottoming out with a 7-15 record, 4.46 ERA, and bad elbow at age 42. After watching Wynn yield more hits than innings pitched in 1962, the Sox had to weigh their options. Could they release a pitcher with 299 career victories?

After soul-searching by a front office afraid to offend its fans, the White Sox dropped Wynn from the roster, but the pitcher received an invitation to spring training and the promise of fulfilling his quest for 300. He pitched well, but his age, girth, and compromised health convinced the Sox to cut ties for good on April 2, 1963, just after Wynn had worked four scoreless innings in an exhibition game.

Nearly three months passed before anyone agreed to add an overweight pitcher to its staff, albeit a pitcher whose ambition possibly could overcome his declining health. It was Wynn's old club, the Cleveland Indians.

After watching him work out for two weeks, the Indians signed Wynn on June 21, 1963. He worked only 55 innings for the Indians in his final summer, but five of those innings came the night he won his 300th game.

Wynn, who changed his diet to enhance his chances to win 300, had been chasing the milestone with all the fury and frustration of a dog chasing its tail. While still with Chicago, he had finished on the short end of a 1-0 no-hitter by Boston's Bill Monbouquette.

"I pitched a dozen or so where I came close," Wynn said years later, when he was broadcasting games for the Toronto Blue Jays. "Joe Pepitone, who didn't hit me too well, hit a home run to beat me. Then Elston Howard hit one into the right-center field stands that beat me in Chicago after I was ahead.

"Luis Aparicio, of all people, made an error in the ninth inning one day, allowing the game to get tied, and it went 11 (innings) before I lost it. I was supposed to pitch in Washington but we bypassed that – I didn't pitch for seven or eight days so I could win the 300th in Chicago. All my friends flew up from Florida, but somebody dropped a line drive in left field."

Donning a Cleveland uniform again didn't prove to be an instant elixir. Ron Hansen homered in the ninth to beat him, 2-0, in his first game with the 1963 Indians. He was also on the wrong end of another shutout, losing 3-0 to the White Sox in a game that Wynn desperately wanted to win.

Finally, on July 13, he captured the big one. Starting the second half of a doubleheader in Kansas City, the 43-year-old pitcher staggered through five innings, trusting roommate Jerry Walker to preserve his 5-4 lead over the Athletics, and had time to shower, change, and make it up to the broadcast booth in time for a post-game interview.

"I never slept last night," he told the radio audience after Walker wrapped up the victory. "The gout was killing me."

Returning to the Cleveland clubhouse, Wynn went straight to Walker and said, "Attaboy, roomie. We kept it in the room. Tomorrow we'll get a Cadillac and we'll both drive it."

Popular and jocular in the locker room, Wynn went to each cubicle, accepting handshakes and congratulations, plus the game ball from catcher John (Honey) Romano.

Wynn said his 300th win was satisfying for several reasons.

"I felt I had it coming to me after pitching so well for so long and losing so many tough ones," said the pitcher, whose career record included 49 shutouts. "I thought I'd never win it. I made about seven or eight starts and was even used in relief, but somehow it always escaped me. I was even ready to give up but Lefty Grove, who won 300 himself, urged me to keep trying. That figure 300 seems to be something special and now that I have it, it is."

Ironically for Wynn, who wanted to celebrate the elusive milestone, his 300th win came on a Sunday – getaway day for the Indians, who flew to Minnesota immediately after the doubleheader in Kansas City.

"They had some sort of blue law in Minnesota that closed all the bars and liquor stores," he said. "If ever there was a time a guy wanted to celebrate something over a couple of beers, that was it. I had waited so long to win my 300th game and I had to wait an extra day to celebrate."

No. 300 was the last win for Wynn, whose 20 appearances for the 1963 Indians included 15 relief outings. He later said he could have lasted longer. "I was throwing harder as [Cleveland's] pitching coach than I did in 1962 or 1963," he said. "I probably could have pitched two or three more years."

Had he not lost a year-and-a-half to wartime Army duty at the peak of his career, Wynn wouldn't have had to struggle. Gabriel Schechter, a library associate at the Baseball Hall of Fame, wrote in 2009 that Wynn projected to 319 victories with his service time factored out.

Such mathematics might have made it easier for Cooperstown to welcome Wynn. Unable to get the required 75 percent of the vote in his first three tries, the outspoken pitcher was vocal in his disbelief. "Hall of Fame?" he said. "Hell, it's a Hall of Shame. I should have been voted in three years ago."

An eight-time All-Star who won the 1958 game and was the starting pitcher a year later, Wynn pitched more seasons (23) than anyone else who worked exclusively in the American League. He also walked more batters (1,775), though he was so adept at escaping jams that he led the league in innings pitched three times.

Never forgetting that he once lifted heavy bales of cotton for 10 cents an hour, Wynn spent hours of his own time trying to increase pensions and benefits for current and former players. A pioneer in the field of players' rights, he retired long before the advent of the players' union and free agency.

"I don't recall ever making big money," he said years after he left the game. "In 1953, I won 18 games and the general manager tried to cut me 25 percent. I wasn't asking for big money; I was more or less trying to maintain the mediocre salary I was making the year before. We didn't have agents. Back then, if you came into the office with an agent, they closed the door on you."

Wynn, whose 1972 election to the Baseball Hall of Fame coincided with a short-lived player strike, supplemented his baseball salary by owning a construction company, bowling alley, and steakhouse near Tampa, where he spent his winters fishing, cooking, flying an airplane, and piloting his own boat. He was all business, off the mound and on – even insisting on staying in a game after a Jose Valdivielso line drive to the chin cost him seven teeth and 16 stitches.

That was one argument that he lost. But he didn't lose many.

"I didn't like losing a ballgame any more than a salesman liked losing a sale," he said. "I had a right to knock down anybody holding a bat."

Box Score of 300th Win

Wynn Baseball Almanac Box Score
Cleveland Indians 7, Kansas City Athletics 4

Game played on Saturday, July 13, 1963, at Municipal Stadium

Cleveland Indians	ab	r	h	rbi	Kansas City Athletics	ab	r	h	rbi
Francona lf	5	0	1	0	Tartabull cf	5	1	1	0
Tasby lf	0	0	0	0	Causey ss	5	0	0	0
Howser ss	5	1	2	0	Lumpe 2b	4	0	1	3
Kirkland cf	5	2	1	0	Alusik rf	3	1	1	1
Alvis 3b	4	1	0	0	Lau c	3	0	1	0
Adcock 1b	4	1	1	3	Charles 3b	2	0	1	0
Romano c	3	1	2	1	Essegian lf	4	0	0	0
Luplow rf	2	0	2	2	Harrelson 1b	3	1	2	0
Brown 2b	4	0	1	1	Drabowsky p	1	0	1	0
Wynn p	2	1	1	0	Willis p	0	0	0	0
Held ph	1	0	1	0	Cimoli ph	1	0	1	0
Walker p	0	0	0	0	La Russa pr	0	1	0	0
Totals	35	7	12	7	Fischer p	0	0	0	0
					Siebern ph	1	0	0	0
					Lovrich p	0	0	0	0
					Edwards ph	1	0	0	0
					Totals	33	4	9	4

Cleveland	0	1	0		0	4	0		1	0	1	–	7	12	0
Kansas City	0	0	0		1	3	0		0	0	0	–	4	9	1

Cleveland Indians	IP	H	R	ER	BB	SO
Wynn W (1-1)	5.0	6	4	4	3	3
Walker SV (1)	4.0	3	0	0	2	2
Totals	9.0	9	4	4	5	5

Kansas City Athletics	IP	H	R	ER	BB	SO
Drabowsky L (0-6)	4.2	6	5	5	5	5
Willis	0.1	1	0	0	0	0
Fischer	1.0	2	0	0	0	0
Lovrich	3.0	3	2	1	1	1
Totals	9.0	12	7	6	6	6

E–Harrelson (6). DP–Kansas City 1. 2B–Cleveland Held (13,off Fischer), Kansas City Lumpe (16,off Wynn); Lau (4,off Walker). 3B–Cleveland Kirkland (1,off Lovrich). HR–Kansas City Alusik (8,4th inning off Wynn 0 on, 0 out). SF–Adcock (1,off Lovrich). Team LOB–8. Team–7. SB–Kirkland (3,2nd base off Lovrich/Lau). CS–Howser (3,2nd base by Drabowsky/Lau); Alusik (1,2nd base by Wynn/Romano). U-HP–Larry Napp, 1B–Bill Kinnamon, 2B–Frank Umont, 3B–Johnny Stevens. T–2:42. A–13,565.

Career Statistics

WYNN, Early	Early "Gus" Wynn; B: 1-6-1920, Hartford, AL; D: 4/4/1999, Venice, FL; BB/TR, 6'/200 lbs.; Debut: 9/13/1939; HOF 1972

YEAR	TM-L	W	L	PCT	G	GS	CG	SH	SV	IP	H	R	HR	SO	ERA
1939	Was-A	0	2	0.000	3	3	1	0	0	20	26	15	0	1	5.75
1941	Was-A	3	1	0.750	5	5	4	0	0	40	35	14	1	15	1.58
1942	Was-A	10	16	0.385	30	28	10	1	0	190	246	129	6	58	5.12
1943	Was-A	18	12	0.600	37	33	12	3	0	256	232	97	15	89	2.91
1944	Was-A	8	17	0.320	33	25	19	2	2	207	221	97	3	65	3.38
1946	Was-A	8	5	0.615	17	12	9	0	0	107	112	45	8	36	3.11
1947	Was-A	17	15	0.531	33	31	22	2	0	247	251	114	13	73	3.64
1948	Was-A	8	19	0.296	33	31	15	1	0	198	236	144	18	49	5.82
1949	Cle-A	11	7	0.611	26	23	6	0	0	164	186	84	8	62	4.15
1950	Cle-A	18	8	0.692	32	28	14	2	0	213	166	88	20	143	3.20
1951	Cle-A	20	13	0.606	37	34	21	3	1	274	227	102	18	133	3.02
1952	Cle-A	23	12	0.657	42	33	19	4	3	285	239	103	23	153	2.90
1953	Cle-A	17	12	0.586	36	34	16	1	0	251	234	121	19	138	3.93
1954	Cle-A	23	11	0.676	40	36	20	3	2	270	225	93	21	155	2.73
1955	Cle-A	17	11	0.607	32	31	16	6	0	230	207	86	19	122	2.82
1956	Cle-A	20	9	0.690	38	35	18	4	2	277	233	93	19	158	2.72
1957	Cle-A	14	17	0.452	40	37	13	1	1	263	270	139	32	184	4.31
1958	Chi-A	14	16	0.467	40	34	11	4	2	239	214	115	27	179	4.13
1959	Chi-A	22	10	0.688	37	37	14	5	0	255	202	106	20	179	3.17
1960	Chi-A	13	12	0.520	36	35	13	4	1	237	220	105	20	158	3.49
1961	Chi-A	8	2	0.800	17	16	5	0	0	110	88	43	11	64	3.51
1962	Chi-A	7	15	0.318	27	26	11	3	0	167	171	90	15	91	4.46
1963	Cle-A	1	2	0.333	20	5	1	0	1	55	50	14	2	29	2.28
TOTAL	23	300	244	0.551	691	612	290	49	15	4564	4291	2037	338	2334	3.54

Almost, But Not Quite

Tommy John – 288 Wins

Bert Blyleven – 287 Wins

Robin Roberts – 286 Wins

Ferguson Jenkins – 284 Wins

Jim Kaat – 283 Wins

If Tommy John hadn't had Tommy John surgery, he would have won 300 games.

If Bert Blyleven and Robin Roberts hadn't pitched for bad teams, they would have won 300.

If bullpen duty hadn't claimed Fergie Jenkins early in his career and Jim Kaat late in his, they would also be members of the 300 Club.

Baseball is a game of what-ifs, especially in making seemingly arbitrary decisions about who achieves fame and immortality.

All eligible 300-game winners have been elected to the Hall of Fame, along with many pitchers who didn't win that many. Roberts and Jenkins are in the Hall, but Blyleven, John, and Kaat are still knocking on the door. Only a handful of games – perhaps reachable in a single season – have made the difference up to this point.

Tommy John played in the majors for 26 years, one short of Nolan Ryan's record, but stopped a dozen wins short of 300.

"I definitely wanted to get there," he said, "but nobody would sign me. I sent tapes to the Cardinals and the Orioles, telling them I would start or relieve. (St. Louis manager) Whitey Herzog told me he really wanted me. But (general manager) Dal Maxvill said, 'Why would you want an old guy like that when we can utilize the younger pitchers from our organization?'

"Whitey thought I would do well because I was a sinkerball pitcher and old Busch Stadium was a huge ballpark. The Cardinals had Ozzie Smith, Terry Pendleton, Jose Oquendo, Willie McGee, and Andy Van Slyke – guys who could track balls down. Whitey told me, 'I could see you being another John Tudor type of guy, coming in and giving us six or seven innings per game.'

"I would have loved to pitch for the Cardinals because they're close to home (Terre Haute, Indiana) and my mom and dad could have seen me play."

Baltimore Orioles manager Frank Robinson never responded to his tapes, John said, and his career was over.

What if he hadn't missed a year as the guinea pig for elbow ligament transplant surgery? "Dr. (Frank) Jobe told me if I didn't have it I would never pitch in the major leagues again," John said. "He said I could throw batting practice to kids but that would be it. I didn't think I was done and wanted to play. I didn't know how difficult the surgery would be but said, 'Get it on.' I had the operation in September and then pitched in a game one year and one day after surgery. I started seven games in 28 days and knew I was okay."

John said the best game of his career came against future 300-game winner Steve Carlton in 1977, three years after the pioneering operation. "I beat the Phillies in a driving rainstorm at Veterans Stadium," said John, who then pitched for the Dodgers. "It poured from the first pitch I threw right to the end. The score was 4-1 but I never would have been allowed to finish it now – the closer would have pitched the ninth inning. But that was my game and why would I want somebody to come in and screw it up?

"Earlier that year, we were in San Francisco with two outs in the bottom of the ninth and Willie McCovey coming up. (Dodgers manager) Tommy Lasorda came out and asked me how I felt. I said, 'Tommy, do you want to win the championship?' He said, 'Yeah.' I said, 'You better get somebody in here because I don't think I have enough left to get him out.'"

A new pitcher came in, threw four sliders, and we clinched the division title. "I knew my stuff had left and was smart enough to figure that out," John said, "but if I still had it, as in the Carlton game, there was no way I wouldn't finish.

"Today, the game has evolved so much, with so much notoriety on set-up men and closers, that it is virtually impossible for any starter to go past seven (innings) anymore."

John threw 167 complete games, a total that will elude virtually all active pitchers. One of them came against Tom Seaver at Shea Stadium.

"It was a Sunday afternoon and I was warming up in the visitors' bullpen during the first inning – on the road, I always warmed up in the first because I didn't like a long sit-down time," he said. "Steve Garvey hit a home run off Seaver that inning so when I got to the mound, somebody said, 'There's your run. Now hold 'em.' That was all I got. I won the game, 1-0."

John also won a bet in a game he started against Nolan Ryan. "He was pitching for the Angels and I was pitching for the Dodgers in a Freeway Series exhibition game. We're in a National League ballpark, Dodger Stadium, and playing by NL rules. So I made a statement in the clubhouse: 'Here's our bet for the day: I'm going to strike out more guys in my seven innings than Nolan will in the same seven.'

"I knew that was a pretty good bet because Nolan had to bat and I knew I could strike him out two or three times. They had four left-handed batters and I knew I could get each of those four guys at least once, and maybe one of them twice, and then somebody else in the lineup once or twice. So I figured I'd get nine strikeouts. That is exactly what happened – and Nolan had eight in the first seven innings. He struck out the last six, for a total of 14, but I still won the bet. I ate free on the road lots of times that year because I was collecting my bets."

John won one fewer game after returning from surgery than Sandy Koufax won in his whole career. Yet Koufax, whose arthritic elbow forced his premature retirement, is in the Hall of Fame. "He struck out a lot of guys and his wins were more spectacular," John said, "but a win is a win. And the other thing I think tips the scales for me is the surgery itself. There are guys I played with and against who saw me pitch and know how well I did. Just look at the record."

Bert Blyleven is in the same boat. "Sometimes guys get overlooked," said Blyleven, who has spent the past 13 years broadcasting games for the Minnesota Twins. "It took Jim Rice 15 years to get in. He must have hit a lot of home runs his last year."

A right-hander whose 242 complete games included 60 shutouts, Blyleven lost his bid for 300 wins by pitching for teams that failed to back him with much run support.

"If you follow the game, you know how difficult it is for a pitcher to win," he said. "Everything has to go your way. I lost 250 games in my career but a lot of them were close. If I lost 1-0, I thought it was my fault. It made me work harder."

Blyleven had a record 20 no-decisions in 1979 and had more 1-0 victories than anyone not named Grover Cleveland Alexander, Walter Johnson, or Greg Maddux. His best years were 1979, when he pitched for Pittsburgh, and 1987, with Minnesota. Both teams won world championships.

"I was hoping to pitch 5,000 innings but ended up 30 innings short," he said. "I wanted 4,000 strikeouts and wanted more shutouts.

I figured if I reached those goals, the wins would come. I knew I was 13 short of 300 but I include my Little League wins, so I'm well over 300 anyway. I went as far as my body could take me. When my mind and body told me I couldn't go nine anymore, I knew it was time to go do something else."

Kaat was among the most influential people in his career, along with Jim Perry, Luis Tiant, and Dave Boswell. "I was young (19) when I came up," he said. "Those guys helped me so much. Their leadership enabled me to look further down and see if I could help someone someday. Back then, if you played four or five years, you felt very fortunate. I played as long as I did because of the foundation I had."

Blyleven was a workhorse who liked to finish what he started. "I looked at going to the mound as an 8-to-5 job," he said. "I didn't work from 8-to-1. I don't believe quality starts are what they say now: six innings and three earned runs or less. To me, a quality start is seven innings and two runs or less. I'm glad I pitched in the era I did, when going the distance meant something to a ball club. Anytime a pitcher can go nine, it helps the next day's starter and bullpen."

Bad ball clubs didn't faze the Netherlands native, one of three pitchers to win a game before his 20th birthday and after his 40th. "I never looked at teams as bad," he said. "Maybe we didn't have the talent other teams did but once you play at the major-league level, there's never a bad team. There are teams that are just better.

"I actually got great run support when I won 19 games for the 1984 Cleveland Indians. Sometimes you get those types of years and sometimes you get no support. Every pitcher would like to be Rick Sutcliffe or Rick Rhoden. When they walked out there, they had runs on their back. Frank Viola was the same way in 1988."

Like Blyleven, Robin Roberts was often the only star in a dark firmament. He still managed to post six 20-win seasons and make the All-Star team seven times.

"I thought I would pitch until I was 45," he said. "I had a good delivery. But I ran into a little arm problem at the end of my career and wasn't able to go out there and pitch regularly, which I tried to do. But if I had made it til age 45, I knew I'd reach 300."

Roberts recalled that *The Sporting News* started speculating about his joining the 300 club after he reached 280 wins. But neither the pitcher nor the publication realized he'd win only six more games.

"I just wanted to keep pitching," said the long-time Philadelphia star. "I wasn't very good at planning (what I'd do) after my career because I didn't know when it was going to end. I just thought I would pitch a little longer than I did."

The star pitcher for the 1950 Whiz Kids team that went to the World Series, Roberts said his career highlight came early. "Starting my very first ballgame was the biggest thrill I ever had," he said. "I was only in the minor leagues two months so it was quite a thrill to be a major-leaguer. That first game was exceptional.

"I also remember the game against Brooklyn on the last day of the 1950 season when Richie Ashburn threw out the potential winning run at home and Dick Sisler hit a three-run homer in the 10th to win it. We won the pennant and the Phillies hadn't done that for a long time."

Roberts once had a 28-7 season that featured 21 wins in his last 23 starts. "I never thought about winning 30," he said. "I was just going out there one day at a time. It added up to 28 at the end."

The right-hander who twice topped 30 complete games said pitchers can still go all the way. "It depends upon their delivery and how they're pitching," he said. "When a guy has a real good game going and seems to be throwing effortlessly, he should stay in. It's no big deal for somebody to go nine when he's really in charge out there."

Roberts might have missed the 300 Club because of an abysmal season with the forlorn Phillies of 1961. He finished 1-10 for a winning percentage not much worse than the team's. "I was pitching bad and we weren't much of a club," he remembered. "We came in last. I bounced back the next season and joined the Orioles in late May. I won 14 one year and 13 another year. I pitched well with the

Orioles and was on a good club. Then I finished with Houston and the Cubs."

Ferguson Jenkins had considerably more success in Chicago. In fact, he gave the Cubs six straight 20-win seasons from 1967-72, winning the National League's Cy Young Award in 1971 and finishing second in 1967. Jenkins later finished second in voting for the American League's Cy Young Award, following his career-best 25 wins for the 1974 Texas Rangers.

Spending his rookie year in the bullpen probably prevented the workhorse right-hander from winning 300.

"I thought about winning 300 for quite a few years," he said, "and was hoping to have that chance with the Cubs. I went to spring training with them in 1984 at the invitation of Dallas Green. There were 15 younger pitchers and me. It came down to a numbers crunch. I pitched only three innings and did fairly well but they wanted some of the younger guys to get a better shot. I decided it was time to retire."

Jenkins became a contender for 300 wins because he pitched in a four-man rotation in 11 of his 18 full seasons. "I enjoyed it," said the 6'5" Jenkins. "I was ready to pitch every three days. There were even times when I pitched three times in a week: Monday, Thursday, and Sunday. That's unheard-of now."

Complete games are also on the decline. "The category of complete games is pretty well forgotten now," said Jenkins, who pitched for the Cubs, Rangers, Red Sox, Rangers again, and Cubs again. "They're trying to protect young men's arms so they don't run into serious problems. But some guys are just getting loose after 100 pitches.

"Sometimes I threw 150, 160 pitches to win a ballgame in nine innings. I just think to get to the 300-win level, a pitcher has to stay in a game longer and have more control so that when he does give it over to a relief pitcher, maybe the score is 3-1 or 4-1 – the run span is a little better so maybe the starter doesn't lose even if the reliever gives up any runs."

Jenkins is among those who think the days of 300-game winners are numbered. "Randy Johnson may be the last," he said. "Because of the situation of not having run production and the age factor, unless somebody really comes along and puts a lot of 20-win seasons together, Randy might be the last. You have to put up some big numbers."

Jim Kaat won only one fewer game than Jenkins, but hasn't won a ticket to Cooperstown. Spending his last six years in the bullpen almost certainly short-circuited his chances for 300 wins.

"I'm pretty sure I would have made it," said the left-hander, who had his best years with the Minnesota Twins and Chicago White Sox. "And 300 wins is an automatic trigger for the Hall of Fame."

Going to the bullpen was the idea of St. Louis manager Whitey Herzog, who wanted a situational left-hander for the late innings.

"I hadn't started a game in about two years but Whitey gave me the ball one day and I beat the Mets, 1-0, in 10 innings," said Kaat. "I felt like I could still start. Pitching out of the bullpen was a fun thing because we won a World Series but I knew my chances of getting to 300 were pretty much done."

Kaat kept trying, though. In 1984, he went to spring training with the Pittsburgh Pirates. "My career was over but Chuck Tanner and Pete Peterson said they thought I could still pitch," he said. "I had a pretty good spring and thought I could still help some teams out of the bullpen. But when you're 45 and they have young prospects they want to look at, your chances are pretty slim. I wanted to give it one last fling and it was fun anyway."

Unlike most of his colleagues, Kaat was a well-rounded pitcher skilled at hitting, fielding, and base running. "I was a baseball player who just happened to be a pitcher," said Kaat, who won 16 Gold Gloves. "I liked to run, I liked to field, I liked to hit, I liked to do everything. With the DH (designated hitter), those skills have been taken away from the pitcher."

Kaat did his best work when Johnny Sain was his pitching coach, in both Minnesota and Chicago. "My dad was the most influential as far as my interest in baseball – he kept my head screwed on straight and pointed me in the right direction. As far as helping me, Johnny was the best," Kaat said. "If I had pitched as well during the rest of my career as I did under Johnny for four years (1965-66 and 1974-75), I might have won 400 games."

Warren Spahn, another left-hander who liked to deceive hitters, once gave the young Kaat a piece of invaluable advice: "To give you an idea how much the game has changed, his parting words to me were, 'Kid, when the game's tied in the seventh inning, the game is just starting.' His theory was pitchers should be able to close games out and pitch the last three innings."

Although Kaat pitched at least 15 complete games in four different seasons, he knows the game has changed. "A starter with a comfortable lead should be able to pitch nine innings and give the bullpen a rest. It's not that they're incapable of doing that, but that the game has become more specialized. Pitchers are trained differently."

Like other pitchers of his generation, Kaat disdains pitch counts. "I don't know why they exist," he said. "Anybody who knows anything about pitching knows there are days when you might throw 50 pitches and nothing feels right. Then there are days when you could go out there and pitch all day. The ball's coming out of your hand nicely and you're free and easy. So pitch counts don't have any relevance in terms of a pitcher getting tired or getting hurt. There's no way you can use that as a barometer."

Because pitch counts and reliance on relievers reduce the win totals of starters, Kaat considers the 300 Club closed.

"I don't think we'll see any more," he said. "What Greg Maddux, Roger Clemens, Tom Glavine, and Randy Johnson did in a five-man rotation has really been remarkable. The bar should now be 250 wins. Which means that Jack Morris should be in the Hall of Fame.

"I'm glad I pitched in a four-man rotation. I wouldn't have known what to do with myself with that extra day's rest."

Kaat called Al Kaline his toughest hitter, Sandy Koufax his toughest mound opponent, and Chuck Tanner his favorite manager. "He saved my career," Kaat said of Tanner, the manager of the Chicago White Sox when Kaat arrived from Minnesota in 1973.

It was also in Chicago that Kaat caught up with Sain, who had helped him with the Twins years earlier. "Johnny was able to get a little faster arm action by speeding up my release," Kaat said. "A quick pitch was illegal but I pitched quickly. It was a quick delivery."

Of the men who did make the 300 Club, Kaat said Maddux made the biggest impression. "He was not known as a power pitcher but he still piled up a huge number of wins," said Kaat. "What he was able to do over a long period of time without being a power pitcher was pretty phenomenal."

What Bob Feller did was pretty phenomenal, too.

"You never know, but I might have won 350 or 375 games if I hadn't been in the service," said Feller, who finished with 266 lifetime victories but missed four years because of wartime military service. "I was at the top of my career when the war broke out. But when there's a world war going on, sports becomes very insignificant.

"The only win that was important to me during World War II was the war. That's why I joined the Navy right after Pearl Harbor. Not that I am a hero – heroes don't come back from wars like that. Survivors return from wars. I am one of those survivors. I was just very lucky that there wasn't a bullet with my name on it when I was a gun captain on the U.S.S. Alabama."

Who's Next? Anybody?

Roy Halladay? CC Sabathia? Johann Santana? The identity of the next 300-game winner – if there's ever going to be one – is anybody's guess.

The only certainty is that no one is going to join the club in the next few years.

Jamie Moyer, who finished 2009 with 258 career victories, is 47 years old and fading. Andy Pettitte, who turns 38 in 2010, is too far away, with 229 wins, and is likely to follow the example of former Yankee teammate Mike Mussina, who retired with 270.

According to Bill James, writing in *The 2010 Baseball Handbook*, Halladay has the best chance, but he'll have to maintain a high performance level for years. At age 33, he has 148 career wins. James gives him a 33 percent chance of reaching 300.

Next on the list, at 23 percent, is Sabathia, who has 136 lifetime wins at age 28. But pitching in too many postseasons could reduce his regular-season effectiveness before he approaches the 300-win circle.

The favorable odds for Dan Haren, like Halladay an accomplished right-hander, are just 21 percent in the opinion of James, citing the 29-year-old pitcher's 79 career wins. Moyer is next at 20 percent, followed by Pettitte at 18 percent.

Only one other pitcher, Javier Vasquez, was given more than a 15 percent shot, James wrote. Vasquez has a 17 percent chance of reaching 300. The 33-year-old has 142 career wins.

Although Tim Wakefield should reach 200 victories in 2010, he's 43 and too far away, even though his best pitch – the knuckleball – puts little strain on his arm. He has no chance for 300, according to James, who also assigned zero odds to Livan Hernandez (156 wins at age 35) and Jon Garland (117 wins at age 30). Even Kevin Millwood, with 155 wins at age 35, and Roy Oswalt, with 137 at 32, have no better than a one percent chance.

Despite the long odds against virtually all players now in the majors, James concludes that "it is likely that one or two pitchers now active will eventually win 300 games."

Few of the pitchers who did it agree.

"It takes 15 wins a year for 20 years to win 300 games or 20 wins for 15 years," Don Sutton said. "More and more pitchers are coming out prior to the decision of a ballgame. People in baseball seem content to use more pitchers, pay more money, and get less out of their investment.

"I don't think anyone else will win 300. Pitchers don't go nine innings because the environment does not encourage it. We glorify 200 innings pitched and a 4.50 earned run average. That level of performance is not conducive to winning 300 games."

Sutton, who worked in a four-man rotation early in his career, once made 41 starts in a season. He also started 750 games without ever missing a turn.

"You can take the pitch counts and shove them."

"I have yet to see any statistical data that tells me somebody is going to fade away and become a scarecrow after 100 pitches," he said. "You can take the pitch counts and shove them. Johann Santana is not going to lose his stuff just because he threw 102 pitches. And Javier Vasquez is not going to turn into a pumpkin at 103 pitches. It is just an arbitrary measure that we're perpetuating because we talk about it all the time."

Like Sutton, Nolan Ryan started his career in an era when pitchers worked in four-man rotations and pitched more innings per start.

"Winning 300 is a bigger challenge today than it was for me," said Ryan, whose pitch count exceeded 200 in several games. "In Texas, we asked our pitchers to work deeper into games. We felt each time we went to the bullpen, we lessened our chances of being successful. If you go to the bullpen three or four times, there's a better chance one of those relievers won't be on that night. And the more you use them, the greater chance you have of wearing down the bullpen for the second half of the season."

Roger Clemens, who spent his youth watching Ryan pitch in Houston, knows longevity is the key to winning 300. "Staying healthy and having the will and desire to continue pitching are important," he said. "When I first got to the majors, I couldn't believe how many people smoked, not only in the clubhouse, on the team bus, and even in the tunnel (from the dugout to the clubhouse) between innings.

"There are so many other things that enter into winning 300. Like when you come out of games with the lead, head for the clubhouse, and all hell breaks loose on the field before you get there. You think, 'Now I understand why it was so difficult to get to that number.'"

According to Tom Glavine, "There are a lot of guys out there who you look at and say, 'Man, they have the talent to win 300 games.' If it was about talent alone, there would be a lot more 300-game winners than there are. But when you start breaking down how long you have to pitch to win 300 games, it comes down to about 20 years.

"In today's game, everything is about power. When I see the effort these guys put in, and the power they are pitching with, it seems next to impossible to me that any of them are going to be able to stay healthy long enough to do it."

The desire is there for most, he said. "I wish I had a dollar for every guy who said, 'Look, I am only going to play 10 years so I can get my pension' or 'I just want to play until I have a couple of good contracts and then I'm going home.' Guys get to that situation and realize they want to keep playing. They are financially sound for life but they realize how much they enjoy the game. You just want to play as long as somebody's going to give you a uniform."

Gaylord Perry, who was literally the "Ancient Mariner" when he won his 300th for Seattle, said pitchers have to pitch well past the usual baseball retirement age. "If a couple of guys played til 45, they could do it," he said, "but they usually don't play that long anymore. They make so much money now they don't need to."

Tom Seaver agrees. "If the system doesn't change, it doesn't look like there will be (any more 300-game winners)," said the three-time Cy Young Award winner. "If a pitcher has the capability of winning 300 games, he's going to have so much money that he's not going to stay when the going gets rough. Otherwise, he might have to go through a year when he's 8-12 or has some physical problem. Plus he'll have to deal with the pitch count and the manager's desire to use a set-up man and closer.

"I had a pitch count but it was self-imposed. My pitch count was 135, Jerry Koosman's was 145, and Nolan Ryan's was 155. It's different today. The corporate arm and the statisticians have come into the clubhouse. The way I look at it, why would you want to find a reason to take a Nolan Ryan out, a Roger Clemens out, or a Steve Carlton out? Instead of looking for a reason to take him out, you should be looking for a reason to leave him in."

Randy Johnson, the newest member of the 300 club, isn't sure he'll be the last.

"When I was in New York," he said, "I won 34 games (in two seasons). But I was still 40-odd games short of 300 so nobody was talking about it. I was already 41 at the time and then I had two back surgeries. So people didn't think I could do it, either."

Greg Maddux agrees that the door to the 300 club has been left ajar. "I think we'll have more members," he said. "When I won 300, I was asked if I was going to be the last. When Tom Glavine and Randy Johnson did it, they were asked the same question.

"This game has been going on for 100 years and will probably go on for another 500. As long as there's a United States, there's going to be baseball. We might even see someone hit 800 homers or maybe have a pitcher win 400 games."

Hall of Famer Robin Roberts, who had six 20-win seasons but still fell 14 short of 300 wins, thinks the 300 club is closed to new membership.

"It would be difficult at best," said the former Phillies standout. "Most of the guys who won 300 pitched with three days of rest and got five to seven more starts per season. Over a long career, that's a lot of additional ballgames.

"To win 300, you need a combination of things. You may be going good but your team may not be a real strong team. On the day you pitch, they have a feeling they're going to win and play like big-league ballplayers. But overall, the better the team, the easier it is."

Former pitcher Ralph Branca, who opened the 1947 World Series for the Brooklyn Dodgers, lists himself among the skeptics.

"It's never going to happen again," he said. "Not with people pitching every five days and getting 32 or 33 starts a year. You have to win 15 games for 20 years and nobody's going to last that long. They pitch five or six innings every five days. In my opinion, they don't throw enough and that's where sore arms and other problems come from."

Chipper Jones, the 2008 National League batting champion, also thinks 300-game winners are on the wane.

"It's going to be tough, especially in this day and age with the number of special pitchers they have and the late-inning relievers," Jones said. "There are a lot more chances for starting pitchers to get their good performances blown late in games because there aren't as many complete games as there were in the 1950s, '60s, or '70s.

"The common denominator of the 300-game winner is that you have to be able to pitch for 20 years or more. There aren't too many guys who pitch 20 years. To go out and be that productive for that long a period of time is a tremendous testament to whomever gets there."

Bobby Cox, in his 25th and final season as manager of the Atlanta Braves, is an expert on the subject of pitching and should be: He managed four 300-game winners in Maddux, Glavine, Phil Niekro, and Gaylord Perry.

"It's probably not going to happen," said Cox. "If I had to take a guess, I'd say no. A lot of the old guys did it on three days' rest. They had more starts and more complete games. Now the bullpens are pretty good (so managers don't mind using them) but in the old days, the guys in the bullpen weren't considered good enough to start."

Cox is positive nobody will replicate Warren Spahn's ability to win 20 games in 13 different seasons, all after World War II.

"Let me tell you," he said. "You can be the greatest pitcher in the world and pitch close to 20 years but you'll only win 20 once or twice. You have be very special yourself and be on very good teams."

Ironically, Cox was managing Toronto when Niekro beat the Blue Jays for his 300th win on the last day of the 1985 season. Since the Jays had clinched the American League East title two days earlier, Cox conceded he had mixed feelings about that game. He wanted his team to win but also wanted his former ace to win his 300th.

Years later, Cox had two future members of the 300 club on his team at once.

"Every manager should have that opportunity," he said of the Maddux-Glavine tandem. "Those guys didn't miss turns. They were always there to pitch. They were team guys, too, and would pitch on three days' rest when they had to, like the old-timers. To win a pennant, it's wonderful having those types of guys."

Dallas Green, a former pitcher who became a manager and general manager, had Steve Carlton as the backbone of the 1980 Phillies team that won a world championship. Like Cox, he doubts whether the 300 club will expand beyond its current 24 members.

"Baseball has changed so much," said Green. "Relief pitching is a major part of the game, managers look at the pitch count, and guys aren't logging the innings. They might leave with a lead but the bullpen can't always hold 'em. So I don't think we're going to have any more 300-game winners."

Mets broadcaster Keith Hernandez, who shared 1979 National League MVP honors with Willie Stargell, agreed.

"Unless something changes dramatically," said Hernandez, "I don't think there will be another 300-game winner. Guys used to start 36, 37, 38 games. But now you're talking 32. I do think, though, that starters should be able to pitch into the eighth inning. We're not going to change the pitch count, which is about money and saving arms, but pitchers could be more economical. If they get through seven innings with 100-110 pitches, they could turn it over to the set-up man and closer. That takes the burden off the bullpen."

Gary Matthews, who played left field in Steve Carlton's 300th win, also thinks the 300-game winner has gone the way of the brontosaurus.

"The guys aren't pitching the innings or staying in as long," said Matthews, a member of the Phillies broadcast team. "I can't think of any guys who are going to be close. Without the four-man rotation, pitchers are not throwing as many innings so they're not going to be big winners. Once a guy wins 15 games, that's considered pretty good – the way 20 wins used to be. And don't forget we were talking about 30-game winners at one time, too. So now winning 20 or 25 will be as rare as winning 30."

Houston Astros radio voice Milo Hamilton, behind a big-league mike since 1953, also predicts Randy Johnson will be the last member of the 300 Club.

"There's nobody with a good shot at it," said the 82-year-old Hamilton, a member of the Hall of Fame's broadcast wing. "With the five-man rotation, all the travel, guys getting hurt more often, there are too many ingredients that will keep anybody from winning 300 again.

"When the manager went to take out Warren Spahn, Spahnie would say, 'Who do you have down there that's better than me?' The Gibsons, Drysdales, and Spahns were there to pitch and finish what they started."

So did Bob Feller, whose 36 complete games in 1946 were the most in the majors since the heyday of Grover Cleveland Alexander in 1916.

Feller finished with 266 wins because he spent four seasons in the U.S. Navy at the peak of his career. "I didn't win 300 games," he said, "but we won World War II and that was a little more important."

The long-time fireballer for the Cleveland Indians collected eight battle stars while participating in five different military campaigns. Had the war not intervened, Feller estimated he would have won 100 more games, perhaps even passing Alexander and Christy Mathewson on the lifetime victory list (at 373).

"There's a lot of luck in this game, just as there is a lot of luck in life," said Feller, still an ambassador for baseball at the age of 91. "Either you live too long or you die too soon. In baseball, you have injuries and bad years. In the rest of your life, you have to avoid all the hazards out there. Everything is a game of inches. If you're lucky, you'll be successful.

"In baseball, much depends on how good your teams are. Over a period of time, though, water usually reaches its own level. A lot of good ballplayers nowadays don't know the fundamentals as well as we did, but the team that wins the World Series is the one that knows the fundamentals the best. If you have good pitching, you'll probably win.

"As for 300-game winners, I think Randy Johnson is the last one we'll have, at least in the foreseeable future – until they get rid of this pitch count nonsense. A pitcher should be in good enough condition to finish his ballgame. That's the kind of pitcher I want on my team – a man who can hold a one-run lead through the seventh, eighth, and ninth innings."

300 Wins Club

In Order By Most Wins / Ties Alphabetized

Victory #300 Details								
Pitcher	Wins	Threw	Pitching For	Lg	Age	Date	Opponent	Score
Cy Young	511	Right	Boston	AL	34	07-03-1901	Baltimore	9-1
Walter Johnson	417	Right	Washington	AL	32	05-14-1920	Detroit	9-8
Grover Alexander	373	Right	Chicago	NL	37	09-20-1924	New York	7-3
Christy Mathewson	373	Right	New York	NL	32	06-28-1912	Boston	10-3
Warren Spahn	363	Left	Milwaukee	NL	40	08-11-1961	Chicago	2-1
Pud Galvin	361	Right	Pittsburgh	NL	31	09-04-1888	Indianapolis	5-4
Kid Nichols	361	Right	Boston	NL	30	07-07-1900	Chicago	11-4
Greg Maddux	355	Right	Chicago	NL	38	08-07-2004	San Francisco	8-4
Roger Clemens	354	Right	New York	AL	40	06-13-2003	St. Louis	5-2
Tim Keefe	342	Right	New York	PL	33	06-04-1890	Boston	9-4
Steve Carlton	329	Left	Philadelphia	NL	38	09-23-1983	St. Louis	6-2
John Clarkson	328	Right	Cleveland	NL	31	09-21-1892	Pittsburgh	3-2
Eddie Plank	326	Left	St. Louis	FL	39	09-11-1915	Kansas City	3-2
Nolan Ryan	324	Right	Texas	AL	43	07-31-1990	Milwaukee	11-3
Don Sutton	324	Right	California	AL	41	06-18-1986	Texas	4-1
Phil Niekro	318	Right	New York	AL	46	10-06-1985	Toronto	8-0
Gaylord Perry	314	Right	Seattle	AL	43	05-06-1982	New York	7-3
Tom Seaver	311	Right	Chicago	AL	40	08-04-1985	New York	4-1
Old Hoss Radbourn	309	Right	Cincinnati	NL	36	05-14-1891	Brooklyn	4-0
Mickey Welch	307	Right	New York	NL	31	08-11-1890	Brooklyn	3-0
Tom Glavine	305	Left	New York	NL	41	08-05-2007	Chicago	8-3
Randy Johnson	301	Left	San Francisco	NL	45	06-04-2009	Washington	5-4
Lefty Grove	300	Left	Boston	AL	41	07-25-1941	Cleveland	10-6
Early Wynn	300	Right	Cleveland	AL	43	07-13-1963	Kansas City	7-4

Bibliography

Adomites, Paul; Greenberger, Matthew D.; Johnson, Dick; Nemec, David; Palmer, Pete; Schlossberg, Dan; Shea, Stuart; and Tully, Mike, *Cooperstown: Hall of Fame Players*, Lincolnwood, IL: Publications International, 2007.

Ballou, Bill, *Behind the Green Monster: Red Sox Myths, Legends, and Lore*, Chicago: Triumph Books, 2009.

Berke, Art, "Atlanta's Fluttering Legend," *Braves Illustrated*, Atlanta, 1978.

Bjarkman, Peter C., *The New York Mets Encyclopedia*, Champaign, Ill.: Sports Publishing, 2001.

Blake, Mike, *Baseball's Bad Hops and Lucky Bounces*, Cincinnati: Betterway Books, 1995.

Broeg, Bob, *Superstars of Baseball*, South Bend, Ind.: Diamond Communications, 1994.

Brown, Gene, *The New York Times Book of Baseball History*, New York: Quadrangle, 1975.

Buckley, James Jr., and Pepe, Phil, *Unhittable: Reliving the Magic and Drama of Baseball's Best-Pitched Games*, Chicago: Triumph Books, 2004.

Caillault, Jean-Pierre, *The Complete New York Clipper Baseball Biographies, 1859-1903*, Jefferson, NC: McFarland & Co., 2009.

Cohen, Richard M. and Neft, David S. and Michael L., *The Sports Encyclopedia: Baseball 2007*, New York: St. Martin's Griffin, 2007.

Cohen, Richard M., Neft, David S., Johnson, Roland T., and Deutsch, Jordan A., *The Scrapbook History of Baseball*, Indianapolis: Bobbs-Merrill, 1975.

Dewey, Donald, and Acocella, Nicholas, *Total Ballclubs: the Ultimate Book of Baseball Teams*, Toronto: Sport Media Publishing, 2005.

Enright, Jim, ed., *Trade Him: 100 Years of Baseball's Greatest Deals*, Chicago: Follett, 1976.

Freedman, Lew, *Early Wynn, The Go-Go White Sox, and the 1959 World Series*, Jefferson City, NC: McFarland, 2009.

Freese, Mel R., *Charmed Circle: 20-Game Winning Pitchers in Baseball's 20th Century*, Jefferson, NC: McFarland, 1997.

Goldman, Steve, editor, *It Ain't Over 'Til It's Over: the Baseball Prospectus Pennant Race Book*, Philadelphia: Basic Books, 2007.

Golenbock, Peter, *Amazin': the Miraculous History of New York's Most Beloved Baseball Team*, New York: St. Martin's Griffin, 2002.

Honig, Donald, and Ritter, Lawrence, *The 100 Greatest Baseball Players of All Time*, New York: Crown, 1981.

Honig, Donald, *The Greatest Pitchers of All Time*, New York: Crown, 1988.

Honig, Donald, *The Philadelphia Phillies: an Illustrated History*, New York: Simon & Schuster, 1992.

Honig, Donald, *The St. Louis Cardinals: an Illustrated History*, New York: Simon & Schuster, 1991.

Horn, Bradford, executive editor, *National Baseball Hall of Fame and Museum Yearbook*, Cooperstown, NY: 2009.

James, Bill, and Neyer, Rob, *The Neyer/James Guide to Pitchers: an Historical Compendium of Pitching, Pitchers, and Pitches*, New York: Fireside, 2004.

Jones, David, editor, *Deadball Stars of the American League*, Dulles, Va.: Potomac Books, 2006.

Kelley, Brent P., *The 100 Greatest Pitchers*, Greenwich, Conn.: Bison Books, 1988.

Kerrane, Kevin, *The Hurlers: Pitching, Power, and Precision*, Alexandria, Va.: Redefinition Books, 1989.

Kuenster, John, ed., *The Best of Baseball Digest*, Chicago: Ivan R. Dee, 2006.

Kuenster, John, ed., *From Cobb to Catfish: 128 Illustrated Stories from Baseball Digest*, Chicago: Rand McNally, 1975.

Lang, Jack, and Simon, Peter, *The New York Mets: 25 Years of Baseball Magic*, New York: Henry Holt, 1986.

Light, Jonathan Fraser, *The Cultural Encyclopedia of Baseball*, 2nd ed., Jefferson, N.C.: McFarland, 2005.

Lyons, Jeffrey and Lyons, Douglas B., *Short Hops & Foul Tips: 1,734 Wild and Wacky Baseball Facts*, Lanham, Md.: Taylor Trade, 2005.

MacKay, Joe, *The Great Shutout Pitchers: Twenty Profiles of a Vanishing Breed*, Jefferson City, NC: McFarland, 2004.

MacLean, Norman, executive editor, *All-Time Greatest Who's Who in Baseball 1872-1990*, New York: Who's Who in Baseball Magazine Company, 1990.

Markusen, Bruce, *Tales from the Mets Dugout*, Champaign, IL: Sports Publishing, 2007.

Marazzi, Rich, and Fiorito, Len, *Baseball Players of the 1950s: a Biographical Dictionary of All 1,560 Major Leaguers*, Jefferson City, NC: McFarland, 2004.

Masterson, Dave, and Boyle, Timm, *Baseball's Best: the MVPs*, Chicago: Contemporary Books, 1985.

Mayo, Jonathan, *Facing Clemens: Hitters on Confronting Baseball's Most Intimidating Pitcher*, Guilford, CT: The Lyons Press, 2008.

Macht, Norman L., *Tom Seaver*, New York: Chelsea House, 1994.

Mazzone, Leo, and Freeman, Scott, *Leo Mazzone's Tales from the Mound*, Champaign, IL: Sports Publishing, 2006.

McNeil, William F., *The Evolution of Pitching in Major League Baseball*, Jefferson City, N.C.: McFarland, 2006.

Meyerhoff, Steve, and Sloan, Dave, editors, *Heroes of the Hall: Baseball's All-Time Best*, St. Louis: The Sporting News, 2002.

Mullen, Maureen, *"Yogi Was Up with a Guy on Third...": Hall of Famers Recall Their Favorite Baseball Games Ever*, Chicago: Triumph Books, 2009.

Nathan, David H., *The McFarland Baseball Quotations Dictionary*, Jefferson City, N.C.: McFarland, 2000.

Palmer, Pete, ed., *The ESPN Baseball Encyclopedia*, New York: Sterling, 2008.

Pearlman, Jeff, *The Rocket That Fell to Earth: Roger Clemens and the Rage for Baseball Immortality*, New York: Harper Collins, 2009.

Pepe, Phil, *Magic Moments Yankees*, Chicago: Triumph Books, 2008.

Pietrusza, David; Silverman, Matthew; and Gershman, Michael, editors, *Baseball: the Biographical Encyclopeda*, New York: Total Sports Illustrated, 2000.

Purdy, Dennis, *The Team by Team Encyclopedia of Major League Baseball*, New York: Workman Publishing, 2006.

Reidenbaugh, Lowell, *The Sporting News Selects Baseball's 50 Greatest Games*, St. Louis: The Sporting News, 1986.

Reidenbaugh, Lowell, *Cooperstown: Where Baseball's Legends Live Forever*, St. Louis: The Sporting News, 1983.

Reisler, Jim, *A Great Day in Cooperstown: the Improbable Birth of Baseball's Hall of Fame*, New York: Carroll & Graf, 2006.

Robinson, Ray, editor, *Baseball Stars of 1975*, New York: Pyramid Books, 1975.

Ross, Alan, *Mets Pride*, Nashville: Cumberland House, 2007.

Rust, Art Jr., with Marley, Mike, *Conversations with Baseball Greats*, New York: McGraw-Hill, 1989.

Schlossberg, Dan, *The Baseball Almanac: Big, Bodacious Book of Baseball*, Chicago, Triumph Books, 2002.

Schlossberg, Dan, *The Baseball Book of Why*, Middle Village, NY: Jonathan David Publishers, 1983.

Selter, Ronald M., *Ballparks of the Deadball Era*, Jefferson City, NC: McFarland, 2008.

Shatzkin, Mike, and Jim Charlton. *The Ballplayers*, New York: Arbor House, 1990.

Silverman, Matthew, editor, *Mets 2009 Annual*, Hanover, Mass.: Maple Street Press, 2009.

Smith, Ron, *The Sporting News Selects Baseball's 100 Greatest Players*, St. Louis: The Sporting News, 1998.

Spatz, Lyle, ed., *The SABR Baseball List & Record Book*, New York: Scribner, 2007.

San Francisco Giants Media Guide, 2009.

Stang, Mark, *Athletics Album: a Photo History of the Philadelphia Athletics*, Wilmington, Ohio: Orange Frazer Press, 2006.

Sugar, Bert, *Bert Sugar's Baseball Hall of Fame: a Living History of America's Greatest Game*, Philadelphia: Running Press, 2009.

Thorn, John, ed., *Total Baseball: The Ultimate Baseball Encyclopedia*, 8th edition, Toronto: Sports Classic Books, 2004.

Total Baseball Trivia, New York: Total Sports Illustrated, 2001.

Vincent, David, *Home Run's Most Wanted*, Washington: Potomac Books, 2009.

Westcott, Rich, Winningest Pitchers: Baseball's 300-Game Winners, Philadelphia: Temple University Press, 2002.

Wilbert, Warren N., *The Arrival of the American League*, Jefferson City, N.C.: McFarland, 2007.

Wilkinson, Jack, *Game of My Life: Atlanta Braves*, Champaign, IL: Sports Publishing, 2007.

Woods, Bob, ed., *The Baseball Timeline*, New York: DK Publishing, 2001.

Periodicals

Baseball America

Baseball Digest

ChopTalk

Sporting News

Sports Illustrated

USA Today

USA Today Sports Weekly

Websites

BaseballAlmanac.com

TheBaseballPage.com

Baseball-reference.com

Baseballhalloffame.org

Baseballguru.com

Goodsportsart.com

LibraryofCongress.com

Miscbaseball.wordpress.com

MLB.com

Retrosheet.com

Index

Alexander, Grover Cleveland — vii, xxiv, 5, 18, 39, 53, 56, 63, 73, 90, 129, 168, 195, 231, 258, 272

Blyleven, Bert — xi, xxi, 255, 256, 258, 259

Carlton, Steve — vii, xvi, xviii, 124, 133, 134, 135, 136, 137, 138, 139, 140, 141, 142, 143, 144, 173, 179, 211, 223, 235, 256, 257, 268, 270, 271, 273

Clarkson, John — vii, 17, 23, 24, 25, 26, 27, 240, 273

Clemens, Roger — vii, x, xi, xv, xvi, xviii, xxi, 82, 88, 93, 99, 100, 101, 102, 103, 104, 106, 107, 108, 109, 110, 111, 112, 113, 140, 173, 191, 232, 234, 238, 240, 263, 267, 268, 273, 277

Cy Young Award xi, xviii, 40, 80, 99, 101, 106, 139, 153, 157, 159, 163, 179, 194, 195, 211, 222, 231, 236, 246, 249, 261, 268

Drysdale, Don — 44, 102, 109, 165, 167, 168, 199, 223

Gaylord Perry viii, ix, xi, xvii, 172, 173, 191, 197, 199, 232, 268, 270, 273

Gibson, Bob — xxi, 109, 137, 141, 195, 214

Glavine, Tom — viii, x, xvii, xxi, 82, 90, 91, 93, 95, 173, 177, 179, 180, 217, 218, 219, 220, 221, 222, 223, 224, 225, 238, 239, 263, 267, 268, 270, 273

Grove, Lefty — vii, 35, 77, 84, 89, 115, 123, 124, 125, 126, 127, 128, 129, 130, 212, 231, 240, 251, 273

Halladay, Roy — xviii, xxi, 265

Jenkins, Ferguson — xi, xxi, 94, 197, 255, 256, 261, 262

John Clarkson — vii, 17, 23, 25, 240, 273

About the Author

Dan Schlossberg is the author of 35 books and more than 25,000 articles about baseball for newspapers, magazines, and online publications. He has contributed to *Baseball Digest, The Sporting News*, MLB.com, the All-Star and World Series programs, *Draft, Hemispheres, Hooters, Red Sox Magazine, US Airways Magazine*, and many other periodicals. The former AP sportswriter is managing editor of BallTalk, a syndicated weekly radio baseball show; travel editor of *The Maggie Linton Show* on Sirius XM Satellite Radio; and Senior contributor of *Travel With Kal*, heard by 500,000 Connecticut residents weekday mornings. In 2009, he contributed weekly baseball radio reports to MLB flagship stations in Dallas, Denver, and St. Louis plus the ESPN affilliate in Cleveland.

The 1969 Syracuse University graduate has also worked for The Associated Press [AP], American Express, the *Bergen Jewish News*, Motor Club of America, the *North Jersey Herald-News, Woman's World*, and the University of Medicine and Dentistry of New Jersey.

Dan is president emeritus and co-founder of the North American Travel Journalists Association [NATJA], past president of the Working Press Association of New Jersey, and a member of the American Society of Journalists and Authors [ASJA] and the Society for American Baseball Research [SABR]. Dan has won awards for writing, broadcasting, and public service.

Wayne Hagin has worked behind a big-league microphone for the A's, Giants, White Sox, Rockies, and Cardinals before joining the New York Mets radio team in 2008.